Little Lodges on the Prairie
Freemasonry & Laura Ingalls Wilder

Shine brightly !
Teresa Lynn

Teresa Lynn

Tranquility Press
2014

Little Lodges on the Prairie: Freemasonry & Laura Ingalls Wilder

Tranquility Press
P.O. Box 170582
Austin, TX 78717
www.TranquilityPress.net

Editing by Faith Lynn

ISBN 978-0-9904977-0-7

For
my Sisters and Brothers
in the Order of the Eastern Star
and Freemasonry.
May your good works never cease.

And for
all of Laura's fans, kindred spirits.
May you keep her legacy alive
to inspire new generations.

Table of Contents

Acknowledgments
and Credits

There are but few Masonic historians in America...a peculiar type of man is required... He must have an absorbing love for research, an almost infinite patience, and an analytical faculty... And then, as Masonry goes in America, he must have abundant private means or steadfast backing...

The above quote was printed by the Editor of *The American Freemason* in the June, 1911 issue. In the case of this book, there is the added dimension of the Ingalls family, so the point is even more fitting.

Although I do have the first qualification of an absorbing love for research, I do not possess the rest in abundance, and I especially do not enjoy the last: "means" or "backing." This has made the work infinitely more difficult, and it has been accomplished only with the support and assistance of many persons and organizations. Some of these have rendered such great assistance that even shouting it to the world from the mountaintop is not equal to what is deserved. There is no such mountaintop, but I do have these pages, which I hope will allow their legacy of kindness to be known and live on.

I first met **David Harris**, Past Master of **De Smet Lodge #55, A. F. & A. M.** in De Smet, South Dakota. Upon hearing about my plans for a book based on the Ingalls' connections to Freemasonry, he not only agreed to help, but

7

enthusiastically encouraged me. He also introduced me to *Shirley Lenz*, Worthy Matron of ***Bethlehem Chapter #13***, Order of the Eastern Star in De Smet. She became a dear friend instantly, and she, too, was very supportive of the idea. David and Shirley, along with ***Mark Harris*** and ***Wade Hoeffert,*** made available the records of the Lodge and Star Chapter in De Smet, as well as acquainting me with some local history, especially in regard to those organizations.

Also in De Smet, I researched in the archives of the museum at the ***Laura Ingalls Wilder Memorial Society,*** where executive Director ***Cheryl Palmlund*** was very helpful in searching for additional tidbits relating to the Ingalls family. ***Jenny and Andy Todd*** at the Prairie House Manor Bed and Breakfast also shared information.

In Keystone, South Dakota, I met equally supportive people. Although the Lodge and Chapter there have closed, the Past Master & Worthy Patron, ***Chuck Childs,*** and Past Matron, ***Grace Childs,*** graciously opened their home and shared the surviving records. They also arranged for ***Lois and Linda Halley*** to come by while I was there and share personal memories of Carrie, as Lois had known her in the Eastern Star. Charles, Grace, and Lois have all been very close friends to other persons who had known Carrie well, and shared some wonderful insights. Another personal friend of both David and Carrie, ***Robert Hayes***, shared his memories of them and of Keystone's history, as well as sharing some of his personal photographs. Mr. Hayes worked with his father on Mount Rushmore, and he gave me lots of information about the creation of that monument.

The ladies at the ***Keystone Historical Museum*** were very helpful, allowing me to document the connections of the Swanzeys to Freemasonry through items they have on file.

It was several months later that I was able to return to South Dakota and resume the search. ***Karen Steptoe***, Grand Secretary of the ***Grand Chapter of South Dakota***, Order of the Easter Star, was preparing for a Chapter-related trip, but she still generously agreed to meet me and allow me to review the Grand Chapter records. Her husband Robert even entertained my husband while I did so. **Richard McCauley** of the **Grand Lodge of South Dakota, A. F. & A. M.** gave up much of his time helping me dig out records there.

Later, my husband and I were visiting our good friends, **Arnold Shute** and **Nancy Durnin**. On hearing about this project, they volunteered to drive us to Columbia, Missouri, where the Grand Lodge and Grand Chapter of Missouri are located, to review documents in those archives. **Brenda Austin**, Grand Secretary of the **Grand Chapter of Missouri**, Order of the Eastern Star, and **Ronald Miller**, Grand Secretary of the **Grand Lodge of Missouri, A. F. & A. M.** took time to assist me in finding records pertaining to the Ingalls family.

In Mansfield, Missouri, I had the privilege of attending Chapter where Laura and Almanzo had been members, and found wonderfully friendly and helpful sisters and brothers. **Colleen Stofer** and **Jo Ann Gray** at **Mansfield Chapter #76**, Order of the Eastern Star and **David Gray** of **Mansfield Lodge #543, A. F. & A. M.** were especially obliging in making those records available.

Many thanks are due **James McCrae, Jack Kellam, Marie Tschop** (www.AllThingsLauraIngallsWilder.com), and **Nancy Cleaveland** for their useful feedback and suggestions on the manuscript.

Roslyn Houghton has been a teacher, mentor, and friend for many years. Without her direction, which put me on the path to writing, this book would not exist.

Faith Lynn had the onerous task of editing the manuscript, which she did with skill, efficiency, and grace. Her guidance was invaluable and her cheering gave me confidence to continue.

Throughout the entire process, my beloved husband **David** was beside me. He made countless sacrifices so that I could work on "the Laura project." He has been my champion and my inspiration. His love and support are what ultimately made this book possible.

A special note of warm, fraternal regard goes to my sisters and brothers in **Kerrville #24, OES**, who welcomed me with open arms when I began my journey in the Order, and have been wonderful friends all these years. Star hugs to you all.

In addition to the foregoing, who were personally helpful to me, I am indebted to **William Anderson** and **John E. Miller**. Their research provided a basis for me to build on.

I have been privileged to obtain copies of records and photographs from many sources. Among these are the Grand Lodge of South Dakota, A. F. & A. M., the Grand Lodge of Missouri, A. F. & A. M., the Grand Chapter of South Dakota, Order of the Eastern Star, and the Grand Chapter of Missouri, Order of the Eastern Star. In addition to these are De Smet Masonic Lodge #55, A. F. & A. M., Mansfield Masonic Lodge #543 A. F. & A. M., Bethlehem #13 (De Smet), Order of the Eastern Star, and Mansfield #76, Order of the Eastern Star. Copies of records of the foregoing printed herein were made by me, and are used with the permission of the respective organization, as listed above. Unless otherwise noted in the caption, photographs were taken by me, or they were obtained from the public domain or from individuals who wish to remain anonymous.

Unless otherwise noted, quotes and images from De Smet, South Dakota newspapers are courtesy of the Laura Ingalls Wilder Memorial Society, and quotes and images from Mansfield, Missouri periodicals are courtesy of the State Historical Society of Missouri.

Cover: Photo of Almanzo courtesy Laura Ingalls Wilder Home Association, Mansfield, Missouri. Photo of Laura courtesy South Dakota State Historic Society, Pierre, South Dakota. Photo of Eastern Star pin courtesy of and copyright Laura Ingalls Wilder Home Association, Mansfield, Missouri. Mount Rushmore pin courtesy National Park Service. Photo of author copyright Marc Bennett, White Oak Studio, Fredericksburg, Texas. Cover design by Teresa Lynn.

Author's Note

As a researcher of both Laura Ingalls Wilder and Freemasonry, I often speak to people about both subjects. Over the years, it has become apparent that few individuals know about the extensive connections between the two. This book will document the many ways various members of the Ingalls family were involved in Freemasonry. The reader must have a basic understanding of Freemasonry to fully understand the role Laura and her family played in the fraternity, and what it meant to them; therefore, some background information is included in this book. However, an organization that has been in existence for over half a millennium cannot be properly distilled into one book. The information on Freemasonry that follows is not a complete history or thorough explanation; rather, it is simply a quick introduction for the reader to have some idea of the organization with which members of the Ingalls family were involved. There is much information available for those who wish to know more; a bibliography can be found at the end of this book.

Similarly, this book cannot cover in detail the entire lives of the Ingalls family members, even just those who were Freemasons or Eastern Stars; the barest of sketches is provided herein. There are many resources available to learn more about the lives of this fascinating family. A few are listed in the bibliography.

It is customary to use the last name of individuals about whom a non-fiction piece is written. I am writing about a family, however, so several people share the same last name. In addition, most readers of the *Little House* books – as well as devotees of the television show based on those books – feel that they know Laura and her family; to fans, they will always be Charles and Caroline, Laura and Almanzo, and so forth. Therefore, after the first introduction of each person, first names will be used.

Regarding the source material, in many cases the documents are over one hundred years old, and this makes them challenging to work with. To begin with, they are frail and brittle; also, many of them have been damaged by things such as flood and fire. Due to their fragile and sometimes damaged condition, the copies herein are not pristine. Some have obvious burn marks or water stains. Most are faded. I did not want to alter or "clean them up" too much (such as with Photoshop or other software) because their age and condition is part of their historic interest, so some are not very clear.

Sometimes, a disaster destroyed records completely. Carrie Ingalls described one such loss in a history of the Mt. Aetna Chapter of the Order of the Eastern Star in Keystone that she wrote on September 30, 1935, for the Grand Chapter of South Dakota:

> *On the night of January 15, 1917 fire broke out on Main Street in a building two doors from Masonic Hall. All buildings were frame and the fire spread rapidly. Two elderly Masons, Spencer Smith and Andrew Marble arrived at the fire among the first and their first thought was of the property in Masonic Hall. They rushed to the hall, and realizing there was not much time, gathered some furnishings and threw them from a window. The large Masonic Bible was the first thing thrown. This was picked up and later returned to the Masons with only its binding loosened.*
>
> *The two Masons gathered up jewels, gavels, etc.,*

placing them in a pile to be gathered up quickly and were getting ready to move furniture near a window when Alice Smith (now Sister Alice McDonald) daughter of Brother Smith, missing her father on the street and guessing where he was, rushed up the stairs and found the two. Her pleadings for them to come down were of no avail, they declaring there was time to save the furniture. Knowing the Hall was on fire and fearing the stairs would be cut off, she seized both men by the arms and with the strength of desperation and terror dragged them to the head of the stairs. There others who had seen her enter the hall and followed, met them and with their help the two protesting Masons were piloted to safety. By this time the flames were so near and the heat so intense no one could enter the hall to get the things so perilously gathered together.

Other records have simply been lost. In most cases, it is believed that when the record keeper died, family members not associated with the Lodge or Chapter disposed of the documents they held. The facts presented in this book are according to the documents available to me at this time; I hope that one day, some of the lost records will be found.

The only way to go is ahead.
But the past is always important.
The past can educate, it can entertain,
and it can inspire new generations.
~Laura Ingalls Wilder

In the Beginning

*We keep moving forward, opening up new doors
and doing new things, because we're curious...
and curiosity keeps leading us down new paths.*
~ Walt Disney, cartoonist, DeMolay

My husband, David, and I were visiting his family one day many years ago when I overheard his brother, Grady, who is a pilot, tell David something about flying a burned child somewhere. That intrigued me, but I couldn't join the conversation just then. Later, I asked my husband about it.

"Yes, he's a Shriner," David said. "You've heard of the Shriners Hospitals for Children, haven't you? He flew burned children to Shriners burn hospitals."

"What are Shriners?" I wanted to know.

"They're a part of the Freemasons."

That didn't tell me much. "What are Freemasons?"

"A group that does charity, like the Shriners Hospitals. I was telling Grady that I was thinking about becoming a Mason," my husband answered.

Of course then I wanted to know all about them; naturally, I turned to the Internet. You can find out anything online, right? In just a few minutes, I had found out that Freemasonry is a satanic religion, and that it is not a religion at all; that it's a secret society so no one can know who's a Mason, and that lots of famous people are known to be Masons; that Masons ride goats, that they worship goats, and that they have nothing to do with goats.

Clearly some more serious researching was needed. I began to delve deeper to find legitimate, accurate information. One of the first things I found out is that there are indeed lots of famous people who are known to be or have been Masons: George Washington's affiliation with Freemasonry is well documented in everything from his own letters and writings to his Masonic aprons.[1]

George Washington portrayed as Master of the Lodge.

I was going down a list of famous Freemasons and came to "John Wayne, actor; Oscar Wilde, writer; Laura Ingalls Wilder, children's author; Lawren –"[2] Whoa, wait just a minute! Laura Ingalls Wilder? I knew that was not possible, as only men can be Masons. A second look revealed an asterisk next to Laura's

Minutes from the meeting at which George Washington was made a Mason. Courtesy De Smet Lodge #55.

name. I skipped the rest of the names on the list to scroll down to the footnote. It said that while Laura was not a Mason, she was a member of the Order of the Eastern Star, and that a woman must be related to a Freemason to join that Order. It went on to say that it was not known (at least by the compilers of that particular list) who her Masonic relative was, so they just listed Laura.

This was extremely intriguing to me. I have been a lover of Laura Ingalls Wilder and her writings almost my entire life. It started with the television show *Little House on the Prairie* when I was just a sprig of five years old. My family, like so many others, enjoyed the heartwarming episodes each week, and we watched faithfully. I believe it took about three seasons before I paid enough attention to the opening credits to notice that they included information that the show was based on the *Little House* series of books by Laura Ingalls Wilder. This opened a whole new opportunity to delight in the stories of the little house. A rapacious reader even then, I raced to the library the very next day, and checked out the books.

I fell in love. I reread the books countless times, and each time, I had cravings – cravings for the food Laura described so succinctly, which always left me hungry; for the music she remembered, which brought such joy to her household; and for the sense of community that the later books in the series portray. I was drawn to the simplicity of their life, the closeness of the family, and their self sufficiency.

Then one day, I read the back of one of the books, something I had never done, and there was a shocking discovery: Laura was a real person! As I pondered that fact, I thought of all the changes she had lived through, and I wondered what happened next in her life.

It was many years before I found the answers to the questions I had. During those years, my love of Laura and her writings never diminished; in fact, I began to look at her family as a model and her writings as full of wisdom that could be applied to my own life. I respected Laura's values as portrayed in her books: honesty, integrity, faith, patriotism, a good work ethic. So the fact that she had chosen to join the Order of the Eastern Star impressed me.

I knew that Laura would never belong to an organization that diametrically opposed her values, but I still had questions. How did Laura come to join the Order? Had she remained a member? What relative was a Mason? How many family members affiliated? How extensive was their involvement? And what are those organizations all about, anyway? I had to find out.

Soon after I began this search all those years ago, my husband became a Master Mason, a Shriner, and attained the 32nd degree of the Scottish Rite. I joined the Order of the Eastern Star. I quickly came to understand why the Ingalls family would associate themselves with Freemasonry. I found that the fraternity promoted the search for truth, justice, charity, faith, patriotism, education – themes which also run through the *Little House* books, and the real lives of Laura and her family.

I am still fascinated by what various individuals think of the fraternity. As shown by my initial Internet search, the reputation of Freemasonry among non-affiliated persons seems often to fall on one of two extremes: either it is believed to be a satanic cult, or it is thought of as an elite, powerful group that secretly runs the world and has access to great treasures (or both). To find the truth of the matter, let us look at how the organization came to be, how it evolved into what it is today, and how members of the Ingalls family were involved with it.

History of Freemasonry

Ancient History

All the ancient histories, in the words of one of our wits, are only fables agreed upon.
~ Voltaire, philosopher, Freemason

The early history of Freemasonry is rather vague, "shrouded in mystery," as they like to say. What this really means is that no one knows exactly how Freemasonry began.

Legend holds that the organization began with the actual stone masons who worked on King Solomon's Temple almost a thousand years before the Christian era. Only masons who were men of the most upright character were allowed to work on that holiest of buildings. To ensure that only the deserving would have a place at the construction site, they devised secret words and phrases to convey the trade secrets of their craft to deserving masons, and to keep those secrets from masons who were not deemed worthy and from other persons who were not masons.

Supposedly, it was from these groups that the men of the Order of Knights Templar were chosen to protect Christians on pilgrimage to Jerusalem during the time of the Crusades, due to the high moral conduct to which they swore. According to legend, they discovered a great treasure in the Temple, which they guarded fiercely and passed on to succeeding generations of Templars. This is an interesting story, but unfortunately there is no evidence to back it up. What we do know is that the Order of the Knights Templar was founded in Jerusalem in 1119 A.D. after a particularly large and brutal massacre of Christian pilgrims by the Muslims during the crusades. The Order – members of which may have been chosen from masonic guilds, although this cannot be documented – was charged with protecting future pilgrims from such atrocity on their travels, and defending the Holy Land. Christian kings, as well as popes, granted them exceptional rights and privileges, enjoyed by no one else, to carry out their mission.[1] The Templars took their duty seriously, and became legendary in their execution of it. Wealthy patrons who believed in the cause donated money and property to them, leading to great wealth within the Order. This is where the fabled treasure of the Knights came from. These very donations and privileges proved to be their undoing, however, as greed and jealousy led King Philip IV of France to order the arrest of all Templars in France, and all their assets confiscated. The order was carried out in coordinated attacks at dawn on Friday, the 13th of October, 1307, with mass arrests of the Templars in their very beds. (Some say this is the origin of the idea that Friday the 13th is an unlucky day.) Under pressure from Philip IV, Pope Clement V issued the Pastoralis Praeeminentiaei a few weeks later. This Papal Bull accused the Templars of gross heresies and obscenities, and commanded all Christian authorities to arrest the Templars and seize their assets for the church. The Templars were put on trial and tortured until confession. A few of them managed to escape. It is from these escapees that the secrets of Freemasonry are supposed to have come.[2]

We know there were stone mason societies in existence in Europe from long before the Templars' time; extant records date them as early as 643 A.D. According to one document, an unnamed son of King Athelstan loved and learned the craft. He convinced his father to provide official recognition of the group by granting them a charter and commission, and authorizing an annual meeting of masons, beginning in 926 A.D.[3]

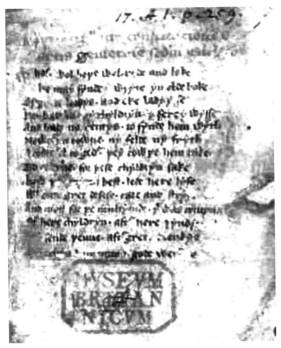

The Halliwell Manuscript is the oldest extant Masonic document.

This and similar documents are called Old Charges.[4] They outline the history of the trade secrets of stone masonry. From these documents, we know that societies of masons existed, that they had instructions in behavior (often taking the form of an oath, from which the obligation that Freemasons today take upon initiation is derived), that they had rituals and secret words, and that they claimed a history going back at least to Euclid, who lived about three hundred years before the Christian era. The importance of geometry is often emphasized in their documents. These masons were the ones who built the great cathedrals and castles of the medieval period. The headquarters for the stone masons at a large building site was a smaller building or tent nearby known as the lodge. In the lodge, the craftsmen received their orders from the supervising master mason and met to discuss the technicalities of their work; it was also the place they could rest and eat.

Suppose you are a stone mason living in 1200 A.D. No ordinary rough mason, who simply lays stone, you are a free mason. The designation signifies that you work with freestone, the fine-grained sandstone or limestone used for the detailed and complex ornamental work. The term also indicates that, due to both the necessity of skilled sculptors and the privileges of membership, you have unparalleled freedom to move about the country in performance of your duties. You have been working at a cathedral outside of London. In the mason's lodge, you have learned new techniques from the masters. These new techniques have been taught to you using mnemonic devices, meaning you have memorized certain phrases and actions to aid memory retention of the skills you have learned. You have advanced your skill and been promoted from apprentice to craftsman. Now you have completed your work on the cathedral and need to find employment elsewhere. You have heard that a large castle is being built in Exeter, so you journey there, seeking work. When you arrive, no one there knows you. You have no resumé or union card. You find the supervising (master) mason and ask if there is a place for you to work. The master can make his decision in one of several ways. He can just look at you and make a decision. Quick, but not very reliable. He can ask you to sculpt something, to prove that you know what you're doing and see your level of skill for himself. Reliable, but not very quick. Or, he can ask you for the secret words and signs. Since you had belonged to a society of masons previously, you know secret words and signs which instantly let the master know that you are trustworthy, that you have vowed to follow certain behaviors and work ethics, and how skilled you are (since there were different words for masters, craftsmen, and apprentices). Quick and reliable. Which do you think the master would most like to use?

This is the origin of Masonic Lodges, with their rituals and secrets. They were "operative masons," that is, working masons by trade, and the oaths and signs and secret words had a practical purpose in the trade at that time.

Modern History

Without continual growth and progress, such words as improvement, achievement, and success have no meaning.
~ Benjamin Franklin, Founding Father of America, polymath, Freemason

How did masonic lodges that began as trade associations become the prestigious gentlemen's societies of our founding fathers? There are not enough surviving records to draw a definitive, unbroken line from the ancient to the modern lodges, but documents do exist which provide a glimpse of the transition.

The Lodge of Edinburgh (Mary's Chapel) #1 of Scotland possesses the oldest minutes of any extant Lodge in the world, from July, 1599. At that time, according to their records, the Lodge was entirely operative; that is, every member was a stonemason by trade. It remained so until the year 1634, when minutes of meetings show that Lord Alexander, Sir Anthony Alexander, and Sir Alexander Stachan – none of whom practiced the trade of masonry – were admitted. Another non-mason, Robert Moray, was initiated into this same Lodge in 1641.

It wasn't long before other Lodges began to admit non-masons as honorary members; in Oxford, Elias Ashmole, one of the founders of the Royal Society, wrote in his diary in 1646 that he was made a Freemason.[5] He lists everyone who was at the meeting, and none of them have been found to have any connection to operative masonry. It is generally supposed that the reason for this sudden surge in accepting non-masons was that toward the end of the Gothic era and the beginning of the Renaissance, there was less physical building and more emphasis on enlightenment and intellectual growth, meaning less work for trade masons and, therefore, a decline in their membership.

One side effect of this decline was a decrease in the masons' box charity. A box charity was a box into which each member periodically placed a set sum of money. In times of personal financial distress, any member could apply for assistance from the box. Remember, this was long before the days of Unemployment or Welfare aid. With fewer masons, and less work for them, the box charity would have been stretched thin as more masons applied to it and not so many contributed. Accepting wealthy, non-trade members of the region into the society served each party: the society's membership and box charity was replenished, and the wealthy patron received the prestige of belonging to a "secret club," with all the benefits of brotherhood, or at least networking, that came with it. Thus, "accepted masons" joined the "free masons." Some Lodges even accepted new members in exchange for a free meal for the Lodge; these were known as "supper Lodges" or "leg of mutton Lodges." (This actually created a problem for the Masons, however, as unscrupulous men found out about it and used the idea to their own advantage: they claimed to initiate others into Masonry without themselves being Masons. The price they charged for these "initiations" was, of course, a leg of mutton, either actual or cash equivalent.[6]) Although the Lodges were perhaps bending the rules a bit to allow non-masons, they only accepted into a Lodge men who were deemed worthy in regard to their moral behavior and who, in harmony with the new ideals of the enlightenment, wanted to work in cooperation with other men to create not only a better Lodge society, but also a better society at large. Also in harmony with the times, when symbolism of all types was enjoying a spurt of popularity, signs and symbols were used to reinforce the teachings. Naturally, these signs and symbols were drawn from the trade mason's craft.

The non-mason men who were initiated into Lodges were known as speculative masons. The word "speculate" comes from the Latin "specere," meaning "to look." These men were merely spectators, or onlookers, rather than workers, or operators, of the craft. Before long, speculative masons began to outnumber operative masons. Some Masons today consider that they are both speculative and operative, even though they have never lifted a trowel. In this case, the term speculative refers to the mental part of a Freemason's life – learning the Craft's lessons – while the operative is putting these lessons into practice and action.

By the early 1700s, so many Lodges were made up of mostly "accepted" speculative Masons, with only a few true "free" operative masons, that the leaders began to see the need for some sort of means to keep them unified in their rituals, words, and so forth. This hadn't been a problem when only operative masons belonged to the society, since using the signs and phrases in their work kept them consistent with one another. These new members, however, were not so familiar with the trade language of the operative masons, and did not have the benefit of repetition or practice through daily work, so they had some trouble remembering everything exactly so. Furthermore, they were forbidden to write anything down to aid their memory, for fear the trade secrets would become publicly known. To solve the problem of uniformity, in 1717, on the 24th of June, the Grand Lodge of London and Westminster (also called the Premier Grand Lodge of England) was organized.[7] As the ultimate authority, its leaders established the ritual and set some basic tenets, called "landmarks," based on the Old Charges, to which all Lodges had to conform in order to be recognized as a true Masonic Lodge. Lodges today must still adhere to those same landmarks.

In outlining the tenets of the society, the Grand Lodge drew inspiration from the tolerance, unity, and advancement of intellectual pursuits promoted by the enlightenment. The founding principles were liberty, equality, and peace. Charity, beginning within the Lodge, Mason to Mason, but also extending outside the Lodge to any in need, was also an important precept.

These were principles with which the nobility and landed

gentry needed to affiliate, to advance their reputation. Many of them sincerely embraced the ideals; a few merely wanted to maintain the appearance of morality for political reasons. The affluent and influential members of society gained admittance to the Lodges, and used their affiliation to promote themselves socially and politically, in addition to promoting their Lodges as organizations of charity and brotherhood. All types of officials, from the highest levels of government to the law enforcement officers patrolling the roughest streets, were attracted to these groups. They benefited in the same way that others did, but law enforcement officers had a special incentive to recruit from within its ranks. The Masons within the Lodge were (and still are) required to take an oath to help and protect one another. To a man who served in harm's way, it made sense that those individuals who had already sworn to aid him are the ones he would most trust and want to be serving alongside him.

With the upper levels of society affiliating with Freemasonry, officials enlisting from within the Lodge, and others who wished to associate with those of higher social classes joining, the local Lodges experienced a period of explosive growth in the early eighteenth century. There's an old saying that in those days, everyone who was anyone belonged to a Masonic Lodge. The majority of Lodges were now speculative Lodges made up of accepted Masons, instead of operative Lodges made up trade freemasons. In 1723, James Anderson, a Presbyterian minister, wrote:

...the British nations indulg'd (sic) their happy Genius for Masonry of every sort, and reviv'd (sic) the drooping Lodges of London...wherein the Forms and Usages of the most ancient and worshipful Fraternity are widely propagated...several Noblemen and Gentlemen of the best Rank, with Clergymen and learned Scholars of most Professions and Denominations, having frankly join'd (sic) and submitted to take the Charges, and to wear the Badges of a Free and Accepted Mason...[8]

Since one of the ancient, established landmarks was that a member must be a free man (not a slave), the term

"Freemason" began to mean any member of a Masonic Lodge, whether a true working freemason or not. The term "Lodge" came to mean the group of individuals, rather than the place in which they met, which was often a tavern or private home. Still today, there are Lodge buildings, and within them Lodge rooms wherein meetings are held, but the "Lodge" is the brotherhood itself. (However, in common usage it is becoming more popular for the building to also be called the Lodge.) Sometimes, Lodges meet in places other than buildings; caves have historically been favored, due to the innate privacy they provide.

Of course, such prestige could not go unchallenged. Rival Grand Lodges sprang up, including the Ancient Grand Lodge of England, the Grand Lodge of Scotland, and the Grand Lodge of Ireland. Each one claimed ties with the trade of freemasonry dating back to antiquity; with this common basis, there was much similarity between them. The Ancient Grand Lodge of England and the Premier Grand Lodge of England eventually merged, creating the United Grand Lodge of England. Today, a Lodge may be designated "A. F. & A. M." (Ancient Free & Accepted Masons), "F. & A. M." (Free & Accepted Masons) or even "F. A. A. M." (Free And Accepted Masons). Each designation indicates which Grand Lodge has jurisdiction over the Lodge so designated. All are considered Freemasons, and all recognize and accept one another's members freely. The differences between them are minimal, no more significant than you might find between the various chapters of any other organization.

Each Grand Lodge has authority over its jurisdiction. There is no one "Grandest" Grand Lodge with authority over all, so each jurisdiction has some differences from the others, but they all abide by the same ancient, established landmarks. For a new Lodge to be recognized as a "true," "regular," or "duly constituted" Lodge, it must be chartered by the existing Grand Lodge in its jurisdiction. For a new Grand Lodge to be formed, an existing Grand Lodge must grant jurisdictional authorization.

Soon after the formation of the Premier Grand Lodge of England, a group of Masons in Boston sent a representative, Henry Price, to petition for a charter for a Lodge in the colonies. The request was favorably received, with Price being named Grand Master for the entire "New England." He subsequently established several Lodges in the colonies.[9]

There is evidence of Masonry in the New World prior to that first, official charter of Henry Price. A grave stone discovered on Goat Island, Nova Scotia in 1827 is inscribed with the year 1606 and an old style depiction of the Masonic square and compasses.[10] It bears no name, so we do not know whether the mason at whose grave it was laid was a free or an accepted mason, but it does provide confirmation that masons were arriving in the New World as far back as the early 1600s, and that masonry was important enough to them for its emblem to be inscribed on their gravestones. We also know that William Penn, who founded Pennsylvania in 1681, was a Freemason, as were many other men of that era.

The Goat Island Stone provides one of the earliest indications of Masonry in the New World.

As it had in the mother land, Masonry enjoyed rapid growth in the Americas. Benjamin Franklin wrote a history of Freemasonry in the December 5, 1730 issue of his *Pennsylvania Gazette* and began it with the following statement: "As there are several Lodges of Free-Masons erected in this Province [Pennsylvania], and People have lately been much amus'd (sic) with Conjectures concerning them; we think the following account of Freemasonry from London, will not be unacceptable to our Readers..."[11]

Since the ideals of Masonry – particularly those of equality and liberty – paralleled the ideals in the establishment of the new country, many of America's founding fathers were Masons. In fact, the role of Freemasonry in the founding of the United States can hardly be overstated. The British Governor of Massachusetts in 1760 wrote that the Masons meeting "at Adjutant Trowel's long garret spewed more sedition and libel than was hatched in all the garrets in Grubstreet," and that they must have "ransak'd Billingsgate and the Stews for muck to sling at the British authority."[12] ("Adjutant Trowel" was a pseudonym for Thomas Dawes, the owner of the long garret, or attic, in which the Masons were meeting at the time. He was one of the leaders of the American Revolution and a Freemason. "Grubstreet" [sic - actually Grub Street] was a street in London where vagrants and starving artists congregated; it was also populated by publishers of hack journals. "Billingsgate" was a well known fish market which, in addition to the normal goods it sold, also sold entrails and other offal to the impoverished, so that reference to it in this context meant "garbage." In addition, the salty language of the fishmongers made the name "Billingsgate" synonymous with profanity. "The Stews" was slang for brothels. Basically, the Governor was saying that the Masons spread more lies about British authorities than gossip journals spread rumors, and that what those Masons said came from the filthiest of places. The point is that they were plotting and promoting American independence.)

By 1773, the Masons had purchased The Green Dragon tavern, where "more Revolutionary eggs were hatched...than in any other spot in Boston."[13] Certainly the Boston Tea Party, a key catalyst of the American Revolution, was planned there, and it is noteworthy that the minutes from the meeting that was to be held on December 16, 1773 (the night of the Boston Tea Party) state that the meeting was not held because there were too few Brethren present.[14] It was no coincidence that Masons were leaders of the rebellion against the Crown. Men who were taken with the ideals of liberty and equality espoused by Freemasonry could not be content to be ruled by far away aristocracy, with no say in the governance.

In the same way that the founding fathers of America wanted to keep as much power within the states and out of the federal government as possible, they eschewed the idea of a Grand Lodge over all of America, and set each state to have its own Grand Lodge, with no other, outside authority over those, except the ancient landmarks, which all must follow. This has remained to be the case; they do, however, recognize and admit each other's members freely, after examination. A Mason who visits a Lodge other than his own will have to prove both his affiliation with the organization and which degree he has attained – just as stone masons in days of old did when arriving at a new building site. In some cases, this can be done by showing a current dues (membership) card along with identification. Other Lodges require the visitor to give the secret passwords and signs.

Prince Hall Lodges

We...desire only that the Supreme Architect of the Universe may diffuse in our hearts the true spirit of Masonry, love to God and to our fellowman, which we humbly conceive to be the two grand pillars of Ancient Freemasonry.
~ Prince Hall, abolitionist, Freemason

It did not escape the notice of abolitionists living in the New World of the 1700s that the most influential men in both politics and society were Freemasons. One abolitionist in particular, Prince Hall of Boston, saw that the principles of liberty and equality were dear to Masons.

Little is known of Hall's early life. It is believed that he was the son Bostonian William Hall and a slave woman from Barbados, but he was given his manumission paper in 1770, which stated he was "always accounted as a free man." Hall became a leather-worker and a caterer, rising to a prominent position in Boston society despite his background. He owned property and businesses, paid taxes, and voted.[15]

Prince Hall as Master of the Lodge.

A tireless advocate for black education, freedom, and equality, Hall petitioned Massachusetts for funds to establish schools for children of color, for the abolition of slavery, and for funds to aid blacks in returning to Africa. All of these petitions failed. Undeterred, Hall started a school for black children in his own home, and continued to work for freedom and equality. He made it his life's work to help other black men and women facing oppression, and he thought that if he were a Mason with a Mason's influence, he would have a better chance of being effective in securing these rights to people of color. He also believed that aiding black men in their efforts to better themselves was the best way to bring them to a more favorable standing in society.[16]

Hall petitioned several Lodges in the area, but, presumably due to his race, was not accepted until he petitioned Lodge #441 of the Grand Lodge of Ireland. This Lodge was made up of men of Irish descent – a people who had faced some prejudice themselves. They accepted Hall's petition, along with the petitions of 14 other men of color. On March 6, 1775, these were the first black men in America to become Freemasons. Their degrees were conferred upon them by John Batt, a Sergeant in the British Army and the Master of Lodge #441.[17] Records indicate that an initiation fee of three guineas was paid to Lodge #441 for each initiation.[18] This seems to be commensurate with the amount other men of the time paid.

A few weeks later, the "shot heard 'round the world" was fired at Lexington, setting off the American Revolution. The soldiers that made up Lodge #441 left with their regiment, but before departing, Master Batt gave the black members a permit to continue meeting as a Lodge, and also to be buried with Masonic rites. They reorganized as African Lodge #1 on July 3, 1776, and were issued a charter from the Grand Lodge of England in 1784.

It was directly due to Masonic connections that three black men were saved from slavery. In February, 1788, three free black men were lured on board a ship in Boston Harbor with a promise of work. One of the men, named Luck, was a member of the African Lodge. The ship set sail, stopping at other ports along the way and deceiving other black men to board the same way, with an ultimate destination in the West Indies. It is unclear exactly how Prince Hall found out about the deception, but upon his discovery of it, he immediately secured the signature of nearly two dozen other Freemasons on a petition to the General Court of Massachusetts, pressuring them to end the slave trade. His impassioned plea prompted the clergy of Boston to add their voices to the cause. In addition, the Masons addressed the case to Governor John Hancock, who was also a Freemason. (This was the same John Hancock who was the first signer of the Declaration of Independence.) Both actions were successful: the Court passed an act to prevent the slave trade and closed the ports to slave ships, and the governor sent letters to the governors of the West Indies isles, informing them of the facts of the crime. Meanwhile, the men who had been kidnapped were offered up for sale as slaves. It so happened that the man to whom they were offered was a Freemason. When Luck made himself known as a brother in the fraternity, the merchant took Luck and his friends to the governor of the island. The men were freed and returned to Boston.[19]

By 1807, the African Grand Lodge had chartered many black Lodges throughout the country. But sadly, the equality espoused by Freemasonry was not extended immediately, either by the Lodges or the citizenry. Prince Hall Lodges, as the Lodges of black men came to be known, were not recognized by any existing Grand Lodge in America as "regular" and "duly constituted," giving as a reason the fact that there already existed Grand Lodges in those jurisdictions, and there could only be one Grand Lodge in each jurisdiction. It made no difference that those existing Grand Lodges did not accept black men, giving them no other recourse. Therefore, for decades, no member of a Lodge formed under the African Grand Lodge was accepted elsewhere in the nation as a true

Mason.

It wasn't until 1994, after many decades of proving lineage to the original African Lodge chartered by the Grand Lodge of England, that the Prince Hall Grand Lodge of Massachusetts was officially recognized, paving the way for further acceptance. Today, there is still some dispute over the validity of Prince Hall Lodges, especially in the American South. Most Grand Lodges, however, do accept Prince Hall Lodges as legitimate, and Freemasonry is largely integrated in both Prince Hall and other Lodges, although there are still pockets that are segregated.

Modern Masonry

Masonry Is...

Freemasonry embraces the highest moral laws and will bear the test of any system of ethics or philosophy ever promulgated for the uplift of man.
~ Douglas MacArthur, General, Freemason

Freemasonry had an auspicious beginning. What has it been in more modern times, and why were the Ingallses interested in joining the fraternity?

Today, Freemasonry is said to be the oldest and largest fraternity in the world. There are approximately five million members worldwide; about half of those are in the United States.[1] Within the organization, all members are equal as individuals; there is no recognition of social status or class among them. The Masonic term is "on the level," and it means that a lowly laborer may meet with the President of the United States, and while in the Lodge, the President has no more prominence as a person than the laborer – they are equal as brothers. Even military courtesies (such as saluting higher officers) are not used in the Lodge room. Although an office in the Lodge, such as that of Worshipful Master, may be a higher office, the individual in the office remains on the level with the other members.

The requirements for membership are simple, yet

meaningful. Freemasonry is by ancient tradition a males-only organization, and gender is the first stipulation for joining. Why is this a meaningful requirement? Remember that Freemasonry is an ancient organization. Women were not stone masons in those times. Also, through most of history, women did not have equal legal standing with men. They were not able to make contracts or act in other legal capacities. Even today, that is still the case in some places. Much of ritual Masonry depends on the obligations made, which has always been considered a contract, and this precluded women. There are some Lodges that admit women, particularly in Europe, but since this goes against the ancient Landmarks that all Lodges have agreed to abide by, none of them are recognized as a "regular," or true, Masonic Lodge by the Grand Lodge of their jurisdiction, and other Lodges will not recognize or accept the female members of gender integrated Lodges.

A further requirement for membership is that the man must have attained the age of majority (18 or 21 years old in most cases, varying by state or region). Again, this is so that he can make contracts or take obligations legally. He must be sound in body and mind, so that he will be able to perform any needed actions, including aiding his fellow Masons in their time of distress. A Mason must be free. He cannot be a slave, although any race or ethnicity may join – and again this is so that he will be able to keep his obligations; a slave does not control his own actions and might therefore be unable to fulfill a commitment made. Finally, the man must hold a belief in a Supreme Being, and be of high moral character. Applicants are screened – investigated by a committee of three Masons, including a background check – and a criminal record will bar admittance unless there are some mitigating circumstances. Generally, a reputation as being anything less than an honest, upright individual will result in an applicant being blackballed. Literally: that's where the expression came from. Applicants are voted on by the membership using a secret ballot of black (rejecting) and white (accepting) balls placed in the ballot box.

An antique ballot box of De Smet Lodge #55 A. F. & A. M.

Many people believe Masonry is a religion. This is a misconception. Freemasonry is a fraternity, not a religion. There is no special God or theology for Masons, and a Mason may be of any religion or faith, as long as he is not an atheist. Many of the founding fathers of America who were Masons were deists.

One reason confusion exists about the nature of the organization is the spiritual aspect of the fraternity. Faith is an important value in Freemasonry. Masons are admonished to seek the blessing of Deity before commencing any important undertaking. Furthermore, they are instructed to diligently study the Sacred Law.

> *Adopting no particular creed, forbidding all sectarian discussion within the Lodgeroom, but urging each to be steadfast in the faith of his profession, Masonry would take every good man by the hand, lead him to its altar, point to the open Bible thereon, and urge that he direct his way through life by the light he there shall find... Read it, study it, and implement in your daily life the precepts contained in it.[2]*

This spiritual aspect of the fraternity was in harmony

with the values of the Ingalls family. The faith of the family is shown from the very first book. In the books which portray the family as living in or near town, church attendance is regular whenever possible; when not possible, they have "Sunday School at home," including prayers and memorizing scriptures from the time they were very young.[3]

In *Little House in the Big Woods*, the family was meant to be far from civilization, so that the story would revolve around the family, all working together, with little distraction from secondary characters or events. Thus, the family does not attend church in the story. Nevertheless, their faith is shown through the religious observance of the Sabbath. Although they did not go out, they all dressed in their best Sunday clothes, and no work or boisterous play was permitted. They read the Bible, and Charles played "Sunday hymns, for even the fiddle must not sing the week-day songs on Sundays."[4]

In *On the Banks of Plum Creek*, the Ingalls family moved to town, and they were able to attend the new church which was built. After the first service,

> On the way home Pa said, "Well, Caroline, it's pleasant to be with a crowd of people all trying to do the right thing, same as we are."
> "Yes, Charles," Ma said, thankfully. "It will be a pleasure to look forward to, all week."
> ...After that they went to Sunday school every Sunday.[5]

When the family moved to De Smet, they again were founding members of the church, with regular attendance. But their faith extended to more than just going to services, as shown by a conversation Laura has with her blind sister, Mary:

> "But – it isn't so much thinking, as – as just knowing. Just being sure of the goodness of God." [Mary said.]
> Everyone knows that God is good. But it seemed to Laura then that Mary must be sure of it in

42

some special way.

"You are sure, aren't you?" Laura said.

"Yes, I am sure of it now all the time," Mary answered.[6]

Laura felt this herself. She wrote in her autobiography, *Pioneer Girl*:

> *One night while saying my prayers as I always did before going to bed, this feeling of homesickness and worry was worse than usual, but gradually I had a feeling of a hovering encompassing Presence of a Power, comforting and sustaining and thought in surprise, "This is what men call God!"*[7]

She was able to face her hardships with renewed strength of purpose. This was important enough to Laura that she wrote of it, even though she felt that a person's faith should be private: "It seemed to me that the things between one and God should be between him and God," she wrote.[8] She didn't think one should speak of their faith publicly, yet faith was so integral to who the Ingallses were that she could not help but include references to it in her books.

Farmer Boy emphasized the faith of the Wilders, with regular church attendance, prayers before meals, and a belief in a Providence that rewarded virtue, exemplified by the story of the stray dog. Mother did not like dogs on the farm, but she showed compassion to a lost dog and fed it a good meal. The dog then chased away a would-be robber that night. Mother explained that Providence sent the dog as a test, and said, "Maybe the Lord was merciful to us because we were merciful to him [the dog]."[9]

Although faith is required of members, this does not make the fraternity of Freemasonry a religion. Masonry imposes no theological creed or doctrine of its own, as a religion, by definition, does. It also makes no claims of salvation.

The founders of the modern Lodges (beginning in 1717) were influenced by the times and culture in which they lived. They believed that there can be no morality outside of that imposed by a Supreme Being. Having this belief as a prerequisite to membership would, they felt, ensure that every member had some basis of good character, and some guide by which to plot his spiritual growth. Thus, Freemasonry urges each Mason to practice the faith of his own choosing, in accordance with a Supreme Being as each member understands the concept.

This is not an uncommon idea for organizations that are not religions: the Boy Scouts of America, for example, has the same requirement. Like the Boy Scouts of America, Freemasonry is merely a fellowship – a fraternity, and one in which members are free to hold any beliefs they choose.

Many individuals who believe Freemasonry is a religion and in some way opposed to Christianity, or even satanic, also believe that America was founded as a Christian nation. Understanding that most of the founding fathers of America were Freemasons, it becomes clear that it is impossible for both beliefs to be true.

An Internet search will provide lists of hundreds of men who have been Freemasons, including influential religious leaders such as Jean-Henri Dunant (founder of the Red Cross and a founder of the Young Men's Christian Association), William Miller (renowned Baptist preacher), Raymond Apple (Chief Rabbi, The Great Synagogue Sydney, Australia), William Howley (90th Archbishop of Canterbury), Robert E. B. Baylor (Baptist minister and founder of Baylor University), and Derwyn Owen (Archbishop of Toronto).[10] These men did not praise God one day and then worship Satan a few nights later at the Lodge. Nor did men such as George Washington, Charles Ingalls or Almanzo Wilder, or their female relatives in the Order of the Eastern Star. It is obvious that the men of the fraternity were – and are – upstanding citizens, of high moral character, industrious in working for positive change, and would never be involved in such nefarious activities as some claim Masonry to be.

It may surprise those questioning the religious attributes

of the fraternity to learn that during Lodge meetings, no religious dogma or creed may be advanced, nor any political agenda. The meetings are "no religion or politics" zones, as Lodges are to promote unity, not discord.

Other people question the titles used within the Lodge, such as "Worshipful Master." These titles are vestigial, as they were designated in an era when such honorary titles were common. Consider titles used for royalty or persons of authority in various places, such as "Your Majesty" or "My Lord." In England, Lord Mayors are even called "Worshipful." The titles of Freemasonry are used in a similar way, and are not literally indicative of worship.

The use of altars within the Lodge building is another area of apprehension to some people. I know of a few persons who believed Masons held some kind of blood sacrifice on the altars. That is certainly not the case. The altar is used in the Lodge in both a physical and a metaphorical sense. Physically, the altar holds the Sacred Law, or Scriptures, of its members. In most Lodges in America, where almost all Masons are Christian, the Bible is openly displayed. Where members are primarily of other faiths, they may display other Scriptures, such as the Torah, Koran, or Vedas. In all cases, the placement of the Sacred Law on the altar is a symbol of the light of Divine Will that should guide a man's life, and the altar's location in the middle of the Lodge room makes it equally accessible to all, so that all may be reminded of the precepts of the scripture it holds and the place its teachings should have in their lives.

Metaphorically, the altar is the center of the gathering as a place of covenant and refuge, and a symbol of union and fellowship where all men are equal beneath the Supreme Being. Altars are traditionally places of sacrifice and dedication. In Masonry, members are reminded to sacrifice their vices, and to dedicate their actions toward betterment of self and society. The altar in the Masonic Lodge is a tangible, though not physically used, expression of these ideas.

Another cause of concern to some is the secrecy of the fraternity. Freemasonry is sometimes mistakenly called a "secret society," but Masonry is not a secret at all. Everyone knows about it, and its Lodges are brazenly marked. It is instead a society with secrets. Supposedly, anyway; there really aren't that many secrets. Benjamin Franklin wrote in 1730, "Their Grand Secret is That they have no Secret at all."[11] In these modern days of the information superhighway, there is more truth to his statement than Franklin would have thought possible, and even the few things that Masons wanted to keep secret are no longer.

Why does the fraternity have secrets at all? Remember that in the beginning there was a practical purpose for the secret words and signs: to convey, without the time, effort and cost of actually sculpting something, a mason's level of skill and trustworthiness in a time when there was no other means to do so.

The secret works (signs, words, and rituals) used today are symbolic of this trustworthiness. If a man cannot keep a mere word or hand signal secret, how is he to be trusted with your business, your wife, or anything else of importance? The ability to know that a fellow Mason will treat you honestly in business, care for your wife or widow, keep his word, and render aid when needed: these were – and remain – important characteristics within the Lodge.

The secret words and signs also give Masons a means to identify one another, and know upon meeting, that this is a brother Mason, who has taken an oath which includes helping fellow Masons or their family if needed. It may be easy to overlook the importance of this, but to those living in times or places that make it difficult to know who can be trusted, such as in Nazi Germany, these secret words and signs can mean safety or even life.[12] There are many stories of Masons recognizing one another in troubled times and coming to each other's aid. During the Civil War, a Confederate soldier named Newton experienced this aid:

> My father had been a soldier in the Union Army...Taken prisoner at Arkansas Post, he was carried up the Mississippi River to Rock Island, Illinois... My father became...desperately ill, and made himself known as a Mason to an officer of the camp. The officer took him to his own home and nursed him back to life. When the war ended, he loaned Father money to pay his way back to his Texas home, and gave him a pearl-handled pistol to protect himself. They remained close friends. This experience of my father, when I learned about it, had a very great influence upon my life...the fact that such a fraternity of men could exist, mitigating the harshness of war, and remain unbroken when states and churches were torn in two, became a wonder...[13]

A paper for the Minnesota Lodge of Research reports many other instances of aid and even lives saved, including the case of Margaret Rea, a Southern woman whose home was plundered by Union soldiers. When she became afraid for her personal virtue and her life, she gave the Masonic sign of distress, which her husband had taught her to give if she was in danger. The soldier in charge was a Freemason, and ordered that her belongings be returned to her and she be left unharmed.[14]

Even when the aid is less than life-saving, it can be life-impacting, as shown by the following account of another Civil War soldier and prisoner of war:

I was a prisoner of war for four months, in the prison at Danville, Virginia... I was not a mason during the war, but what I saw there of masonry, induced me to join the beneficent order, and I was made a mason in 1866. I saw what the order did for a brother, as several of those who were masons were treated much better than others; they were taken out of prison on their word as a mason, that they would not attempt to escape – most of the Confederate officers being masons, and they faithfully observed their vows.[15]

"Friend to Friend: A Brotherhood Undivided" is a sculpture by Ron Tunison located at Gettysburg field. It depicts Union General Winfield Scott Hancock rendering aid to his friend and brother in Freemasonry, Confederate General Lewis Addison Armistead. General Armistead is entrusting his personal effects to his friend.

As important as this benefit has been to Masons, the fraternity's primary purpose is not saving lives. Rather, the goal of Freemasonry is, as it was in days of old, building. Today Masons are building not structures and a physical society, but rather character and a better communal society. Freemasonry is often defined as "a system of morality, veiled in allegory and illustrated by symbols." The stated aim of the fraternity is "making good men better." The organization seeks to meet this goal by focusing on lessons that strengthen relationships; promote honesty and brotherly love; encourage education, tolerance, and charity; and seek meaning in the universe and nature, and man's place in it.[16]

This is accomplished through association with like-minded men also seeking personal growth and truth, and by learning from the ancient wisdom of the craft, whose degrees, or stages of advancement within the society, represent movement from darkness and ignorance to light and knowledge. The steps through the degrees include self-examination, determination of values, resolution to keep those values, and making all actions consistent with them. The lessons of each degree are taught through ritual dramas in which the initiate takes part in acting out various scenes from the building of King Solomon's Temple. The continual use of signs and symbols from those dramatic rituals reinforces the lessons.

When a man who has been approved for membership is initiated into the first degree of the Craft, he is known as an Entered Apprentice. He is a Mason, but is only beginning his journey of becoming a "better man." The lessons he now learns in the Lodge lay the foundation for his ascent to a higher character. He is taught the importance of trust and keeping secrets, and takes an obligation to protect the secret parts of the Craft. He is also taught the importance of seeking and obtaining knowledge, and given tools which aid his quest for it. Furthermore, he is shown how to apply that knowledge to his life. When he has learned these lessons, he may be passed to the second degree, that of Fellowcraft.

In the second degree of Fellowcraft, a Mason is taught how to apply the lessons previously learned beyond himself, to his relations with his brethren. The obligation for this degree stresses assistance to brother Masons. He is encouraged to be an active builder of society, and receives guidance as to various ways this may be achieved. When ready, he is then raised to the third degree of Master Mason.

In days of old, a mason did not sculpt his masterpiece (the piece that proved he possessed the skill of a master) and then say, "Now that I'm a master, there's nothing more to learn." On the contrary, he worked harder than ever before, and, if he was a true master, continued to learn and improve and refine his craft. So today, reaching the degree of Master Mason does not mean a man has learned all there is to learn or achieved all there is to achieve. Instead, it signifies that he is ready and able to live his life in harmony with the virtues extolled by Freemasonry, even as he continues to learn, and he is also equipped to help others do the same.

In this way Freemasonry helps men learn and practice their duties in an expanding realm, from self, to fellow Lodge members, to community and society at large. Those duties are expressed in the Masonic principles of Brotherly Love, Relief, and Truth – the "golden tenets" of the Craft.[17]

Brotherly love refers to the concept that the whole human race is one family, bound to aid, support, and protect each other. It unites men of every country, sect, and opinion in true friendship, and reminds members that they are to work together toward a peaceful society in which all people are treated with courtesy and respect. This brotherly affection is the "cement," or "mortar," which bonds the brotherhood together, and each member acts as a symbolic trowel, distributing this mortar to build a harmonious civilization.

Relief alludes to soothing and comforting the sorrow of others, and relieving distress whenever possible. It also implies charitable assistance to those in need, whether with financial aid or in service to them.

Truth can be thought of as the sum of knowledge and wisdom. As such, shows a Mason how to adhere to his high moral standards and fulfill his obligations to himself, his brothers, and his community. Because truth banishes hypocrisy and deceit, it is considered the foundation of every virtue.

In addition to the three golden tenets, Freemasonry promotes the "cardinal virtues" of temperance, fortitude, prudence, and justice. Temperance is due restraint that frees the body and mind from the allurements of vice. A Mason should avoid excess, as well as any licentious habit that could subject him to contempt. Fortitude is defined in the Craft as the steady purpose of mind which enables a man to endure pain, peril, or danger when necessary. Prudence guides Masons to wisely judge all things based on future as well as present consequences. Justice is that standard of right which allows him to render to every man his due, without distinction. Masons are instructed to cultivate these virtues everywhere and at all times.[18]

These same virtues were important to Laura and her family. Fortitude was purposely cultivated by practicing self-denial, even at times they did not need to, such as by putting aside much desired stories until a future date. In addition, although the family members look out for one another, no one is coddled; even young children must do their part to help. The result is shown in their ability to persevere through so many calamities, such as loss of crops, loss of home, entire winters (even years) of deprivation, and illness. After a series of events leaves the family in poverty and one daughter blind, Caroline, though heartbroken, is able to carry on. Her reaction to such hardship is shown in this passage from *By the Shores of Silver Lake*:

> *"Sometimes it is hard to be resigned to God's will. We all had scarlet fever in our place on Plum Creek, and for a while it was hard to get along. But I'm thankful that all the children were spared to us. Mary is a great comfort to me, Brother Alden. She has never once repined."*

> *"Mary is a rare soul, and a lesson to all of us,"*
> *said Reverend Alden. "We must remember that*
> *whom the Lord loveth, He chasteneth, and a*
> *brave spirit will turn all our afflictions to good."* [19]

Even in great difficulties, Caroline looked for something to be thankful for, and was comforted when she found it. Reverend Alden's words convey the message that fortitude is rewarded. Caroline puts it another way in *Little Town on the Prairie*: "'This earthly life is a battle,' said Ma. 'If it isn't one thing to contend with, it's another. It always has been so, and it always will be. The sooner you make up your mind to that, the better off you are, and the more thankful for your pleasures.'" [20]

Since they were written primarily for children, the *Little House* books do not address adult issues, such as temperance, a great deal; still, they leave no doubt as to the Ingalls' stand on alcoholic beverages:

> *"Two saloons in this town are just two saloons*
> *too many."*
> *"It's a pity more men don't say the same," said*
> *Ma. "I begin to believe that if there isn't a stop*
> *put to the liquor traffic, women must bestir*
> *themselves and have something to say about it."*
> *Pa twinkled at her. "Seems to me you have plenty*
> *to say, Caroline. Ma never left me in doubt as to*
> *the evil of drink, nor you either."* [21]

The value lessons of Freemasonry are reinforced by the symbols and rituals of the craft. Probably the most widely recognized symbols in Freemasonry are the square and compasses. In the craft of masonry, the square is a tool with an angle of 90 degrees, and is used to ensure that the edges of a stone subtend the same angle for accuracy. In the Craft of Masonry, the square symbolizes morality, truthfulness, and honesty; the duties of a Mason to his Brothers and neighbors. Masons are obliged to square their actions by the square of virtue. The symbolism of the square has become so ingrained that it has become common to speak of "a square deal" for any honest transaction.

Likewise, compasses, to the trade mason, are a set of implements used for the admeasurements of the blueprints, to ensure precise proportions which will lend stability and aesthetic beauty to the finished work. In Freemasonry, this tool is emblematic of circumscribing passions and keeping desire within due bounds; the duty of a Mason to himself, and the measure of his life. The square and compasses, along with the Sacred Law – which outlines a Mason's duty to his Creator – are known as the Three Great Lights of Masonry.[22]

Square and compasses, left; 24-inch gauge, right.

The lesson of balance in one's life is illustrated by the 24-inch gauge. This tool is a 24-inch long rule, divided into three parts of eight inches each. For a working mason, it is used to take the measurements of the stone to be sculpted. For a Freemason, the divisions of the tool symbolize hours in the day, and teach him to divide his day into three parts, devoting one portion to the service of others, another portion to his occupation, and the final portion to sleep and refreshment: time management lessons from a 24-inch gauge. There are many more such symbols used in the character building lessons of the Craft.[23]

These symbols remind Masons of their obligation to apply the associated value lessons in their daily lives. Being symbolic, there is room for each individual to add his own interpretation to the lessons based on his personal experiences, and discover even deeper meanings. Thus he may find new ways to implement the values into his life; he may even share his insight with his fellow Masons so that they, too, may benefit from it.

Does this mean that all Masons are perfect men, or nearly so? Not at all. As with any group, there are those who join simply for prestige, and give no more thought to their values and morals than the "libertine" that Masons are advised to avoid. You may look throughout history and find men of unsavory character who were Masons. You may even find that some of the best men – and Masons – had (and have) beliefs or ideals that are opposed to the ideals of the Craft and of human decency, such as those men of old who supported slavery. George Washington did great and wonderful things, but he was also a slave owner. However, as the primary goal of Freemasonry is self- and societal improvement, those who have no interest in such ideals do not generally have an interest in affiliating with the organization. Perhaps the tenet of equality in Freemasonry was one factor which influenced Washington into eventually freeing his slaves. Furthermore, although most all Masons, like most all men, struggle with various aspects of their character, Masonry provides them a useful tool to use in the challenge. Thus, despite the few exceptions which may be found, the vast majority of Masons are men of honor and integrity, who adhere to and promote the tenets of brotherly love, relief, and other principles of the fraternity.

When is a man a Mason? Joseph Fort Newton answered:

When he can look out over the rivers, the hills and the far horizon with a profound sense of his own littleness in the vast scheme of things, and yet have faith, hope and courage, which is the root of every virtue. When he...seeks to know, to forgive and to love his fellow man. When he knows how to sympathize with men in their sorrows, yea even in their sins - knowing that each man fights a hard fight against many odds. When he has learned how to make friends and to keep them and above all, how to keep friends with himself...

> *When he can be happy and high-minded amid the meaner drudgeries of life...When no voice of distress reaches his ears in vain, and no hand seeks his aid without response...in his hand a sword for evil, in his heart a bit of a song; glad to live, but not afraid to die! Such a man has found the only secret of Freemasonry, and the one which it is trying to give to all the world."* [24]

Readers of Laura Ingalls Wilder's works recognize these same themes. Consider the titles of some of her articles for the *Missouri Ruralist*: "Making the Best of Things;" "Learning to Work Together;" "If We Only Understood;" "Do the Right Thing Always;" and "Your Code of Honor," to name just a few. It is becoming clearer why Laura and other members of her family were drawn to the fraternity of Freemasonry.

Charity

> *What is the use of living, if it not be to strive for noble causes and to make this muddled world a better place for those who will live in it after we are gone?*
> ~ Winston Churchill, U.K. Prime Minister, Freemason

In ancient masonic societies, the box charity was an important part of the fraternity. It provided a way for the members to care for one another, and each other's families, in a time when there was little to no other means of doing so. Due to this precedent, "relief," or charity, became one of the main tenets of Freemasonry, and it remains so today. This tenet is taken seriously by most Masons. In harmony with its stated aims, Freemasonry has broadened its realm of charity through the years from only members and families to the world at large. Today, in the United States alone, Freemasons collectively contribute an average of over $2.6 million every single day to charitable causes, in addition to rendering service as relief.[25] The charitable efforts of the fraternity draw many new members seeking a way to make a difference and work in concert with others to the betterment of both self and society.

Probably the best known Masonic charities are the Shriners Hospitals for Children. There are 22 of these Hospitals in three countries. They specialize in treating children with orthopedic conditions, severe burns, cleft lip and palate, and spinal cord injury. Until recently, the operation of every Shriners Hospital, from the building to the care, from the doctors to the equipment, was paid entirely by Masonic charity. During the recession of 2008, the Hospitals began collecting payments from the insurance company of patients who have insurance; however, they never bill or collect any payment from any patient. All costs not covered by the insurance are paid through charitable donations, the majority of which come from Freemasons.

Other well-known charities of Masons include Scottish Rite Children's Medical Centers, RiteCare clinics, which aid children in language development, and the many educational grants and scholarships of Scottish Rite Masons. Lesser well known charities include grants and foundations providing support to groups such as The Humanitarian Foundation, the Alzheimer's Association, State Mental Health Associations, Autism programs, the Deafness Research Foundation, Military outreach programs, child identification programs, cancer research projects, The Arthritis Fund, and programs for at-risk children, to name just a few.

In addition, the Masonic Service Association of North America has donated over $9.5 billion since its inception in 1923 for relief to those affected by disasters such as earthquakes, floods and terrorism.[26]

These are mind-boggling numbers, especially when one considers that the total charity of Freemasonry has increased steadily through the years, even at times the fraternity itself declined in membership. When the contributions of Masons in the rest of the world are added, the picture of Masonic charity is monumental. But financial aid is only one part of the philanthropy; service to others is equally important.

Again, there are many ways Masons fulfill this standard. Most Lodges have service programs that might include such things as volunteering at local shelters or soup kitchens, cleaning highways or other areas of the community, visiting those in extended care facilities, or volunteering in mentoring programs. Many Lodges support organizations such as law enforcement, fire fighters, and first responders, the military, or other groups or individuals working in service to others, such as by funding life insurance programs for them, providing needed items, or lending a helping hand however they can. Some Masons go as groups to areas of natural or human-caused disasters to work in any way they are able. On a more personal level, home-bound or ill members can generally count on visitations from their fraternal brothers; widows may rely on their late husbands' fellow Masons to help care for yard work, home maintenance, or other chores; and other people of the community may depend on Masons to extend whatever aid they may reasonably be able to give.

It is wonderfully evident that by and large, the men of the Craft live up to their ideal of "relief."

Education

Next in importance to freedom and justice is popular education, without which neither freedom nor justice can be permanently maintained.
~ James Garfield, U.S. President, Freemason

As seeking knowledge and truth is so fundamental to Freemasonry, one would expect education to be highly valued among Masons, and that is indeed the case. If making better men is the primary goal of Masonry, education is a primary means of doing so. The education of life lessons received in the Lodge is an important way to accomplish this, but Masons also value traditional education, and they have championed its promotion for hundreds of years. The fraternity has been instrumental in organizing the free public educational systems in Europe and in the United States, so much so that one man wrote of Benjamin Franklin and his fellow Masons, "The people who are the promoters of the free schools are Grand Masters and Wardens among Freemasons, their very pillars."[27] He was right. Historically, education was available only to those able to pay for private schools or tutors, but Masons of those days believed every citizen should be educated, to provide the best opportunity for success, both individually and collectively. That is why Franklin and other Freemasons were among the most ardent promoters of education for all, to be brought about by schools which were free to all citizens. As Samuel Adams (signer of the Declaration of Independence and Freemason) wrote to his cousin, John Adams (second President of the United States):

> *Wise and judicious modes of education, patronized and supported by communities, will draw together the sons of the rich and the poor, among whom it makes no distinction; it will cultivate the natural genius, elevate the soul, excite laudable emulation to excel in knowledge, piety, and benevolence; and, finally, it will reward its patrons and benefactors, by shedding its benign influence on the public mind. Education inures men to thinking and reflection, to reasoning and demonstration. It discovers to them the moral and religious duties they owe to God, their country, and to all mankind...Education leads youth to "the study of human nature, society, and universal history," from whence they may "draw all the principles" of political architecture which*

ought to be regarded. All men are "interested in the truth." Education, by showing them "the end of all its consequences," would induce at least the greatest numbers to enlist on its side. The man of good understanding, who has been well-educated, and improves these advantages, as far as his circumstances will allow, in promoting the happiness of mankind, in my opinion, and I am inclined to think in yours, is indeed "well-born." [28]

More than merely advantageous, Masons believe that a free system of public education is absolutely essential to maintain a free society, as it is the only means of ensuring equal opportunity to all. This idea is so entrenched within Freemasonic principles that the very rituals of the Masonic degrees stress pursuing knowledge in the various branches of science, mathematics, and the liberal arts.

W. E. B. Du Bois, a renowned educator and Freemason, once remarked that "education among all kinds of men always has had, and always will have, an element of danger and revolution, of dissatisfaction and discontent."[29] While some people feared that providing an education to the so-called "lower classes" would cause them to be dissatisfied with their lot and attempt to displace the "upper class," Masons recognized that these same feelings of discontent are what inspire people to work and fight for a better life, and that persons striving for that better life are less likely to allow tyranny to rule over them. This is why the public education system is so valued and ardently promoted by Masons: it is the desire to advance equal opportunity and access to knowledge as a means of ensuring our society's continuing freedom.

How has Freemasonry lived up to its ideal of enabling all to seek knowledge? Here are a few of the ways:[30]

"The Grand Father of Texas Education," Republic of Texas President and Grand Master Mirabeau Lamar, convinced the legislature to set aside three leagues of land for each county to equip schools, paving the way for public schools in Texas. In addition, he allotted 50 leagues of land for the support of two universities: Texas A. & M. and the University of Texas. Many of Texas' first grade schools and schools of higher education were operated in buildings owned and erected by Masonic Lodges.

Freemasons in Tennessee established the Masonic University of Tennessee, which later became Rhodes College.

Grand Master Benjamin Franklin urged the adoption of a public school system in Pennsylvania, and helped organize the University of Pennsylvania.

West Point Military Academy was proposed by Henry Knox, founded by Henry Burbeck, and supported by George Washington, all Masons. Washington also founded a free school in Alexandria, Virginia.

Philadelphia Lodge #2 states the following in their minutes for February 13, 1781:

> *A Representation of the unfortunate situation of the family of Brethren of Bro. Ad Betten deceas'd being laid before this Lodge from the Brethren of No. 29 it was therefore unanimously agreed that this Lodge pay Ten pounds specie, annually towards the Education of our deceased Bros. Eldest son until he is able to procure a subsistence for himself.*

This is but one example among too many to count of Masons offering financial assistance for education.

The first normal school in America was opened in a portion of the Masonic Temple at Lexington, Massachusetts.

The Grand Lodge of Virginia set up the first Grand Lodge Educational Fund in 1812.

Prince Hall petitioned the Massachusetts legislature on two separate occasions for a school program for African American children. When these attempts failed, he opened a school in his own home. Since then, Prince Hall Lodges have contributed greatly to the education of African Americans, including numerous scholarships. Just between 1991 and 2013, the Prince Hall Memorial, Education and Scholarship Fund gave over $400,000 in scholarships to California students.

The University of Georgia was founded by Freemason Abraham Baldwin.

A group of Masons laid the cornerstone for the University of North Carolina, the first state-funded college in the country. They were presided over by William Davie, a state legislator and Grand Master of North Carolina, today remembered as the father of the University of North Carolina.

Other colleges founded by Masons include Dickinson College (John Dickinson), Oneida Academy (Michael Myers), Hamilton College (Samuel Kirkland), Baylor University (R. E. B. Baylor) and Girard College (Stephen Girard).

Freemason Francis Bellamy wrote the Pledge of Allegiance specifically for a celebration honoring patriotism and public schools. In a speech for that same program, he referred to public schools as the "great American institution that united the nation."

Various Grand Lodges in the United States have founded 88 public colleges in eleven different states. These were among the first universities to accept students regardless of religious affiliation, and often offered free tuition to deserving students.

California superintendent of public instruction John Swett, Freemason, organized teachers' institutes, established a teacher certification system, won support for school taxes, revised school law, and provided for textbooks in public schools throughout the state.

The Grand Lodge of Arkansas established one of the state's first institutions of higher education, St. John's College, in 1859; in 1853, it had established the second public library in Arkansas.

Grand Master De Witt Clinton, when Governor of New York, espoused the cause of public schools so fervently and successfully that he became known as the Father of Public Schools in New York.

Today, millions of dollars each year are collectively given by Freemasons to scholarships, teacher awards, and other aids to education.

These are but a few examples illustrating the efforts of Freemasons to ensure that all citizens are able to acquire an education.

Throughout the series of *Little House* books, education is shown as a privilege, to be taken advantage of whenever possible. Education is one point Caroline was firm on, eliciting a promise from her husband that they would settle down where the girls would be able to attend school. Charles explains to Laura in *On the Banks of Plum Creek*:

> "...it isn't everybody that gets a chance to learn to read and write and cipher. Your Ma was a school-teacher when we met, and when she came west with me I promised that our girls would have a chance to get book learning. That's why we stopped here, so close to a town that has a school...Be thankful you've got the chance, Laura." [31]

When they were not near a school, Caroline taught the girls at home, just as she provided religious training when they could not attend church. That she was diligent in her instruction is proved by the fact that whenever the girls were able to return to school, they were not behind in their classes. [32]

As a schoolteacher herself, Laura was reluctant to let even 30 minutes of education be lost, as shown in this passage from *These Happy Golden Years*: "At half past three they were all so cold that she thought of dismissing school early. The mile that Martha and Charles must walk, worried her. On the other hand, she should not cut short the pupils' opportunity for learning, and this was not a blizzard." At the end of the term, she reminded her students of the importance of an education, telling them that if they "cannot have much help in getting one, you can each help yourself to an education if you try," just "as Lincoln did." [33]

Mary and Laura first attended school in Pepin, Wisconsin.
Mary was six years old; Laura was only four.

Patriotism

> *True patriotism springs from a belief in the dignity of the individual, freedom and equality not only for Americans but for all people on earth, universal brotherhood and good will, and a constant and earnest striving toward the principles and ideals on which this country was founded.*
> ~ Eleanor Roosevelt, First Lady of the U.S., member of the Order of the Eastern Star

Patriotism is an ideal that has always been advanced by Freemasonry. Among the very first lessons a newly initiated Mason learns is loyalty to one's country. In the first charge he receives, he is instructed to be "a quiet and peaceful subject, true to your government, and just to your country; you are not to countenance disloyalty or rebellion, but patiently submit to legal authority, and conform with cheerfulness to the government of the country in which you live." This is reinforced in each degree within the Craft. Master Masons are told that they should be exemplary in the discharge of their civic duties, never losing sight of the allegiance due their native land.[34]

How was it that America's founding fathers, many of them Freemasons who were supposed to remain loyal to their government, became so involved in promoting the Revolution? The answer may be found by considering the service of Freemason John Paul Jones, who became America's first naval hero.

Jones was a Scotsman, who arrived in the Americas just as the Revolution was breaking out. Though not a colonist, he joined the Continental Navy. His reason: "Though I have drawn my sword in the present generous struggle for the rights of men, yet I am not in arms as an American. I profess myself a citizen of the world, totally unfettered by the little mean distinctions which diminish the benevolence of the heart and set bounds to philanthropy," he wrote to one friend, and to another, "I have drawn my sword only from motives of philanthropy, and in support of the dignity of human nature." His service stemmed from "a love of liberty, a concern for 'the Violated rights of Mankind,' and a sense of universal philanthropy," ideals promoted by Masonry.[35]

Similarly, George Washington considered himself a loyal British subject with no wish "to set up for independency," and he was "as well satisfied as I can be of my existence that no such thing is desired by any thinking man in all North America; on the contrary, that it is the ardent wish of the warmest advocates for liberty, that peace and tranquility, upon constitutional grounds, may be restored, and the horrors of civil discord prevented."[36] He believed that if war came, it would be a civil war, among British subjects on each side of the Atlantic, but he hoped for reconciliation instead. In 1775, the Continental Congress sent an "Olive Branch" letter to King George III, suggesting a peaceful resolution. This was in harmony with Freemasonry's ideals. It was not until the king rejected this overture and hired Hessian soldiers – foreigners – to fight the colonists that Washington fully committed to the American cause. The importance of liberty and justice for all outweighed the duty of loyalty to the Crown. While every Revolutionist had his own turning point, each one had to become convinced that continued British governance was detrimental to the colonists, and that the greater good of society was served by revolution. Love of country is admirable, but love of man, and striving for the best for all men, is even more admirable and noble.

That is why patriotism is not in conflict with an organization that claims to be a universal Brotherhood of men from every nation. True patriotism is not a boastful pride and feeling of superiority; rather, it is a recognition of all that is good and honorable in one's own country. Patriotism and nationalism are often confused. Patriotism has been defined as a charitable and generous love of country; nationalism, as an unconditional loyalty and exclusive attachment to the nation.[37] Nationalism can be manipulated and used to the detriment of the people, the way Hitler was able to use the normal patriotic instincts of the people as tools to further his agenda. Reich Marshall Herman Goering said, "Naturally the common people don't want war...the people can always be brought to the bidding of the leaders. That is easy. All you have to do is to tell them they are being attacked, and denounce the pacifists for lack of patriotism and exposing the country to danger. It works the same in any country."[38]

That is not the ideal espoused by Freemasonry. The patriotism advanced by the fraternity involves duties and responsibilities as well as privileges. As two Past Grand Masters put it:

> *Loyalty carries with it the highest obligation of citizenship – obedience to law, respect for constitutional authority, a recognition of the right of every human being to the enjoyment of life, liberty and the pursuit of happiness. The rights we enjoy as citizens carry with them corresponding duties. Among these duties is the careful and intelligent consideration of men and measures coming before the people for approval in our nation's electoral process. No good Freemason will fail to be a good citizen, and to be found on the side of decency, civic righteousness, and public order... Order has been and must continue to be the greatest force of all time on the*

*side of individual liberty and the dignity of man,
and fighting against tyranny and usurpation…
As Freemasons, our field is the whole world, but
our solicitude is to our own country – as it makes
its unique and priceless contribution to universal
good. With due reverence for other nations, and
by loyalty to our own flag, we best serve the whole
human race.*[39]

Lodges support many patriotic activities, and there are many Masonic clubs devoted to those who serve their country. Masons have also formed groups to promote patriotism in the public, such as the National Sojourners, which are military veterans of the fraternity, who travel the country presenting programs on American history and ideals. Veterans groups and similar organizations are often the recipient of Masonic charity, receiving both donations and volunteer work.[40]

Patriotism is also stressed in the *Little House* books, with several chapters in various books devoted to Independence Day. "Hurray!" Charles shouts one Fourth of July. "We're Americans!" The reason for his sentiment is demonstrated in both *Farmer Boy* and *Little Town on the Prairie*, which describe the celebration and quote parts of the Declaration of Independence. "It gave them a solemn, glorious feeling to hear the words;" even the children are proud to be Americans. The pride they felt was not in believing they were better than other peoples, but in the ideals of their country – freedom, liberty, and independence: "everyone was happy because they were free and independent." [41]

Organization

*The achievements of an organization are the
results of the combined effort of each individual.*
~ Vince Lombardi, Pro Football Hall of Fame
coach, Freemason

It takes a lot of organization to accomplish all that

Freemasons achieve in their charitable and other efforts. Internal structure is not usually the most exciting thing to learn about, but it is necessary to understand the role various Ingalls family members played in the local Lodges and Chapters, so let's look at how the organization is arranged.[42]

At the top is…no one. Not only is there no one person at the head of the organization, there is no one committee, group, or Lodge above all either. Instead, there are a number of Grand Lodges, all of whom have agreed to abide by certain ancient "Landmarks" derived from the Old Charges. Each Grand Lodge has authority within its jurisdiction, so the Grand Lodge of New York, for example, can't make rules for a local Lodge in Texas. The Grand Lodge of New York has authority over all, and only, the local Lodges of New York. This authority is defined and delineated in each Grand Lodge's Constitution. New Grand Lodges are given authority from the nearest existing Grand Lodge when there are enough local Lodges in a geographic area to warrant it.

Beneath the Grand Lodge are its jurisdictional local Lodges, often called "blue Lodges." Although the definitive origin of the term has been lost to history, the most commonly accepted theory is that it came from the color of the heavens, symbolic of eternity and immortality. Today, blue reminds Masons that their virtues should be as expansive as the blue dome of heavens. Each blue Lodge has its own constitution, approved by its Grand Lodge.

The officers which make up a Lodge may vary between jurisdictions, but since they are based on the oral tradition of antiquity, there is much similarity. Following is a brief description of the most common offices, so that when records show, for instance, that Charles Ingalls held the office of Junior Deacon, that will be understood.

The highest office is the Master of the Lodge, called the Worshipful Master. The term is honorific, not religious. The Master is elected by his Lodge each year, and he has unequaled authority within his Lodge. As long as he operates within the

Constitution and By-Laws of his Lodge, he may run things the way he sees fit, and he has final say regarding anything pertaining to the Lodge. His duty is to "set the Craft to work and give them wholesome instructions for their labor." In addition to presiding at meetings, the Master is responsible for the initiation and training of new members, the instruction of all members, and outreach to others. In fact, the Master is responsible for every facet of the Lodge, its work, and its members. Of course he has help: the other officers and usually a few appointed committees assist in carrying out the various duties. Also, in actual practice, blue Lodges are run democratically, in accordance with their by-laws, and votes are taken to decide most issues. Still, the Master is ultimately in charge. One thing he may not do, however, is "make innovations in the body of Masonry." In other words, even the Master of the Lodge cannot change the rituals or ancient customs and traditions of the Craft.

Each office has a corresponding "jewel" or symbol. These derive from the custom of officials, such as Mayors or

Jewels of De Smet Lodge #55. Top: Worshipful Master;
second row: Senior and Junior Warden; third row: Senior and Junior
Deacon; fourth row: Tyler, square and compasses, Secretary.

Earls, wearing a particular jewel so that the populace would recognize them and be sure to bestow upon them the honor of their office. The jewel of the Master is the right angle of a square, symbolizing virtue.

Each officer also has a particular seat in the Lodge room that he occupies during the meeting. The Master sits "in the east." Although generally in the actual East according to the cardinal points, even when a building is not properly aligned, the seat of the Master is referred to as being "in the east." All other officers' places are relative to the Master's chair.

The Senior and Junior Wardens are similar to the first and second Vice President of a company. Their duties are to assist the Master in supervising the members – the Senior Warden in their work, meaning Lodge-related activities, and the Junior Warden in their refreshment, or non-Lodge-related pursuits. If a dispute arises among members, the Senior Warden may work with them to resolve it. In so doing, he may show no favoritism – all Masons are treated equally, "on the level." The jewel of the Senior Warden is therefore the level, which is used in the trade of masonry to align horizontal surfaces. His seat is in the west, or opposite the Master. The Junior Warden's duty is to ensure that the members "do not convert refreshment into intemperance or excess" but rather "observe the just medium between intemperance and pleasure." A good party is no excuse to abandon virtue; rather, the upright character expected of a Mason shall be adhered to at all times and in all places. Thus, the Junior Warden's jewel is the plumb, used by stone masons to align vertical surfaces. His chair is in the south. No meeting may be opened without at least one of these three officers present.

Every Lodge has a Secretary and a Treasurer. Their duties are exactly as within any organization, including record keeping and financial concerns. Their jewels are crossed quills and crossed keys respectively, congruent with their position.

The Senior and Junior Deacons may be thought of as the messengers. The Senior Deacon relays messages from the Master to the Senior Warden. In addition, he makes sure that all persons attending a meeting are truly Masons, and introduces new or visiting Masons. The Senior Deacon is also the one who guides new initiates through the ritual dramas of the degrees. The Junior Deacon ensures that the Lodge is properly guarded from inside the Lodge room during meetings, and gives messages to the Tyler stationed outside the door. The Junior Deacon is the only one who may open the door once a meeting has begun, until the meeting is closed; anyone wishing to leave the meeting, even to get a drink or answer nature's call, must go through the Junior Deacon. The Senior and Junior Deacons both have a jewel of the square and compasses; the Senior Deacon's also has a sun, and the Junior Deacon's, a moon. In some jurisdictions, the jewels of the Deacons are doves, symbolic messengers of peace.

Next is the Tyler, also spelled Tiler. The word originates from the Latin *tegere*, to protect or cover, as a roof does a building. This became 'thatch' in Old English, and finally 'tile.' Thus, a tiler lays tiles, or covers the roof, or – in more ancient usage and in Masonic usage – protects the building. Ancient spellings, especially within societies of workers, tended to use a "y;" in the London Ordinances of 1382, the earliest known written use of the word, it is spelled "tylere." Today, some Masons prefer the older spelling of "tyler" in deference to the antiquity of the Lodge; others prefer to use the modern spelling. As the historic documents relating to the Ingalls family use the older spelling, that is the one used herein. The Tyler stands guard at the outside of the Lodge room door to prevent entrance or interference from anyone unqualified to attend the meeting. He makes sure the door to the Lodge room is never opened from outside the Lodge room. The Tyler and the Junior Deacon communicate by signal knocks on the door, and the Junior Deacon will never open the door until the proper signal from the Tyler has been received. As protector of the Lodge, the Tyler's jewel is the sword, and he does carry an actual sword, drawn at all times while a meeting is in session.

While never actually used, this would certainly discourage anyone wishing to enter without authorization!

The Steward of the Lodge is the worker bee. Many Lodges have a Senior and a Junior Steward; some very large Lodges may have even more. They are to assist the other officers as necessary, and are often the ones tasked with both cleaning the Lodge building and providing meals as required, to see that "the brethren are suitably provided for." Thus, the cornucopia is a fitting jewel for this office.

Most Lodges have a Chaplain. As may be expected, he says the (non-denominational, ritually-prescribed) benedictions at the opening and closing of the meetings and at other times as prescribed by the rituals, and may also say grace before meals. His jewel is the open book of Sacred Law, as determined by the Grand Lodge of the jurisdiction; in the U.S., this is generally a Bible.

Although not utilized by all Lodges, when a Marshal, Master of Ceremonies, Director of Ceremonies and/or Ritualist are among the Lodge's officers, they have the duty of assisting the Deacons in preparing candidates for initiation into the Craft, including teaching the secret signs and words. They ensure proper etiquette and procedure in all proceedings, and as such they are often among the most knowledgeable regarding the history and meaning of the rituals. The jewels of these offices may be crossed batons or crossed swords, indicating outstanding service.

While not essential to the operation of a Lodge, the Musician adds "genuine pleasure to the brethren." The ritual dramas of the degrees are greatly enhanced when accompanied by music. The Musician's jewel is the lyre.

Different jurisdictions may have some variation in the officers and their duties. They may also have additional officers, such as Historian or Almoner. These positions are less common than those listed above.

There is no requirement for a Mason to serve in an office, and no set order of office for those who wish to. The only exception to this is for the Worshipful Master, who, in most cases, must have previously served as Junior or Senior Warden.

The collective of local Lodges within a jurisdiction make up a Grand Lodge, and the Grand Officers – officers in the Grand Lodge – are elected by those local Lodges. As with blue Lodges, since there is no final authority over all, there are differences among the Grand Lodges, even in regard to the offices. The Grand Offices are correspondent to the local Lodges' officers, but the Grand Officers' duties are expanded to have authority over all local Lodges in that jurisdiction.

The Grand Lodges and the blue Lodges within their jurisdictions are the basic body of Freemasonry; however, other organizations have been formed with the aim of further study in various, differing areas of Masonic life. These groups are known as appendant or concordant Masonic bodies. Some of them, such as the Scottish Rite and Shriners, have the third degree of Master Mason as a prerequisite for membership. Others, like the Order of the Eastern Star, require some familial relationship to a Master Mason. There are even a few which have no requirement of Masonry but are still affiliated, such as the Rainbow Girls and DeMolay.

The goals of these appendant bodies are also varied. Some focus on the history of Freemasonry, others on the meaning of certain symbols, perfecting the rituals, or other such related activities. While these appendant organizations may offer additional degrees for those who wish to pursue the lessons of Freemasonry further, they are not superior or "higher" degrees in any way other than number. In addition, since only men can join a Masonic Lodge – and only men of a certain age, at that; no "old man in his dotage or young man in his nonage" is allowed either – some of the appendant organizations were created to allow others such as women or children to study and learn to practice the same virtues that Freemasonry teaches. There are at least 35 such organizations in existence today. Laura and her family had extensive connections with one of them.

Order of the Eastern Star

It is ridiculous to attempt to exclude women from this good work...because that in Jerusalem and its vicinity 3000 years ago women were excluded from participating with men in good works is no reason why a woman today should be kept in exclusion.

~ Rob Morris, author, historian, Freemason

A fairly progressive view for a man living in the 1800s, these words were spoken by Rob Morris on August 21, 1880 about why he felt the need to create a Masonic-related Order to which women could belong. (The "good works" in Jerusalem to which he refers was the building of King Solomon's Temple, the builders of which are supposed to be the original "Masons.") He recognized that men are not alone in their desire to improve themselves, help others, and better society; women share these desires.

Morris was born in 1818 and was raised a Master Mason on March 5, 1846 in Oxford, Mississippi. A teacher by trade, he had a keen interest in the history of Freemasonry, as well as the virtues it promotes. After joining a Lodge, he began to travel as much as possible and visit as many Lodges as he could. His travels took him over much of the United States, as well as overseas. His interest was piqued by the Adoptive Rites he witnessed in France.[1]

Adoptive Rites had their origin in 1653, when Christina,

Queen of Sweden, established the Royal and Exalted Order of the Amaranth. This Order was unique in that not only were men accoladed into it as knights for their good deeds, but so were those knights' ladies. Across Europe, and particularly in France, the idea that women had influenced or enabled men to do good deeds gained ground, and it became popular for Lodges to "adopt" worthy women and bestow the honor of various Rites upon them. The Rites were never truly Masonic, as the ancient Landmarks to which all Grand Lodges must adhere prohibit both women from receiving them and Masons from giving them – or even being present at such a ceremony. Lodges which give Masonic degrees to women are not recognized as legitimate by any Grand Lodge.[2]

Some attempts had been made for Adoptive Rites in America, but they had never really caught on. Contemporaries spoke of them as vague, not well written, dull, and lacking in both motivation and meaning.[3] Most Adoptive Rites in America had a big spurt of growth and then died out; they simply were not as popular in America as they were in Europe, which was peculiar given that Freemasonry itself was much more popular in the States than it was across the sea.

One Lodge that did accept women was the Good Templar's Lodge.[4] The ritual and regalia of the Good Templar's was based on Masonic ritual – specifically from the Scottish Rite – but it was not a true Adoptive Rite because it did not require a man to be a Master Mason, or a woman to be related to a Mason, to join. The Good Templar's was a temperance lodge, hoping to make good men better by convincing them of the evils of drink. This Order was popular through the prohibition, although it went through some changes in name and eventually dropped the degree ritual work altogether, but with the prohibition people began to turn their attention to other causes and membership dropped dramatically. Today, this Lodge is known as the International Order of Good Templars. It is still a temperance Lodge, not affiliated with Freemasonry.

At the time Rob Morris was creating the Order of the

Eastern Star, the Good Templar's Lodge was just beginning, so it had not yet grown to the favored organization it later became, and no Adoptive Rite was, in his opinion, fulfilling its mission of aiding women in their endeavor to better society, while at the same time expanding and bettering their own role in that society.

Rob Morris.

Morris set out to change all that. The reason was two-fold: what Masonry could bring to women, and what women could bring to Masonry. Morris believed that having the wives and daughters of the men involved in their Masonic life would exert a gentling influence and "bring the performance of Freemasons closer to their profession."[5] He promoted the idea that women should be in charge of the charities of the Lodges, as he thought they would be more likely to know how best to make use of these, being more in tune with the circumstances of the community's households. This was perhaps stereotypical, but probably not far off the mark.

He believed bringing women closer into the fraternity would benefit the women as well: "...if the gratitude of the Craft were once fairly awakened toward their female relatives for such benevolence as I have suggested many methods would be opened to women for self-support that are now sealed up. Many a clerk-ship, many a copyist's desk, many a situation in post office, library, public bureau, etc., now filled by men alone, would be equally available to women, and so the circle of female occupations would be vastly enlarged." It would also remind the families of Masons that the members of a Lodge had all taken a vow to care for, assist and protect their brethren's widows and orphans, and embolden those family members needing assistance to take advantage of such when needed, thus bringing the orphan and widow "nearer to charity." "All this I had pondered for several years," Morris said.[6]

Thus it was that in February, 1850, Morris created the Order of the Eastern Star, a fraternity in which both Masons and their female relatives could participate. According to Morris, he did not base the theme, symbols, or any other part of the degrees upon those of any previous order, but devised every aspect of it himself. There is some evidence that he in fact did base at least parts of some of the degrees on other, lesser known Rites – or at the very least, was greatly inspired by them – but this is inconclusive, giving the true origins a bit of the mystery associated with Freemasonry. In any case, the degrees come from stories of women in the Bible that promote virtues in harmony with Freemasonry, as determined by Morris. The mission was to "relieve distress, administer to the suffering, and carry healing balm to the sorrowing and disconsolate."[7]

Once complete, he communicated the degrees to his wife, and to a fellow Mason and his wife. Thereafter, as he traveled from Lodge to Lodge, he spread word of the Order, advocating its mutual benefits. This time, the Adoptive Rite caught on, with both men and women joining its ranks quickly. For several years, Morris was the sole leader and authority, and the only one to confer the degrees. It soon became so popular that Morris created "Constellations" of Stars to organize them; however, these proved to be too complicated to garner much interest, and that project was abandoned.[8]

A friend of Morris, Robert Macoy, had the solution. Macoy developed the organization for these groups, to be called Chapters, with a delineation of officers and duties. In 1866, Macoy published *A Manual of the Order of the Eastern Star*, in which he not only outlined the Chapters, but also, with the approval of Morris, refined the degrees and ceremonies. About 1867, Morris left the U.S. to travel abroad, researching Freemasonic origins in the Holy Land. Before departing, he transferred full authority for the Order of the Eastern Star to Macoy.[9]

Chapters began to spring up everywhere, thanks in great part to the extensive traveling of both Macoy and Morris, both in the States and abroad. Soon, the inevitable happened: people needed guidance to continue. When Morris or Macoy came into a town, they conferred the degrees on a group of Masons and their families; then they left for the next town, leaving the new inductees with no real guidance or authority when questions or issues arose. Also, there began to be confusion over the signs and passes. Since there was no common practice to reinforce the work, as there was in Masonry, different people remembered the signs and rituals differently. It became necessary to establish an authority with an official version of the ritual to which Chapters could turn when Morris and Macoy were not available.

It was only natural to form jurisdictions with a Grand Chapter to govern the local Chapters, just as the local Lodges were governed by the Grand Lodge of their jurisdiction.[10] The same jurisdictions were used for the Star Chapters as were used for the Masonic Lodges, with each state in the U.S. to have one Grand Chapter as they gained enough local Chapters to warrant the need, and other countries to have one or more depending on size and population. This worked well, but eventually even more uniformity was desired, as each Grand Chapter made different rules. In 1875, the Grand Chapter of Mississippi sent a communication to the other existing Grand Chapters, requesting delegates from each to meet together for the purpose of creating a Supreme Chapter to have final authority. All but one answered in the affirmative (that one was not against the idea but only unable to send a representative), and in November, 1876 the selected delegates met and formed the General Grand Chapter. The General Grand Chapter formed committees to answer questions and make rules, and they met every three years to review, revise, and add to these as necessary. There was no permanent location for the General Grand Chapter for many years, and the meeting was held in a different city each time. In 1935, the General Grand Chapter purchased the Belmont Mansion in Washington, D.C. for $100,000, and it is still headquartered in that historic building.[11]

Today, the Order of the Eastern Star is said to be the world's largest fraternal organization that men and women both may join, and the General Grand Chapter governs over more than 10,000 chapters. To join, men must be Master Masons in good standing, and women must be related to a Master Mason in one of the following specific ways: wife or widow; daughter, stepdaughter, or daughter-in-law; granddaughter or great granddaughter; mother, stepmother, or mother-in-law; sister, stepsister, or sister-in-law; aunt, niece, or great niece.[12]

Another requirement for membership, in accordance with Freemasonry, is the belief in a Supreme Being. Again, so long as this belief is professed, a person may belong to any religious organization he or she wishes, or none at all. What "Supreme Being" means to each person is for that person, alone, to determine.

When an individual qualified by both these requirements petitions a Chapter for membership, the applicant will be investigated to determine good character. A vote of the Chapter is taken after hearing the report of the investigating committee.

The emblem of the Order is a five-pointed star. Many people wonder why it appears upside-down, even claiming that it is a symbol of the devil. It is interesting to note that equating the inverted star with Satanism is a relatively new phenomenon. Early in the Christian era, an upright star was meant to symbolize the wounds of Christ, and thus his humanity, while an inverted star was meant to represent His condescension (hence pointing down), and thus emphasized His divinity.[13] Perhaps that is why inverted stars appear as decoration in so many of the ancient churches and cathedrals, such as the Amiens Cathedral and Chartres Cathedral in France and the Marktkirche in Germany. Outside of Christianity, inverted stars are found in many places that have nothing to do with any religious meaning, much less the devil, such as the Congressional Medal of Honor and the stars in the elephant of the GOP symbol. In the Order of the Eastern Star, the inverted star represents the Star of Bethlehem which the wise men saw in the East, pointing the way to the Christ Child. Thus, the white ray of the star points downward, as toward the manger, and reminds members to seek Him.

The degrees are themed around the familial roles of women: daughter, wife, mother, widow, sister. Each role illustrates certain virtues as exemplified by the heroines 'Adah,' 'Ruth,' 'Esther,' 'Martha,' and 'Electa.'[14] These heroines are referred to as the "star points," and the ladies in these offices within the Chapter present the lessons of the degrees to initiates. The star points begin with the upper right point of the emblem and go clockwise.

Adah was the name Rob Morris assigned to the heroine representing Jephthah's daughter.[15] She is based on the unnamed daughter in the story from the book of *Judges*, chapter 11, in the Old Testament. This is one of the lesser-known biblical stories: Jephthah promised the Lord that if he could have victory in battle, then "whatsoever cometh forth of the doors of my house to meet me, when I return in peace from the children of Ammon, shall surely be the Lord's, and I will offer it up for a burnt offering." His daughter was the first to go out and greet him. Upon learning of the vow her father had made, she "said unto him, My father, if thou hast opened thy mouth unto the Lord, do to me according to that which hath proceeded out of thy mouth." So Jephthah "did with her according to his vow which he had vowed."[16] While this is a dark and tragic story, it certainly does illustrate obedience to one's convictions of right and duty, and the binding effects of a vow, which are the lessons of Adah. She typifies the ideal daughter because of her sense of duty and her devotion to her father. The color associated with Adah is blue, symbolizing fidelity. Her badge is the sword and veil, representing the idea that the sword must sometimes be taken up with courage, in defense of right and the performance of one's duty. The story of Adah challenges members to carry through life the willingness to solve problems as directed by their conviction to what is right.

The Old Testament book of *Ruth* tells the story of the title heroine, who represents the widow in the Order of the Eastern Star. The story tells of Ruth, a Moabite woman, who married an Israelite that was living for a time in Moab with his family. The man and his father both died, prompting his mother to return to her homeland of Israel. Although she urged Ruth to stay in her own homeland of Moab, "Ruth said, Intreat me not to leave thee, or to return from following after thee: for whither thou goest, I will go; and where thou lodgest, I will lodge: thy people shall be my people, and thy God my God: Where thou diest, will I die, and there will I be buried: the Lord do so to me, and more also, if ought but death part thee and me."[17] Thus she teaches the lessons of constancy and devotion. That wasn't the end of the story, however. Upon arriving in Bethlehem, Ruth needed to provide for herself and her elderly mother-in-law. She did this by gleaning grain behind the reapers (according to Jewish law, harvesters were to leave a bit ungathered for those in need, and anything that fell to the ground was left for the same reason). Thus, she shows, by fulfilling the duty of her work, that patient industry brings the reward of plenty. Ruth's color is yellow, representing constancy. Her badge is the sheaf of wheat, representing the collective worth of small acts combined. She represents the ideal widow because she cherished her family above her every personal ambition and even her original native allegiance. The story of Ruth challenges each member to serve others and extend the hand of friendship to those in need.

Esther, the heroine of the book which bears her name, was a young Jewish girl who, through an unusual twist of events, became wife to the king, making her queen of Persia. When she learned of a plot to exterminate her people, she approached the king – at risk to her own life – to plead their case. Her courageous efforts saved the Jews from genocide.[18] This story teaches courage and loyalty to kindred. The color of Esther is white, for purity. The crown and scepter is her badge, representing justice in power. Esther represents the ideal wife, because she succeeded in fulfilling her duty to her husband but also maintained her high standards and performed her duty to God and her nation. Her story reminds members of the Order today to do the same.

Martha, the sister of Lazarus from the Gospel of John, illustrates unwavering faith through trials. Though her brother died, she believed and trusted in Jesus, and as reward for her faith she witnessed her brother's miraculous resurrection.[19] Faith and trust are her lessons. Martha's color is green, representing new and everlasting life. Her badge, the broken column, represents her faith even when her brother's life was broken. Martha represents the ideal sister: she assumed responsibility for the care and comfort of her brother Lazarus and her sister Mary.

Electa, the name given to the typification of the "Elect Lady" of the Second Epistle of John, has the role of mother, as she was traditionally described as fervent in charity and hospitality.[20] Lore indicates that she was a pagan who converted to Christianity, and was martyred for her refusal to denounce the Christ, thus sacrificing her very life to establish a Christian heritage for her children. She exemplifies the courage one should have in holding to truth, and the love members should have for one another. Red, for fervency, is Electa's color. The cup is her badge, representing both hospitality, and the allotted portion of joys and sorrows which make up the fullness of life. The ideals of Electa are love and hospitality, and she reminds Stars to emulate these virtues by acting with charity toward all.

Emblems of the Order.

The lessons of these five degrees are meant to enrich the lives of members and guide them to higher virtue. It has been customary since the beginning of the Order of the Eastern Star for all five degrees to be conferred consecutively at the same meeting. This is different from the Masonic Lodge, in which initiates traditionally must learn the "work" – lessons and signs – of each degree before proceeding to the next one, so that each degree is conferred at a separate meeting. (Recently, some Lodges have begun consecutive conferring.)

There are thirteen offices in addition to the star points in each Chapter of the Order of the Eastern Star. The Worthy Matron is the presiding officer, similar to the Worshipful Master of Lodge or the President of a company. The Worthy Patron, who must be a Master Mason, is her partner in leadership. He is often the husband of the Worthy Matron, but not necessarily. The Worthy Patron is the one who leads initiates in their obligation. The Associate Matron and Associate Patron are the assistants of the Worthy Matron and Worthy Patron. If the Worthy Matron or Patron must be absent, the Associate Matron or Associate Patron will take their place during the meeting. The Secretary and Treasurer handle the correspondence and money. The Conductress leads initiates through the degrees, with the assistance of the Associate Conductress. Prayers are said by the Chaplain, and the Marshal acts as master of ceremonies. Music is provided by the Organist (or Musician). The Warder and Sentinel guard the door from inside and outside, respectively, to guard against unauthorized entry. The offices of the star points, Worthy Matron and Associate Matron, and Conductress and Associate Conductress must be filled by women; the Worthy Patron and Associate Patron are, of course, men. Other offices may be filled by either gender.[21]

Like Freemasonry, the mission of the Order provides for promoting charity and education, and these are actively advanced through many programs and activities. Members provide scholarships and donations of both time and service to many charitable organizations, including Cancer Research

Project, Arthritis Fund, Heart Fund, Knights Templar Eye Foundation, Shriners' Charities, orphanages, and many others. According to statistics shared at the 2012 Assembly, the Order had contributed $14 Million in the previous three years just to Masonic care centers. These are senior centers and retirement homes for Freemasons and Eastern Stars, which are run with donations in lieu of fees to residents. In addition, hundreds of thousands of dollars are given in scholarships each year to deserving students, in accord with their emphasis on the importance of education.[22]

Family, faith, courage, conviction, industry: these themes also run throughout the *Little House* books, and are a large part of the books' timeless appeal. Laura was able to write about them in such an engaging way because these were the principles her family really lived by. A look at the lives of the Ingalls family will reveal the importance of these values to them.

Early Years

*Exploration is wired into our brains. If we can
see the horizon, we want to know what's beyond.*
~ Buzz Aldrin, astronaut, Freemason

Long ago – January 10, 1836, to be exact – in a small
village in upstate New York, a little boy named Charles Phillip
Ingalls was born. Although he looked like any ordinary baby
boy, there was something different about Charles...or about
one of his feet, anyway. It had a condition called "wandering
foot," which caused an itch, especially when things were not
going well, that could be relieved only by moving to a new,
preferably undeveloped, location. The condition would manifest
only later.

Charles was the third of ten children (second of nine that
lived) born to Lansford and Laura Ingalls. Charles would later
name his daughter after his mother. They lived some years at
Cuba, New York, but, as the family grew, Lansford was unable
to wrest enough of a living from the land to provide for them
all. Several of his family – including at least two brothers and
a nephew of Lansford, among others – had moved to Illinois,
and in the mid-1840s Lansford took his wife and five children
there to join them, settling about 40 miles to the west of
Chicago, near the new and growing town of Elgin, in Campton
Township.[1] Here was Charles's first experience with prairie,
as the land around the town was flat and grassy, unlike the
wooded, rolling hills the family had left behind in Allegany

County of New York.

Although the exact date of the move is unknown, we know they were living in Illinois by July, 1845, when Charles's sister Laura was born in Kane County, and they remained through at least the second day of October, 1850, when the census was taken. They most likely stayed through the winter, moving the next spring. This means Charles lived on the prairie this first time about half a decade, certainly long enough to form an opinion regarding the ease of farming it.

The U.S. Census of 1850 lists Lansford as a "laborer." He did not purchase a farm in Illinois, and the family most likely stayed with one of Lansford's brothers as he hired out to help area farmers or took other work as he could find it. The Census also has something interesting in the line of information regarding Charles. There is not a check in the column to mark for a person who had "attended school in the past year," indicating that Charles had already ended his school days to help support the family. This may indeed be the case; however, there is no occupation listed for him, as there is

The Lansford Ingalls family in the 1850 Census. Notice that Lansford and Peter are marked "Laborer," but Charles is not.
Notice also the check marks in the tenth and eleventh columns; the tenth column is the "married within the year column," and the next column is the "attended school in the past year" column.

for his 17-year-old brother, who was, like their father, marked as a "laborer." No doubt Charles did work on the family farm, and may even have hired out occasionally, but the record is ambiguous enough that it is impossible to say definitively whether he was working full time permanently or still had some school days yet. (It's also hard to say why almost every name on the page seems to have a check mark in the "married within the year" column. Certainly none of the Ingalls family fit that description, yet Charles, his parents, and three of his six siblings are all marked thus.)

Though the economy boomed for awhile, things did not work out for the Ingallses, and in 1851, Lansford packed them all up again and took them to Wisconsin, where they settled outside the town of Concord. They were living there at least by July of that year, when Charles's brother George was born, so they were gone from Elgin by the time the Masonic Lodge was established there in 1852.

At Concord, living on a neighboring farm to the Ingallses, were Frederick and Charlotte Holbrook with her young ones, the Quiner children. Charlotte's first husband, Henry Quiner, had been lost at sea (it was really Lake Michigan), as he and his brother-in-law were going up the Strait of Mackinaw on a trading trip with the Native Americans, in 1844. Following that disaster, Charlotte moved her family, and settled in Concord in 1848. She married Frederick Holbrook the next year, and he became the children's step-father.[2]

The Holbrooks and Quiners became good friends with the Ingallses – and then they became even more than good friends. Three of the Ingalls offspring – Polly, Charles, and Peter – married three Quiners: Henry, Caroline, and Eliza, respectively. So there was joy even though times were hard. And times were hard. There was a financial panic throughout the nation in 1857, which was felt by them all. Charles's father attempted to save his land by obtaining a mortgage on it. He was unable to increase his income, however, and lost the farm when he could not pay off the mortgage. It was in the midst of these troubles that Charles Ingalls wed Caroline Quiner on February 1, 1860, at Concord, Wisconsin.[3]

Wedding photo of Caroline and Charles Ingalls.

Searching for greener pastures, Lansford decided to move his large family (he and his wife had seven children still at home). The town of Pepin, about 240 miles away, was experiencing a boom, with logging a major industry. There were stores, at least one church, a school, and a Masonic Lodge.[4] Lansford relocated there, and his three married children with their spouses, including Charles and Caroline, all chose to move with him. In 1863, the Ingalls clan arrived and began to look for land on which to make their homes and sustain their families.[5]

At first, Charles earned money working for other farmers, helping them bring in the harvest. He often swam across the Mississippi River to work on farms in Minnesota. By September, he had saved enough money to make a down payment on a piece of land, on halves with his brother-in-law Henry.[6] He built a small home and began to farm, supplementing the farm income by trapping and selling furs. About two years after arriving in Pepin, Charles and Caroline experienced the wondrous joy of welcoming their first child, Mary. A couple of years later, on February 7, 1867, Laura joined the family.

About that same time, yet another economic depression hit the country. Early in 1868, Charles and Henry each decided to sell their share of the farm, on an installment sale. The brothers-in-law each used his share of the proceeds to obtain his own farm. Charles signed papers to purchase a plot of land in Missouri in May, 1868. However, he evidently had a flare-up of wandering foot, as he moved his family to Kansas in 1869. They settled not far from the new town of Independence – and on the Osage Diminished Reserve. Although the Reservation was not open for settlement, many pioneers were anticipating that it soon would be, and were trying to arrive early for first choice of the land. Charles and his family were among the first white settlers in the area.[7]

There, Charles built another home for his family, and planted another crop. Again, he needed to supplement his farming income, and he was able to help the few other new settlers with carpentry work to earn enough to purchase necessary supplies. Laura's book *Little House on the Prairie* describes a fictionalized account of these years. It was in 1870, in Kansas, that Charles and Caroline's third child, another daughter, Carrie, was born. Soon after that, however, they received word that the man to whom they had sold the farm in Pepin could not make the payments. About the same time, Charles heard the erroneous message that the U.S. government would not reach a settlement agreement with the Osage Nation, and that the whites who had settled on the Reservation would have to leave. So, he moved his family back to Pepin and took over the old farm once again.

By this time, Mary was six years old, so when they settled down again in Pepin, she began attending the nearby Barry Corner School, with four of her cousins – there were still many Ingallses living there – and other area children. Laura was only four years old, so she was really too young for school, but in the fall term she went with Mary anyway.[8]

89

Education was important to Caroline. Her mother, Charlotte, had been a teacher before she married, and after Caroline graduated, she, too, became a schoolteacher, until she married Charles. Wherever they went, Caroline always took her books, and whenever possible the family received newspapers and church papers. Caroline spent her rare leisure time reading, often aloud to the family. She wanted to be sure her girls received a respectable education, and although she was the one who emphasized a formal education for the children, it was important to Charles as well. At the age of seventeen, he purchased a set of *The Life of Napoleon* for $1.50.[9] At a time when books were hard to come by, the Ingalls family amassed a decent library through the years; evidently the books were important enough that they warranted hard-earned payment, and they were not left behind in their many moves, as was the usual practice among the pioneers. Books were given as gifts within the family, and were always treasured; even periodicals, such as the *Advance, Youth's Companion*, and newspapers, were highly prized. Charles was well-read and knowledgeable about many subjects, informing himself however he was able from the time he was a teenager. He also served as Treasurer on the school board of Barry Corner School for a time while the family lived in Pepin.[10]

Charles and Caroline remained in Wisconsin until 1874. These years before the final move from Wisconsin are related in the book *Little House in the Big Woods*. The family seemed to be doing fairly well in Pepin, but Charles's wandering foot began to itch again, prompting him to seek out a better living for his family. This time, he moved the family to Walnut Grove, Minnesota. Their years there are chronicled in *On the Banks of Plum Creek*, Laura's fourth book.

When they first arrived in Walnut Grove, the family lived in a dugout on their new farm. Charles worked for a neighbor for several months, while he tried to save enough money to purchase the seed wheat for his first crop and begin building a home.

Charles and Caroline were both civic minded and religious, and they demonstrated these ideals in their daily lives. They were present at the August, 1874 organizing meeting when the decision was made to establish the Union Congregational Church in Walnut Grove. They became charter members, and were baptized at the first service. Charles was made a trustee of the church the following February.[11] The family attended regularly, and Laura and Mary went to Sunday School. *On the Banks of Plum Creek* tells a story which shows the priority of church in the Ingalls' lives. Charles saved for several weeks to purchase a new pair of boots, as his old pair was worn completely through. Before he was able to purchase the boots, a request was made for donations toward a bell for the new church. Charles donated the money he had saved for boots toward the bell instead. In *On the Banks of Plum Creek*, the story is told that he gave his last $3, but church records show that in actuality it was more than $26 – and was probably all he had.[12] Faith, family, charity, education: these were always the priorities of the Ingalls family.

The spring of 1875 was a hopeful time for the Ingallses. Charles built a small home and planted his crop. Caroline devoted herself to caring for the new home and the children. Young Carrie stayed home with her mother while Laura and Mary again attended school. Soon they all looked forward to a new addition to the family.

Then the locusts came, like a biblical plague. They decimated all the crops in the area, forcing Charles to leave the family to the mercy of neighbors while he traveled on foot to another county to find work. He was gone several weeks, working the harvest for farmers in areas unaffected by the locusts. When he returned that fall, Caroline was nearing her time of delivery. To have her more conveniently located, Charles rented a house in town, directly behind the church, for the winter. This is where their son, Charles Frederick, was born. The new baby, called Freddy by his sisters and parents, brought joy to the family, but it was short-lived.

Soon after they moved back to the farm the next spring, Caroline became very ill.[13] The doctor came three times, and she eventually recovered, but the medical bills were an added burden. Charles planted a small crop, but, for the second year in a row, the locusts destroyed it. Although he took odd jobs as he could find them, he was unable to provide a sufficient living, especially now that he had to pay the doctor's bills. One of their friends and neighbors, William Steadman, planned to purchase a hotel in Burr Oak, Iowa. He offered Charles the opportunity to manage the hotel for him, and with such bad luck in Walnut Grove, Charles accepted. He sold the farm in July, 1876, and the family spent the harvest with Peter and Eliza Ingalls near South Troy, Minnesota, before going on to Iowa. Sadly, baby Freddy became ill while there. The doctor could do nothing for him, and he died, taking his last breath on August 27, 1876. He was nine months old. Contrary to the television portrayal of the Ingalls family, there was no other son ever born to or adopted by Charles and Caroline.

The Burr Oak House that Charles managed. The family lived in the hotel for the first few months they were in Burr Oak.

Burr Oak was one place that Charles did not try farming. Instead, he and Caroline ran the Burr Oak House (often referred to as the Masters Hotel). Even Mary and Laura helped out, after school and on weekends. Only ten and twelve years old, they were already learning the lessons of selflessness and industry. In school, they learned elocution in addition to the other, regular subjects, and Laura was later grateful for these lessons, as they benefited her many times.[14] The girls did have time for play, too, and Laura spent time splashing in Silver Creek behind the hotel or wandering through the old cemetery on the edge of town. She also spent some time each week taking singing lessons. Laura did not wish to do this, but the man who gave the lessons was influential to Charles's position at the hotel. They felt the man "must be pleased," so Laura took the lessons.[15] In addition, the family was active in the Congregational Church.[16]

The school house in Burr Oak that Laura and Mary attended.

The Ingalls family lived in Burr Oak for about a year and a half. Laura did not write about this time in the *Little House* books. While there, the family first stayed in the crowded hotel, but Charles moved them to a room above the neighboring grocery store as soon as he could. This also proved less than ideal, as it was next door to the saloon, so he rented a small house a few blocks away. Their fourth daughter, Grace, was born there on May 23, 1877. Then, Mr. Steadman sold the hotel, leaving Charles without a job. According to letters Laura later wrote to Rose, the owner of the hotel cheated Charles out of the money he was due from managing the hotel, and so, despite trying several other business ventures, Charles could not make ends meet.[17] He also did not like his family living in the town, for, although they all appreciated the school that the girls attended, which was providing a much desired education, the influence of the saloon was too powerful throughout the town.

The Congregational Church the family attended in Burr Oak.

In 1878, the Ingallses backtracked for the second time, returning to Walnut Grove. They stayed with friends for a while, and Charles worked at various jobs, including keeping a store, operating a butcher shop, helping out at the local hotel, and carpentry.[18] In the midst of these jobs, he also purchased some land – in town, this time – and built another home for the family.

A Masonic Lodge was chartered in Walnut Grove on January 15, 1879, and it is believed to have met on the second floor of William Masters' store building.[19] Charles had worked on the construction of the building, thereby helping the establishment of Freemasonry in the town. Even so, he did not join the Lodge in Walnut Grove. He and Caroline did, however, join the Good Templar's (temperance) Lodge when it was founded at the end of 1878. They did so even though they did not approve of the man who founded the group in the town, believing him to be a hypocrite. But the cause was more important than the man, so they put aside their anger at him and were active in the Lodge.[20] They also became re-affiliated with the Union Congregational Church. Mary was soon baptized, and Charles was again made a trustee.[21] Mary and Laura attended Sunday School at the Congregational Church, and Mary joined the Sunday School Temperance League, solemnly promising at the age of thirteen "to abstain from the use of all intoxicating liquors as a beverage" for her entire life, in harmony with the family's stance on alcohol.[22] Laura may also have joined this Temperance League. Although the family belonged to the Congregational Church, Laura also attended Sunday School at the Methodist Church. This was not due to extra religious fervency, but rather the desire to win a contest for a new Bible. The Sunday School leader at the Methodist Church promised a prize of a new Bible to the person who memorized the most scriptures. Laura and her sisters were raised committing Bible passages, as well as other works, to memory, and it served her well: she tied for first place, and did receive a prize Bible, which is in the possession of the Laura Ingalls Wilder Home Association in Mansfield, Missouri. Civic duty also called, and Charles was elected as a Justice of the Peace of Walnut Grove in March, 1879.[23]

Once again, however, misfortune followed the Ingalls family, and once again, illness struck. Now it was Mary who was suddenly taken ill, coming down with a delirious fever and suffering a stroke.[24] This time, there was not complete recovery: Mary went blind. Once again, doctors' bills piled up, and Charles was not able to pay. Laura put the skills she had learned in Burr Oak to use and took a job at the local hotel, but this did not provide enough additional income to meet the needs of the family. Caroline wanted to stay near "civilization," where there was a church and a school, but when another opportunity to move – with a guaranteed job with good pay – arose, Charles's wandering foot could not be denied, and he moved the family again. Destination: De Smet, Dakota Territory.

De Smet

America was not built on fear. America was built on courage, on imagination, and unbeatable determination to do the job at hand.
~ Harry Truman, U.S. President, Freemason, and member of the Order of the Eastern Star

The move to De Smet (in what later became the State of South Dakota but at this time was still a Territory) in 1879 was the last move Charles and Caroline made. This is not because Charles had found a cure for his wandering foot. It still itched, and he had dreams of Florida and Oregon, at least, at various times, but he learned to control it for practical reasons. The era of the pioneer was coming to a close, and Charles had probably realized by this time that it was easier to make a living where there were other people around who could pay a day's wage for a day's work. Charles and Caroline weren't getting any younger, either, and Laura indicates in the *Little House* books that Caroline was tired of moving "from pillar to post" and was not open to the idea of another move, especially to an unsettled area with no school or church.[1]

The Ingallses were the first family to settle in De Smet. Laura writes about the founding of the town in *By the Shores of Silver Lake*. The final four books of the series are *The Long Winter, Little Town on the Prairie, These Happy Golden Years*, and the posthumously-published *The First Four Years*. These books describe the Ingalls family's early years in the new town.

The Ingalls' early arrival was due to the fact that the job Charles had taken when leaving Walnut Grove was working as storekeeper and paymaster for the railroad being built through the area. When the railway was complete that fall, the workers moved on, but Charles and his family stayed. The town of De Smet was built up the following spring.

The family never had much money, but they were charitable when possible, both with finances and in service. Laura recounts one instance of this in *Pioneer Girl*: "One Irish family, ready to leave, had a sick baby and could not go. Ma heard of it and went to see if she could help. By great good luck she did know what to do and cured the baby. They wanted to pay her but of course she would take no pay."[2]

The Ingallses spent a quiet winter looking after the railroad's equipment, using the surveyor's building as their home.[3] There were no near neighbors, but once winter waned enough for travel, the rush of people was immediate. Before the town was built, newcomers needed a place to stay; it was still too cold to camp out. Charles and Caroline opened their home to these men. They could not afford to give away their own family's sustenance, however, so Charles prudently set a price for a meal and for a night's lodging.

Among the first to come through was a Congregational minister. He stopped in to visit the Ingallses, and while there he held a service in the Ingalls home – the first church service of De Smet. It wasn't long before a church was established, with services held in the depot until a church building could be built. Along with the Reverend Brown and his wife, Charles, Caroline, and Mary were founding members of the First Congregational Church. The other founding members were Mr. Gilbert and his wife (the Gilbert family name is familiar to readers of Laura's books: the mail carrier in *The Long Winter* is said to be a Mr. Gilbert), and V. Barnes (known to *Little House* readers as Lawyer Barnes, who gave Charles firecrackers on the Fourth of July). Charles, Caroline, and Mary all remained life members of this church.[4]

The First Congregational Church building as it looked when the Ingalls family attended, above;
below, as it appears today, home of Christian & Ministry Alliance.

Because of his early arrival, Charles was able to secure a homestead site in a good location near the new town, and due to his good wages from working on the railroad, he was also able to purchase a lot in the town, on which he constructed a building. The structure was meant to eventually become a store, but the family used it as a home first, and lived there for several months while Charles put in a well and built a shanty out on the claim. When the family moved to the farm, Charles rented the building in town to Judge John Carroll, who later purchased the property from Charles and Caroline. Carroll moved the building Charles built to the back of the lot, erecting a new bank in front. Eventually, the little building was dismantled, and the lumber is rumored to have been used to build another structure in town.[5] The building Carroll built is still standing, and currently houses a law firm.

The store building Charles built is the small building on the far left; it's white with a dark roof and lean-to built on the side.

Due to the time, work, and expense that Charles had spent on the building in town and at the homestead, the wages he had earned with the railroad were soon spent. That first year, they were just breaking in the ground on the farm, so not much would grow on it and the crop was small. The family was rationing their food even before the first blizzards of the hard winter of 1880-81.[6]

That winter remains notorious to this day. The area was assailed with blizzards and severe snow storms, which began in October, and brutally low temperatures for eight months. Townspeople ran out of supplies, including both food and coal. For fuel, they burned hay. For food, they rationed and went hungry. According to Laura's book, *The Long Winter,* and her unpublished autobiography, Almanzo Wilder and another young man from town risked their lives to leave the town and try to find, with only estimates as to location, a homesteader with some extra seed wheat. They were successful, and what they purchased kept the town alive.[7]

The situation of the Ingalls family was worse than most others in De Smet. They had been hungry before the blizzards. Then, when they moved back to town for the winter, they agreed to board the pregnant Maggie Masters while her husband George was working for the railroad. George came back to visit her, and was caught by a fierce storm while at the Ingalls' place. In a display of true charity, Charles and Caroline allowed George and Maggie to stay with them through the winter. George considered his wife and himself to be boarders, so they ate the food but did not help with the chores. This meant two additional mouths for Charles to feed, and one of those was "eating for two." At the end of that winter, on May 23, 1881, in the Ingalls' store-building-turned-home, Maggie gave birth to a son, Arthur Kingsbury Masters, the first child born in De Smet. After the hungry, crowded winter, they were all glad when the storms stopped, spring came, and the young Masters couple left. The Ingalls family moved to the homestead for the spring and summer, returning to town in the winter.[8]

In November, 1881, Mary was enrolled in the Iowa College for the Blind. College educations have never been inexpensive, and the Ingalls family would not have been able to send Mary to college had it not been for Section 5, Chapter 13 of the Laws of 1879, Dakota Territory. This law gave the right of education to deaf, dumb, and blind persons, at the expense of Dakota Territory. The blind school that the State paid for Mary to attend was located in Vinton, Iowa. Mary learned the things any sighted student learned in school, such as arithmetic, history, chemistry, literature, and political economics, among other subjects. Moreover, she learned how to do things that sighted persons might take for granted: sewing and knitting, bead work, and music, including the organ. She gained a reputation as an excellent organist, playing all songs from memory. Learning to tie horsefly nets proved useful to her later, providing a way for her to contribute to the family's income. (The term "horsefly net" may refer to a screen that is placed over open doorways and windows of a barn; or it may refer to a net that is placed over a horse's head to keep the flies out of its eyes, nose, and ears. In addition to being uncomfortable, the bites of horseflies could become infected. In the days when horses were essential for both travel and farm work, taking good care of them was a priority.) Mary excelled in all of her classes.[9]

Laura and Carrie attended school in De Smet as they were able, and Laura also kept busy contributing to the family income with various jobs. She was already showing her fortitude when she worked for Mr. Clayson and Mrs. White sewing shirts. She did not enjoy sewing at all, but the family needed the additional income, so Laura did her duty without complaint. She spent some weeks with Mrs. McKee, a new settler, helping her get settled onto that family's homestead while Mr. McKee was busy at work. Another job Laura held was in Florence Bell's millinery. There, she worked with another Laura: Laura Wilder, Almanzo Wilder's oldest sister, who became her sister-in-law.[10]

The year 1883 brought changes. At the upper levels of government, Governor Ordway moved the Territory's capitol from Yankton to Bismarck, further to the north. The majority of the population lived in the southern part of the state, and they were outraged. It was the beginning of the movement toward statehood.[11]

The year 1883 also brought changes locally. That year the town of De Smet incorporated. By then, there were several stores, banks, newspapers, hotels, attorneys, and real estate agents, in addition to the school and churches. As one of the earliest settlers, Charles was able to take a leading role in the community. He served in De Smet in various ways through the years, including as Justice of the Peace, Deputy Sheriff, School Board member, Town Clerk, and Street Commissioner. He held several different occupations over the years as well, including farmer, storekeeper, carpenter, and insurance salesman.[12]

Another sign of growth in De Smet was the establishment of a Masonic Lodge. The first Lodge in Dakota Territory was formed in 1863. Four more Lodges were chartered in the next decade, and in 1875, delegates from each of the five Lodges met together and formed the Grand Lodge of Dakota. When the Territory was divided and admitted to Statehood in 1889, North and South Dakota each formed their own Grand Lodge.

Dakota was still a Territory, however, when a group of men met on December 10, 1883, and organized De Smet Masonic Lodge #55, A. F. & A. M. The thirteen men who met were all already Masons, having received their degrees at other places prior to moving to De Smet. The Lodge was chartered June 18, 1884, with the first officers listed as George Annis, Worshipful Master; W. E. Whiting, Senior Warden; F. W. Collins, Junior Warden; J. E. Smith, Secretary; E. G. Davies, Treasurer; C. L. Dawley, Senior Deacon; L. E. Sasse, Junior Deacon; and T. C. Wilkins, Tyler.

The Masons met on the second floor of J. W. Hopp's *Kingsbury County News* building for several years, then met for a few months in the school building. With the completion of the Kingsbury County Abstract Company building in 1889, the Lodge moved to the second floor of that building, a room which was shared with other fraternal groups such as the Odd Fellows. This building is still standing; it is located at the northeast corner of Calumet and Second Streets, and currently houses the Heritage House Bed & Breakfast. Several years later, the Odd Fellows built a new lodge building for themselves in the next block, and they rented the hall to other fraternal groups for their use as well. The Masonic Lodge was one of those groups, and met there beginning December 19, 1898. In fact, the Masonic Lodge was actually the first group to meet in the building when it was completed, even before the Odd Fellows. Charles was among the men who repaired and readied the Masonic Lodge's furniture for the move. De Smet Masonic Lodge #55 finally received its own building when it was able to purchase what had been the Evangelical Church on the corner of Calumet and Third Streets in 1917. The Lodge still meets in that same building at the same location today.

The first initiates of De Smet Lodge were G. C. R. (Gerald) Fuller (of the hardware store mentioned in the *Little House* books) and Thomas Ruth, the banker.

This Lease, made and entered into the 1st day of November 1893, by and between L. E. Sasse, Lessee of the Kingsbury County Abstract Company, party of the first part, and De Smet Lodge # 55 A. F. and A. M. of De Smet, South Dakota, party of the second part, is as follows:

The party of the first part, for and in consideration of Fifty-Five Dollars, to be paid by said party of the second part, hereinafter mentioned, hereby sub-lets to the said party of the second part, for every First and Third Monday of each month, for and during the term of one year from and after November 1st 1893, the following described premises, to wit: All the rooms on the second floor of the Kingsbury County Abstract Company's Building, situate on Lot 8, in Block 2, in the City of De Smet, Kingsbury County, South Dakota, said rooms to be used by said party of the second part, at the times hereinbefore mentioned, as a lodge or society hall.

The said party of the first part hereby reserves for himself the right to sub-let the said rooms or premises to other lodges or societies on all days and nights not above mentioned.

The said party of the first part hereby agrees to properly heat and light the said rooms, so as to be comfortable to be used by said party of the second part on the nights of the days above mentioned for lodge meetings, and also to keep said rooms at all times cleaned, swept and dusted.

The said party of the second part hereby agrees to pay to the said party of the first part for the use and occupation of said rooms or premises, properly heated, lighted, cleaned, swept and dusted as aforesaid, the sum of Fifty-Five Dollars, to be paid as follows, to wit: $13.75, at the ensealing and delivery of this contract; $13.75, on February 1st 1894; $13.75, on May 1st 1894, and $13.75, on August 1st 1894.

It is hereby mutually agreed by and between the parties to this contract, that before this contract shall be absolutely binding upon the said party of the second part, the ceilings and wood-work of said rooms must be painted, and the side walls papered, at the expense of the said Kingsbury County Abstract Company.

Signed, Sealed and Delivered, this   day of December 1893.

De Smet Lodge # 55 A. F. and A. M.

By

Copy of the Lodge's lease of a room in the Kingsbury County Abstract building, signed in December, 1893.

NAMES OF MEMBERS. 3

Insert here the names, **alphabetically**, of all who are members of the Lodge at the time of making out this report, excluding all who have, from any cause lost membership since the last report, and who are mentioned under the proper heads on pages 9 and 10.

OFFICERS.

1	Geo. N. Annis	W. M.
2	W. E. Whiting	S. W.
3	F. W. Collins	J. W.
4	E. Gomer Davis	Treasurer.
5	J. E. Smith	Secretary.
6	C. L. Dawley	S. D.
7	L. E. Sassac	J. D.
8		S Steward
9		J. Steward
10	T. C. Wilkins	Tyler.

NAMES OF MEMBERS—CONTINUED.

11	Joseph L. Baker
12	C. S. G. Fuller
13	John B Morrison
14	John E. Reisdorph
15	Isaac Trone
16	
17	

NAMES AND DATES OF INITIATIONS. To be entered here only. 6			NAMES AND DATES OF PASSINGS. To be entered here only. 7		
Insert here the names of all who have been INITIATED since the last report, whether you have received fees of them or not.			Insert here the names of all who have been passed since the last report, whether you have received fees of them or not.		
NAMES.	DATES.		NAMES.	DATES.	
1 G. C. R. Fuller	Jany	7	1 G. C. R Fuller	Feby	4
2 T. H. Ruth	Mar	3	2 T. H. Ruth	mar	24
3			3		

Blue Lodges send an annual "return" to their governing Grand Lodge each year, reporting officers, members, initiates, and similar information. This is from the first return of De Smet Lodge #55.

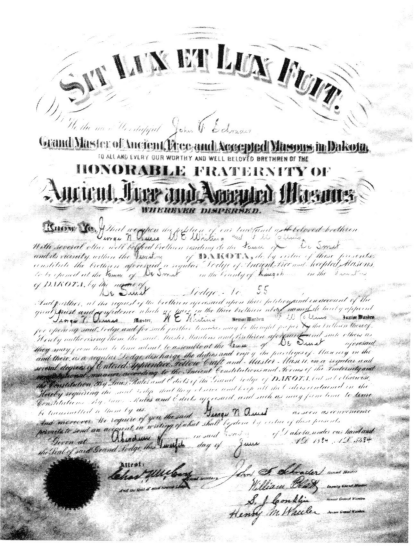

The original Charter of De Smet Lodge #55, A. F. & A. M.

—The new Odd Fellow hall is expected to be ready for occupancy next Monday evening. The masonic fraternity will be the first society to hold a meeting in the new hall.

*The De Smet News published notice when the Lodge moved to the Odd
Fellows hall in 1898. From the December 16, 1898 issue.*

The large, white building in the center was the Kingsbury County Abstract Company building. The Lodge met upstairs for several years, including many years Charles was a member. Today it is the Heritage House Bed and Breakfast. Photo courtesy Kim Ernst.

The current building of De Smet Lodge #55.
They have owned this building and met here since 1917.

In 1883-4, Charles was trying to prove up the homestead, which was required to receive title to the land. Since he had not had great success with farming, he was also working as he could in town. Therefore, it is likely he did not then have the time to invest to join the Lodge and learn the work. Part of the ceremony involves asking the initiate a series of questions, each of which he must answer exactly with the prescribed answer in order to proceed. The phrase "giving the third degree" for an interrogation comes from the ritual of being raised to the third degree in the Masonic Lodge. It can be very time-consuming to learn the work exactly right. There are usually two or three men in a Lodge who help new initiates learn the rituals. One of the most proficient ritualists in the area was Charles Dawley, who married Laura's teacher Miss Garland.

The year 1883 was an important one for Laura personally, as well. She earned her teacher's license that year, on the 10th of December, following in the steps of her mother and grandmother, and began teaching her first term of school that same month. She was also courted by a young man from a neighboring farm, Almanzo Wilder, who had courageously helped save the town by bringing wheat during the hard winter. This winter, each Friday afternoon Almanzo drove Laura home from her teaching position to be with her family for the weekends, and drove her back on Sunday evening. Soon, he was taking Laura on buggy rides in the spring.

Almanzo was born outside Malone, New York on February 13, 1857. The fifth of six children, he spent his younger days there, on the prosperous farm of his parents, James and Angeline Wilder. His boyhood on the family farm is described in Laura's book, *Farmer Boy*. In 1871, his parents sold the farm in New York and moved west to Spring Valley, Minnesota. Almanzo went with them, and most of his teen years were spent in Spring Valley. In 1879, Almanzo headed even further west, to De Smet. Two of his older siblings, Royal and Eliza Jane, accompanied him. They each filed claims, and when not working the land, they worked in town. Almanzo worked as a laborer on the railroad for a short time. Royal opened a feed store, which Almanzo helped run at times. Eliza Jane taught a term of school in De Smet, with Laura as one of her students.[13]

Almanzo was an ambitious young man and filed on not only a homestead claim, on which he resided and farmed, but also a tree claim. According to the 1878 amendment of the Timber Culture Act, he had to "plant, protect, and keep in a healthy, growing condition for ten years" at least ten acres of trees in order to receive title to the land. In drought-dried Dakota, this was no easy feat. Almanzo was also known as an expert horseman, and he raised and trained horses on his farm whenever possible. He was partial to Morgans, and his teams were the envy of the town.

Almanzo courted Laura for about three years. During that time, she worked for the town dressmaker and alternated between being a schoolgirl and a schoolteacher. In those days, one did not need to be graduated oneself to be a teacher, but only needed to be able to pass the teacher's examination. Laura passed the examinations, so she was able to teach even though she herself was still a schoolgirl. She would teach for a term, then return to school for a term. Laura continued this pattern until the year she was to graduate. Three schools employed her: Bouchie School, Perry School, and Wilkin School. When Laura agreed to teach at the Wilkin School, she was not aware that by so doing she herself would be unable to graduate. She later explained that she had been ready to graduate at the end of the previous term, but the school master had decided not to have a graduation ceremony for only one student. He did not know that Laura would be getting married instead of returning to school after she taught the term at Wilkin School, and he planned to graduate an entire class after the following term; but that was the term Laura would miss while she was teaching. She was given the opportunity to decline the position with Wilkin School, even though it was too late to hire someone else. As a testament to the importance she gave education, Laura denied herself a graduation ceremony to ensure that the Wilkin School would have a teacher and the children an education. She wanted to graduate, but knew it was the education, not the ceremony, that was important.[14]

While Laura was teaching and sewing, Almanzo was busy working his tree claim and homestead. When he enjoyed a visit from his family, he surely introduced Laura to them, although there is no record of the fact. In the autumn of 1884, Almanzo took a few months off farming to take a peddler's trip with Royal, selling notions from his brother's store on an extended route through neighboring states. Although their original plan included going to the New Orleans Exhibition after a stop to visit their parents, Almanzo did not go that far; he returned to De Smet early, and resumed his courtship of Laura.[15]

Laura and Almanzo were married on August 25, 1885. The notice in the *De Smet Leader* read:

Married. WILDER-INGALLS- At the residence of the officiating clergyman, Rev. E. Brown, August 25, 1885. Mr. Almanzo J. Wilder and Miss Laura Ingalls, both of De Smet. Thus two more of our respected young people have united in the journey of life. May their voyage be pleasant, their joys be many and their sorrows few.

The *Kingsbury County News* also announced the marriage:

MARRIED at the residence of the officiating clergyman, Rev. E. Brown, August 25, 1885, Almanzo J. Wilder and Miss Laura E. Ingalls, both of De Smet. Both the contracting parties are well and favorably known in De Smet, both having located here before there was a town and they will start in their new career with the best wishes of all. May their pathway be ever bright with no clouds to dim the sunshine of their happiness is the wish of the NEWS.

A little over three months after Laura's wedding, Charles embarked on a new phase in his own life: that of a Freemason. On December 7, 1885, Charles P. Ingalls, 49-year-old farmer of De Smet, petitioned the Lodge to become a Mason, submitting $1 of the initiation fee with his request. He was recommended by C. S. G. (Charleton) Fuller, C. L . Dawley, and L. E. Sasse. The Master of the Lodge assigned George Masters, J. E. Smith, and George Wilmarth to investigate the petitioner. The report being favorable, and the vote of the Lodge being taken, Charles was initiated into the first degree as an Entered Apprentice Mason in De Smet Masonic Lodge, No. 55, A. F. & A. M. on January 18, 1886. The primary focus of this first degree is the importance of seeking knowledge, something with which Charles was in complete agreement.

His petition shows that Charles had requested to join the Lodge at some point earlier, but was unable to do so due to illness. There is no indication or record as to when the first request was made, or what the illness was that prevented his joining.

It is likely that Charles received a good bit of bantering before his initiation. It is customary for the Masons to tease candidates in the days leading up to the ceremony. "Better watch out for that goat – he'll take you for a wild ride!" and similar comments portend things such as riding goats, being buried alive, and other alarming activities. It is believed that the idea of a goat in the Lodge has its origin in the mythical Greek god Pan, who was goat-like in form. When Christianity began to spread, Pan was transformed into Satan (which is why the devil has historically been pictured with horns, hooves, and tail). As Freemasons held secretive rituals, rumors abounded about them consorting with the devil. Nor were the Masons the only group subject to this theory: Odd Fellows, Woodmen of the World, Elks, and other such societies suffered the same accusations. Although there have always been those who persist in believing such claims, the idea mostly petered out, and as it did so the Masons and other groups were able to turn it into a joke (similar to the way the patriots of the American Revolution turned the derogatory phrase "Yankee Doodle" into a positive rally song). There is evidence of some groups such as the Odd Fellows and Elks putting initiates through a light hazing, which might include such things as being led

PETITION ✠ TO ✠ BE ✠ MADE ✠ A ✠ MASON.

To the W. Master, Wardens, & Brethren of _DeSmet_

Lodge No. _55_ , A. F. & A. Masons:

The petition of the subscriber respectfully represents that, having long entertained a favorable opinion of your Institution, he is desirous, if found worthy, of being admitted a member thereof. If accepted, he pledges himself to a cheerful obedience to all the requirements of your By-Laws, and to the established rules and regulations of the Order.

He has ~~never~~ petitioned ~~any other~~ Lodge for the degrees in Masonry. _but owing to sickness was unable to take the degrees_ His age is _49_ years; his occupation is that of a _Farmer_ ; his residence is _DeSmet_

Dated at _DeSmet_ this _Seventh_ day of _December_ 188_5_

Charles P. Ingalls

The petitioner must sign his full name.

Recommended by

C. S. G. Fuller

C. L. Dawley ⎫ Master Masons.

L. L. Sass

Frank Hudson, Jr., Dealer in Masonic Books, Blanks, etc., Springfield, Ill.

Ten Dollars with This

Charles's petition for membership in the Masonic Lodge.

around the room on a mechanical goat or being sprayed with trick mirrors, but these stunts were never part of the initiation itself. As far as I have been able to discover, stunts are not pulled today in any of the societies, but the joke of riding a goat persists. The more popular and well-liked a man is, the more teasing he often receives.[16]

THE BUCKING GOAT

From a 1907 advertisement of a stunt goat.

It is also important to note that Charles was not asked to join the Lodge; he approached them. It is a rule in Masonry that members are not to ask others to join. The works of the fraternity and the lives of the members themselves are to stand as testimony on their own, causing other men to desire to join. That is why they have the expression, "To be one, ask one." Charles evidently saw something in the men of the Lodge that prompted him to petition for membership. As he once remarked, "It's pleasant to be with a crowd of people all trying to do the right thing."[17] Charles would not have joined the Lodge without truly embracing their ideals. Not only would his personal integrity have prevented that, but so would his finances: the initiation fee was $3, and Charles worked hard for every cent.

The brothers of De Smet Lodge #55 were pillars of

the community who embodied the ideals of Freemasonry. They provided relief to those in need, and promoted faith, education, and patriotism. A few of the ways they did this were through charitable aid, special Easter services to celebrate the resurrection of Christ, and annual dinners on George Washington's birthday, at which historical and patriotic recitations were given. Since these were causes Charles supported, they no doubt influenced his decision to petition the Lodge for membership.

A man must ask to join, but what about leaving? If a man decides he wants to discontinue his association for any reason, he may do so by simply writing a letter to his blue Lodge informing them of that fact. There is no pressure to remain or special requirements to leave. If his dues are currently paid, he will be granted a demit, which gives him the right to rejoin at a future time if he wishes. (If he owes on his dues, he can still terminate his affiliation, but will be required to pay the delinquent amount before rejoining.) A man may also cease to pay his annual dues, and he will be dropped from membership by suspension.

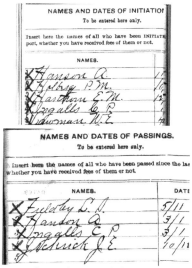

The book of returns was bound too tightly to allow full copies, but I was able to verify the dates of Charles's initiation, passing, and raising.

About six weeks after being initiated, Charles was passed to the second degree of Fellowcraft on March 1, 1886. The precepts of assistance to others and building society are ideals with which he was already living in harmony, as his public service in the town of De Smet, and his willingness to lend a hand to a neighbor whenever he could, attest.

NAMES AND DATES OF RAISINGS.

Insert here the names of all who have been RAISED since the last port, whether you have received fees of them or not.
These names must also appear among the names of members.

NAMES. FIRST NAME IN FULL.	DATES.
Hawthorn, Eaelbert M.	Sep. 27 1886
Ingalls, Charles P.	Feb. 7 1887
Lawman William S.	Sep. 27 1886
Mills, Robert B.	Oct 3 1886
Sanford Eawin P.	Jan 3 1887
Van Hook, David A.	June 7 1886

In 1886, the little town underwent some big improvements. A new mill was built, along with two new bank buildings and various other businesses and homes. The crowning glory, however, was the Couse Block and Opera House, built on the second floor of a new store.[18] It is likely that Charles Ingalls worked on at least some of these buildings. He was also busy on his farm, a full-time job of its own. His concentration on these projects may explain at least in part why Charles was not raised to the sublime third degree of Master Mason until February 7, 1887. An illness Charles suffered may also have been at least part of the reason for the delay: on March 26, 1887, Grace noted in her diary that "Laura has not been here for two weeks nor we their (sic). Pa has been sick a long while we had the doctor and he has just got well."[19] It is unclear whether it was Charles's illness that prevented visits with Laura, or Grace was just stating an unrelated but noteworthy

OFFICERS.

FIRST NAME IN FULL.

1. *Jacob E. Jickrick* — W. M.
2. *George E. Masters* — S. W.
3. *Edward A. Morrison* — J. W.
4. *John E. Risedorph* — Treasurer
5. *Edwin P. Sanford* — Secretary.
6. *Charles L. Dawley* — S. D.
7. *William A. Lawman* — J. D.
8. *David A. VanHook* — S. Steward
9. *Isaac M. Trone* — J. Steward
10. *Charles P. Ingalls* — Tyler.

From the annual return to the Grand Lodge of South Dakota for 1888.

fact. As officers for the year 1887 were already installed in De Smet Lodge, Charles did not hold an office upon being raised. He held his first office, that of Tyler, in the year 1888, and remained in that position in 1889.

Through these years, Charles had been working various carpentry and other jobs in town, in addition to serving as Deputy Sheriff. He finally gave up on farming entirely, and built a home for the family in town, on Third Street. When the house was complete, the family moved into it, and Charles and Caroline remained there for the rest of their lives. Caroline minded the home, as she always had, stretching the thin resources as far as could be done. Mary had been studying at the College for the Blind, but she did not attend the 1887-88 year for unknown reasons. She returned the following year for her final terms. Mary graduated from the blind school on June 12, 1889, and returned home, surely an occasion of celebration.[20]

Grace was still attending school in De Smet. She and Carrie were also involved in the Young People's League at the

The final home of Charles and Caroline Ingalls.

Congregational Church, and other activities of the young folks in town. Carrie was in her later teen years and, although her health was always frail, she was evidently a popular girl. She served as Secretary of the Good Templars society in De Smet in 1889. The entire family were prohibitionists, and, according to Grace's diary, they were involved with and enjoyed many of the lectures and entertainments of the temperance campaign that fall. They were all pleased when prohibition passed by a substantial majority in the November election.[21] As a closing to the year, on December 2, 1889, Charles was installed as Junior Deacon of the De Smet Lodge for the coming year.

> De Smet Lodge, No. 240, I. O. G. T., meets every Friday evening at 7.30, in the old county building at corner of Third St. and Calumet Ave. P. LAWRENCE, C. T.
> CARRIE INGALLS, Rec. Sec'y.

From the December 7, 1889 issue of the De Smet Leader.

The public installation of the officers of the Masonic lodge on Monday night was a very pleasant affair. The hall was well filled with people, mostly of our city, but a few from Lake Preston. The opening ode was sung by a male quartet consisting of Messrs. Hamilton, Seelye, Trousdale and Morrison, with Mrs. Hamilton at the organ. The following officers were installed by District Deputy C. S. G. Fuller: E. A. Morrison, W. M.; Geo. B. Wilmarth, S. W.; E. P. Sanford, J. W.; W. L. Seelye, Sec'y; C. L. Dawley and C. P. Ingalls, deacons; E. R. Rilling and J. L. Barker, stewards; J. F. B. Masters, tyler; C. S. G. Fuller was afterward installed treasurer. After another ode by the quartet, Rev. C. C. Marston of Watertown came forward and gave an address upon the subject of Masonry. After a closing ode, the meeting became informal and refreshments were served. All voted it a very pleasant entertainment, and departed with very friendly feelings toward this the most ancient of all orders.

The De Smet Leader published notice of Masonic installations, as this example from December 7, 1889 shows.

While Charles was turning away from farming and moving his family into town, Almanzo was busy trying to make his farm prosperous, and not having much success. Mother Nature thwarted him with a hail storm that destroyed his entire wheat crop just before it was ready for harvest in 1886, so he lost a year's income. Despite the hardships, the year ended with a joyous event, when Laura gave birth to their daughter, Rose, on December 5, 1886. It was evidently a hard birth (most likely due to Laura's small size and the baby's large size), for they had to have the doctor come to help, which added to their bills. The newspaper announced:

The good angel called at the home of Mr. and Mrs. A. J. Wilder last Monday night, and left a bright little nine-pound girl to cheer their solitude. Dr. Cushman reports mother and daughter doing nicely. Grandpa Ingalls is entitled to wear gray hairs and numerous wrinkles now. 'Manley' says they have named the little one Rose and if she don't cause him many a 'rose' during the cold, stilly watches of night 'ere the balmy zephyrs of spring arrive, he may thank his lucky stars.

"Manley" (sic) was Laura's nickname for Almanzo; he called her Bessie. Others sometimes used these names as well.

Almanzo reaped a fair crop in 1887, but it was not enough to eliminate all of their debt. Trying to expand their portfolio, so to speak, he and Laura invested in a flock of sheep with her cousin, Peter. It did pay off in the end, but still not enough to pay off their debts.[22] Then came the worst of times for Laura and Almanzo, when grief of every sort assailed them.

In the summer of 1887, their barn and haystacks burned down. Almanzo and Laura happened to be returning from visiting some friends at the time, and, with neighbors' help, were able to stop the flames from spreading to their home.[23] It was a major setback, but the young Wilders had hope that they would be able to overcome the loss with the next harvest. It was not to be.

The next spring, Almanzo and Laura both contracted diphtheria.[24] It was debilitating, and Laura and Almanzo were bed-ridden for several weeks. Charles and Caroline kept Rose while Royal looked after his younger brother and sister-in-law. Eventually they improved, but Almanzo suffered a stroke soon after. The medical profession was not yet very advanced, so the diagnoses of those days are always subject to reevaluation; some believe that he may actually have had polio.[25] Whatever the cause, it left him permanently crippled, with a lifelong limp and pains in his hands and feet, particularly in cold weather. There were now more medical bills added to their debt. Their weakened condition made farm work difficult, so they could not count on income from a good harvest.

Laura was pregnant when the illness struck, and that probably contributed to the most terrible blow of all. She gave birth to a son in the summer of 1889, but the baby was not healthy. He lived only days, not even long enough to be named. Baby boy Wilder died on August 5, 1889 and is buried in De

Smet Cemetery.[26]

As though fate was testing just how much the young couple could take, less than three weeks later the Wilder's home was burned to the ground in a freak fire, a complete loss.[27] That was the final stroke: having been besieged by calamities in their first years of marriage in De Smet, Laura and Almanzo thought it prudent to leave Dakota with its memories of heartache for some place that would be beneficial to their health, in addition to providing a means to make a living. They probably made their first plans when Almanzo's parents visited that December, and Laura and Almanzo arranged an extended stay with them in Spring Valley, Minnesota, where the elder Wilders still resided on a successful farm. Until then, Laura and Almanzo stayed with Charles and Caroline for a few weeks, then boarded with a neighbor in return for keeping house for him.[28]

In 1890, the young Wilders packed up and traveled to the home of Almanzo's parents. There, Almanzo's mother could help Laura care for her crippled husband and young daughter, and Almanzo did not have the entire responsibility of running a farm in less-than-optimal health. Almanzo was already familiar with the town and many of its residents, as he had spent his teen years there. Laura may have met some kinfolk, as distant Ingalls relatives resided in the area.[29]

Just over a year later, in October, 1891, they moved to Westville, Florida, at the urging of Laura's cousin, Peter. Peter had gone there with Almanzo's brother, Perley, the previous year. They believed that the warmer climate would be better for Almanzo, as the cold winters up north increased the pain in his hands and feet.[30]

While the young Wilders were still in Spring Valley, Bethlehem Chapter #13 of the Order of the Eastern Star Chapter was formed back in De Smet, on June 1, 1891.

After establishment of the General Grand Chapter in 1876, Chapters of the Order of the Eastern Star spread rapidly. Within just thirteen years, the six existing Chapters in Dakota Territory met in Watertown, North of De Smet, and formed a Grand Chapter for the Territory. This was in July, 1889 – only four months before statehood. At that time, each state organized its own Grand Chapter. A mere two years later, De Smet was forming a Chapter.

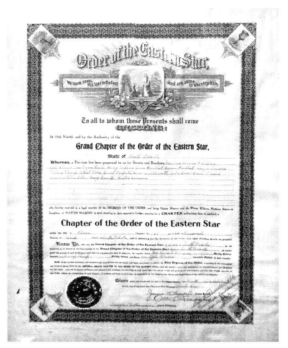

Charter of Bethlehem Chapter #13, De Smet.

It is no surprise that Mrs. C. P. Ingalls – Caroline – should be among the charter members. She was a well-respected, founding member of the community, and the virtues of faith, devotion, industry, and fortitude promoted by the Order matched her own values.

Also among the charter members was Miss Carrie Ingalls. In fact, Carrie was not only a charter member, but was immediately installed into the office of Warder. Laura's good friend Mary Power, who was now Mrs. Edwin Sanford, joined at this same meeting and was installed as the officer of Marshall. George and Margaret (Maggie) Masters, who had stayed with the Ingallses during the hard winter of 1880-81 and had a baby in their home, were also charter members and charter officers: she as 'Esther' and he as Worthy Patron. The office of Treasurer was filled by charter member Mrs. C. L. Dawley, who had been Laura and Carrie's teacher, Miss Florence Garland. Other well-known members of the community who joined the new Chapter included Mrs. G. C. R. Fuller, who was installed as the charter 'Martha.' She was the wife of Gerald Fuller, of the hardware store from which Laura and Carrie purchased a mowing machine part for Pa and then got lost in the Big Slough on the way home, thereby providing Laura's first interaction

From the list of charter members of Bethlehem #13.

with Almanzo, in *The Long Winter*. Mrs. Thomas Ruth (the wife of banker Ruth, also mentioned several times in *The Long Winter*) was installed as 'Electa' (mistakenly called 'Electra' in the minutes of the meeting).[31]

*From the minutes of the first meeting of Bethlehem #13;
Carrie was voted into the office of Warder.*

Charles did not join when the Chapter was formed, and Laura, living out of state, of course could not. Grace was not old enough to join, and even when she did attain that age, she never did. Mary never joined either, almost assuredly because her blindness made her ineligible. At that time, there were physical requirements related to the ability of an individual to perform certain signs and so forth. Mary, being blind, would not have been able to see when signs were made and so could not have made the proper response. Today, such requirements have been eliminated, and blind persons, as well as individuals with other disabilities, are able to join the Order. If she had been able to join, Mary no doubt would have done very well and taken great pleasure in it. "Think of being able to study and learn – Oh, everything!" Mary says in *Little Town on the Prairie*, and the book later says, "Mary had always so loved to study. Now she could revel in studying so much that she had never before had a chance to learn."[32]

At this meeting, Carrie was in her office as Warder,
and Caroline was in the station of Electa as a Pro Tem officer.

It is hard to determine to what extent Caroline was involved with the Order. She did not hold any office; however, there are many other ways to serve. She may have been active behind the scenes, or she may have simply attended the meetings. Existing records do not provide definitive information, although they do show that she filled in as a Pro Tem officer on occasion.

Carrie embraced the Order whole-heartedly. She held an office almost every year and very seldom missed a meeting; there were even times that she filled two offices at the same meeting, due to lack of sufficient members to attain the full eighteen. The meetings of the Eastern Star were held on the second and fourth Mondays of each month. Lodge meetings were held on the first and third Mondays of each month. Since this was alternate Mondays from Eastern Star meetings, every week the Ingalls were involved with the fraternity in some way.

Charles had not yet joined the Eastern Star, but he was active in the Lodge. Records show that he was faithful in attendance and held office regularly. On November 30, 1891, he was again installed as Junior Deacon, for the coming year of 1892, his third year in that office.

The following is intended to provide a general yet accurate representation of what happens in a typical Masonic Lodge meeting, such as Charles would have attended, and such as is still held today – without revealing any secrets of Freemasonry; however, keep in mind that procedures vary slightly between states.[33] All persons in the following meeting were members of De Smet Lodge #55, holding the office portrayed.

It's Monday evening and Charles is leaving the house. Wearing his good suit, he walks to the Lodge, since it is a nice May evening and the Lodge building is only a few blocks away. Making his way upstairs, he enters the outer door of the building and goes first to the dining area, where he finds many men already there. Among them is Charleton Fuller. Charles does not yet know that his daughter will marry the brother of Fuller's wife, connecting the two families; tonight, they are simply brothers in the Lodge. With Charleton is his brother Gerald, and Mr. Dawley, who had married Laura's teacher, Miss Garland. They are engaged in conversation with Mr. Harthorn and Mr. Wilmarth, local merchants. Over there is Will Whiting, who, along with Charles and a few others, had helped organize Kingsbury County. Mr. Whiting is talking to Thomas Ruth, the banker, and Mr. Wilkin, at whose home Laura stayed when she taught school in that district. Wilkens had served as Tyler the charter year.

Charles greets the other men, shaking hands with them as he makes his way to an empty chair at a table. There is much conviviality. Charles takes a plate from the center of the table and helps himself to bread, cheese, a slice of ham, and a sugar cookie. The men are jovial as they enjoy the refreshment. It has always been traditional for Lodges to enjoy a meal before the meeting (sometimes after), if possible. There are many ways this has been funded: in old days when Lodges met in taverns, each man might purchase his own meal. Later, some places charged for the meal; this got to be controversial as it sometimes proved to be either a hardship or an embarrassment (or both) to those men with limited means. Most often, there is a donation box, and those who are able, donate to fund the meal. If Charles had enough to spare, he may have dropped a coin or two into the box. If not, no one begrudged him a few bites.

Soon, the men begin leaving the table and preparing for the meeting. On another table against the opposite wall lies a stack of white aprons; next to them are the jewels of the Lodge. Since Charles is Junior Deacon, he finds the jewel of the square and compasses with moon, and arranges it over his collar. He ties on one of the white aprons. This is a Master

Mason's meeting, so all the men wear their aprons the same way: fully spread over their suit coats. (If it were a Fellowcraft or Entered Apprentice meeting, Masons of those degrees would tuck up one or both corners into the waistband of the apron, in accordance with their degree.) Charles enters the inner door to the Lodge room and makes his way to the seat of his office, on the west wall, beside the door and near the Senior Warden. The camaraderie enjoyed in the dining room continues in the Lodge room. The Secretary takes note of all who are there, so he can mark down in the minutes which of the officers are present and if there are any visitors.

The chairs in the Lodge room are arranged along the North and South walls, except for the chairs of officers that sit in the east and west. The Master and Senior and Junior Wardens' chairs each have a podium before them. Hanging on the wall behind the Master's chair is a large, capital G. The Charter of the Lodge and a portrait of George Washington also hang on the wall in the east. The altar sits in the middle of the room. On it are a closed Bible, and a square and compasses. Three unlit candles stand at the right of the altar. In the Northwest corner stand two fluted pillars.

Interior of De Smet Lodge, facing the east. The Master's chair is beneath the "G" on the wall. The altar is in the center.

At the designated time, the Worshipful Master, Edwin Sanford, puts on the master's hat. The Master of the Lodge must wear a hat in meetings, and he is the only one allowed to do so. Then, bam! The sound of the striking gavel from the podium in the east calls the brothers to attention. The Master announces that he is about to open the meeting, and directs that all men be "properly clothed," meaning that they should all be sure they have tied on the appropriate apron, in the correct manner, and officers should be wearing the jewel of their office. He instructs all to take their positions, then asks if all present are Masons. Brother Whiting, as Senior Warden, quickly identifies everyone present, and answers Master Sanford in the affirmative. The Tyler, Brother Wilmarth, stands before the altar with his sword drawn. Upon being questioned by the Master, the Brother Wilmarth affirms his duty to guard the Lodge against those unauthorized to enter, and then takes his position outside the inner door to the Lodge room, leaving the door open.

The view from the east. The room has been set up for an Eastern Star meeting; the chairs and pedestals around the altar would not be present in a meeting of the Masonic Lodge.

Master Sanford then addresses Charles, "Brother Junior Deacon, what is your duty?"

"To see that the Lodge is properly tiled, Worshipful Master," Charles replies.

"You will inform the Tyler that I am about to open a Master Mason Lodge for the dispatch of business, and he is directed to Tile accordingly," Master Sanford instructs Charles.

Charles approaches the door, takes hold of the handle, and relays Master Sanford's message to Brother Wilmarth. He then closes the door, and raps a signal knock with his knuckles. On the other side of the door, the Tyler raps a reply, "sealing" the door. Charles informs Master Sanford when the door has been sealed.

Bam! Bam! Bam! Upon the third strike of the gavel, all rise and the meeting opens. It begins with a review of the offices of Junior and Senior Warden and Worshipful Master, stating their position and duties within the Lodge. An invocation by the Chaplain and the Pledge of Allegiance to the flag follow. At the prompt of the Worshipful Master, all members give the secret Masonic signs.

The meeting is now open, and Worshipful Master Sanford again addresses Charles, "Junior Deacon, you will inform the Tyler that a Master Mason Lodge is now open for the dispatch of business and he is directed to tile accordingly."

Charles again approaches the door and taps, a different pattern than what he had done previously. After the Tyler taps the appropriate response, Charles opens the door and states, "Brother Tyler, the Worshipful Master has now opened a Master Mason Lodge for the dispatch of business. You are directed to tile accordingly."

Brother Wilmarth replies, "Duly noted."

Charles closes the door, gives the signal knock, and, upon receiving the answering knock which seals the door, returns to his chair.

Meanwhile, the Senior Deacon, Brother Dawley, has approached the altar, opened the Bible to the appropriate passage for a Master Masons' meeting, and placed the square and compasses in the proper configuration. A Masonic Lodge may be opened on the first degree, the second degree, or – most commonly – the third degree of the Master Mason. The scripture to which the Sacred Law is opened, the configuration of the square and compasses, and which signs are given all depend on the degree on which the Lodge is opened. The Senior Deacon then lights the three candles. Today, Lodge rooms are wired with appropriate lights over and beside the altar. In Charles's day, before electric lights were available, candles or lamps were used.

Charles again informs the Master that the duty has been performed. Bam! The gavel signals that all may now sit down.

Next, any visitors are introduced. Then the Secretary reads the minutes of the previous meeting. The Master asks if there are any corrections to be made. No one answers, so he asks for a vote to approve the minutes.

As Master Sanford announces the pass of the vote, a rap sounds on the door.

The meeting comes to a halt as Charles immediately jumps to his feet and addresses the Master, "Worshipful Master, there is an alarm at the door!"

"Brother Junior Deacon, determine the cause of the alarm."

Charles approaches the door, and raps a signal knock. The answering rap from the Tyler outside the door informs Charles that it is safe to open the door. When he does, Brother Wilmarth tells him the reason for the alarm: a latecomer has arrived. The Tyler has already ascertained that the new arrival is a Master Mason, approved to attend the meeting.

Charles closes the door before announcing, "Worshipful Master, the alarm was caused by a Master Mason wishing to enter the Lodge room."

"See that the Master Mason is properly clothed and allow him to enter," instructs Master Sanford.

Charles opens the door, verifies that the latecomer is wearing his apron, and admits him.

While Charles and Brother Wilmarth seal the door again, the arriving Mason proceeds directly to the altar and gives the sign of the Master Mason. After this is confirmed by the corresponding sign from the Worshipful Master, the new arrival may take his seat.

The meeting then resumes. Thomas Ruth, the Treasurer, gives a financial report, followed by the Secretary, who reads any new correspondence, including any petition for membership. When a petition is received, the Master appoints a committee of three masons to investigate the petitioner, and at the next meeting the committee will report on their findings. Charles served on several of these investigating committees through the years. After hearing the results of the investigation, the Lodge will vote on the petition using black and white balls in a secret ballot.

Next, announcements are made. These may include community events, illness or achievements among members, friends, or family, or any other item of interest; however, there may be no discussion of political or religious topics. Then it's down to business.

Minutes of the meetings from Charles's day show that the business of the meeting was often initiating new members, as the Lodge was growing rapidly. They also cared for the furniture of the Lodge and engaged in charitable activities. On rare occasions, the Lodge had to handle unpleasant business, protecting the reputation of the Craft when a brother strayed from the strict moral code. For example, Charles and Royal Wilder were among those called to testify in a Masonic trial against a member who had been accused of "borrowing" an item from Royal's store and not returning it when promised. Evidently the accused man was a friend, and Royal did not wish to take the matter to the civic authorities, but at the same time he could not afford to have things taken from his store and not paid for. Even though Royal was not a member of the Lodge, he knew that the members would deal with their brother fairly, and brought the matter before them. Royal's own testimony is given as a "profane," or non-mason. The word comes from the Latin *pro*, meaning before or outside, and *fanum*, meaning temple; literally, "outside the temple." The accused man admitted his error and made restitution. In Charles's day, De Smet Lodge investigated other accusations of

Opening of Royal's testimony. The name of the accused has been erased. When he completed his testimony, Royal signed his statement.

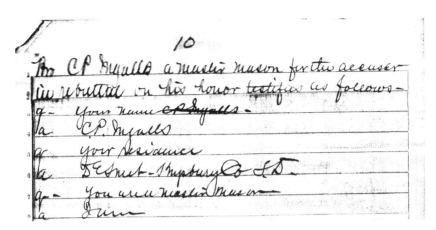

Charles was a witness at the trial.

conduct unbecoming a Mason, such as slander and "consorting" with a lady in a hotel, unmarried. This type of conduct was not tolerated, and men found guilty of it were expelled from the Lodge. Lodges may still expel those who "breach good morals" and act in a way to bring dishonor to the organization, although the interpretation of what constitutes a breach of good morals has evolved with the changing times.

Most of the business of the Lodge today is taken up by discussion of the charitable and civic activities of the Lodge: fundraising, disbursement of aid, community events, approval of scholarships, and other such philanthropic concerns.

After the business is completed, it is time to close the Lodge. Charles and Brother Wilmarth engage in a reversal of the opening ritual, going through the prescribed knocks to unseal the door. The ceremony of closing involves questions and answers of officers, giving the secret signs, and a closing prayer. After the meeting is declared closed, Charles opens the door, then approaches the altar, sets aside the square and compasses, closes the Bible, and extinguishes the candles. The men leave their jewels and aprons on the table in the adjoining room for the next meeting. After more visiting, Charles makes his way home.

As he walks home, Charles notices the full moon over the trees. He doesn't dream that one day man will walk on that very moon; he would also have been surprised to know that event would spur a special Lodge. The Apollo 11 landed on an area of the moon known as the Sea of Tranquility on July 20, 1969. On that historic date, the first man to set foot on the moon was Neil Armstrong. Right behind him was Edwin Eugene "Buzz" Aldrin, Jr., who was a member of a Masonic Lodge in Texas. Aldrin carried with him a Scottish Rite flag and a Special Deputation from the Grand Lodge of Texas, authorizing him to claim Masonic Territorial Jurisdiction on the moon. Contrary to some reports, Aldrin did not leave any Masonic paraphernalia on the moon or perform any Masonic rituals there. However, through the Special Deputation, the Grand Lodge of Texas established jurisdiction over the moon and was able to charter Tranquility Lodge #2000, A. F. & A. M. The flag that Aldrin carried on the flight was donated to the Supreme Council of the Southern Jurisdiction of the Scottish Rite. This all happened within a few decades of the Masonic Lodge meetings Charles attended.[34]

Many of the townspeople mentioned in Laura's *Little House* books were members of the Masonic Lodge and Eastern Star. Extant records reveal a little about their Masonic lives. Laura's dearest friend, the one who witnessed her marriage to Almanzo, was Ida Wright. She was called Ida Brown after her adoption by Rev. and Mrs. Brown. Laura describes Ida's engagement to Elmer McConnell in *These Happy Golden Years*. They married in December, 1885, and had five children. The McConnells moved to Wisconsin by the turn of the century,

where Elmer worked as school janitor. Later, the family moved to Sacramento, California. It is undetermined where or when Elmer joined a Masonic Lodge, but that he did is evidenced by the square and compasses on the headstone at his grave site. Ida died in 1929 and Elmer in 1942. They are buried in the Masonic Lawn Cemetery in Sacramento, California.[35]

Another of Laura's good friends was Mary Power. She was beginning to go out with "the new clerk in Ruth's bank" in *These Happy Golden Years.* The new young banker was Edwin Sanford. Edwin had moved to De Smet in 1884 and began work as bookkeeper at the Kingsbury County Bank. Soon he was a cashier and stockholder. He and Mary Power wed on April 3, 1886, and they lived across the street from Charles and Caroline Ingalls on Third Street. Both Edwin and Mary led active social lives, including activity in the Lodge and Eastern Star Chapter. Edwin joined the Lodge in 1886, and held several offices throughout the years. These included Secretary, Treasurer, and Junior Warden. He also served as Master of the Lodge for five terms. Mary was a charter member of Bethlehem Chapter #13, and held the charter office of Marshall in 1891; later, she filled the Star Point stations of 'Esther' and 'Martha.' They were active in both the Lodge and Chapter for many years, through 1906. Edwin paid his Lodge dues for 1907 but did not attend any meetings in that year, and on March 2, 1908, he demitted from De Smet Lodge. This was because he and Mary had moved to Washington State, where Edwin continued in the banking business. Mary died in 1929 and Edwin in 1932. They are buried in Bayview Cemetery at

Bellingham, Washington.[36]

Mary was not the only Power girl that Laura knew. Although not mentioned in the *Little House* books, there were two other sisters, Susie and Lizzie, as well as three brothers, James, Thomas Jr., and Charles. In addition to being Mary Power's sister, Susie Power had another connection to Laura: she married Jake Hopp, the newspaperman from whom Laura bought her name cards in *Little Town on the Prairie*. Jake and Susie married in 1883. The couple moved to Idaho in 1892 and Jake ran a newspaper there for a few years, but in 1902 went into the hardware business. He and Susie moved to Bellingham, as Mary and Edwin had, in 1930. They had no children.[37]

For a short time Jake Hopp boarded in and ran his printing press out of the back of a local hardware store, that of Charleton Fuller. In 1882, Charleton Fuller partnered with his brother Gerald, who was mentioned in the *Little House* books. The brothers each married in 1883, Charleton to Chloe Dow, and Gerald to Luella Burns. Charleton remained in De Smet. He served in the Dakota National Guard when it was formed, attaining rank of Lt. Colonel. He and Chloe ran the store in De Smet and remained in the town their entire lives; they are buried in the town's cemetery. Gerald and Luella moved to California a few years later; they sold their farm in De Smet to the county for $1000 to be used as the "poor farm." Charles Ingalls worked on the construction of the buildings there, and was paid $6 for his labors. While in De Smet, however, both Fuller brothers were active members of the Masonic Lodge. Gerald joined De Smet Lodge #55 in 1885, being its first initiate on January 7 when he became an Entered Apprentice. He was passed to Fellowcraft on February 4, and raised as a Master Mason on August 18. He was a regularly attending member. Gerald's wife Luella served as 'Ruth' in the Bethlehem Chapter of the Order of the Eastern Star in 1895. Gerald's brother Charleton had been a member of a Lodge in Chicago; he transferred his membership to De

Smet and is listed as a charter member in 1884. Charleton held several offices, including Worshipful Master in 1885 and Secretary for several years. He later became a District Deputy for the Grand Lodge of South Dakota. His responsibilities in this office included installing officers in the blue Lodges in his district, and visiting each Lodge to ensure compliance with the constitution and by-laws of the Grand Lodge, as well as the ancient landmarks. Charleton was appointed as the special deputy for the purpose of constituting Bethlehem Chapter #13; he was already a member of the Order. Charleton served as Worthy Patron in 1902. His wife Chloe held several offices: charter 'Martha' in 1891; 'Ruth' and 'Esther' for several years; Secretary in 1905; and five years as Worthy Matron. When Charleton died in 1905, he was given a Masonic burial.[38]

Laura's sister Grace married Nathan Dow, the brother of Chloe Dow Fuller, connecting the families. Another relative of Nathan's was the famed painter Harvey Dunn. Harvey was the son of another one of Nathan's sisters, making him Nathan

Harvey Dunn, at far right, with brothers in De Smet Lodge.
Notice Dunn's paintings on the wall behind them.
The painting on the top left, "The Badlands," still hangs there.

and Grace's nephew. He was also a Freemason, and attended Lodge in De Smet on occasion.

The first teacher Laura had in De Smet was Miss Florence Garland. Miss Garland married Charles Lansing Dawley in December, 1887. Dawley was a clerk of courts at that time, but soon opened a real estate and insurance agency, which became his life's career. Civically, he served on the city council of De Smet, and on the school board. Dawley was a charter member of De Smet Lodge #55, and served as Senior Deacon its first year. He soon took the office of Senior Warden, and held that office for many years. In addition, he was known as a proficient ritualist, helping many Masons learn the Masonic degree work. Dawley also joined the Scottish Rite and the Shrine in Sioux Falls, attaining the thirty-second degree in Freemasonry. In fact, he was awarded the rank and title of Knight Commander of the Court of Honor on October 20, 1903, for commendable service to the Rite. In the Eastern Star, he and Florence were among the most active members. Offices Dawley held include Worthy Patron during four years and Sentinel for two. He had the honor of being deputized by the Worthy Grand Matron in 1894 for the purpose of installing two members of his Chapter as Grand Officers – Emma Gipson as Grand Organist and Jesse Masters as Grand Sentinel. For her part, Florence served in several positions through the years, including Treasurer, 'Ruth' and 'Adah', Warder, Conductress, Associate Matron and Worthy Matron. The Dawleys had two children; their son Walter joined De Smet Lodge in the early 1920s, and father and son were members together for about a decade, until Dawley's death. Walter remained an active member for many years. Charles and Florence Dawley lived in De Smet until their deaths in 1933 and 1935, and they are buried in the De Smet cemetery.[39]

Thomas Ruth is known in *The Long Winter* as "Banker Ruth," who was rich enough to buy lumber to burn and pay $50 for a bag of wheat. He was an early settler in De Smet, establishing Kingsbury County Bank in 1880. In 1889, he was elected Mayor of De Smet, and from 1890-1894 he served as South Dakota's Commissioner of School and Public Lands. When a fire department opened in De Smet, Ruth served as the organization's secretary, and when the Territory of Dakota was moving into statehood, he served on the committee of the Southern Dakota Convention for the framing of the new State's Constitution. Ruth had served in the Civil War, and later belonged to the National Guard for many years, rising to the rank of Colonel. Col. Ruth was an early member of De Smet Lodge and served a year as its Treasurer. His wife Lora was a charter member of the Bethlehem Chapter of the Order of the Eastern Star in De Smet, serving as the charter 'Electa.' She died shortly thereafter, in 1893. Col. Ruth remarried in 1895, to Amelia Bell, who joined the Chapter shortly before their marriage. Amelia was sister to Florence Bell, the dressmaker for whom Laura worked. Col. Ruth and Amelia had one son.

Colonel Ruth, the banker, left; Amelia Bell Ruth and baby Edwin, right.
Photos courtesy Jenny Todd.

The Ruths moved to Pennsylvania in the early 1900s; soon after that, Ruth's nephew moved to De Smet and joined the

139

Lodge. This nephew was also named Thomas H. Ruth, and was sometimes called "Jr." to differentiate him from his uncle. The younger Thomas Ruth petitioned for membership on June 3, 1907 and was initiated that August. On February 10, 1908, he was raised to the sublime degree of Master Mason. He was very active and held many offices through the years, including Master of the Lodge in 1922. Meanwhile, Col. Ruth died in 1908, and Amelia took their son Edwin and moved to West Virginia.[40]

Another local businessman was George Wilmarth. Wilmarth was born in Pennsylvania in 1844. He served in the Union Army during the Civil War, reenlisting twice. He had one child with his first wife; he later remarried and fathered nine more children. Upon moving to De Smet, Wilmarth opened a general store. He and his family, and his store, are mentioned several times in the *Little House* books. Wilmarth's daughter Mary Alice was the first girl born in De Smet. George Wilmarth was active in De Smet Lodge and held office several years. These include Senior Stewart for two years, Junior Warden for three years, and Senior Warden in 1890. He received a letter of condolence from the Lodge upon the tragic death of his two-year-old son, who died when his mother, who had been nursing another sick child in town, unknowingly brought the germs of the disease home. Wilmarth died in 1897 and is in buried De Smet.[41]

George Wilmarth. Courtesy Peggy Ward.

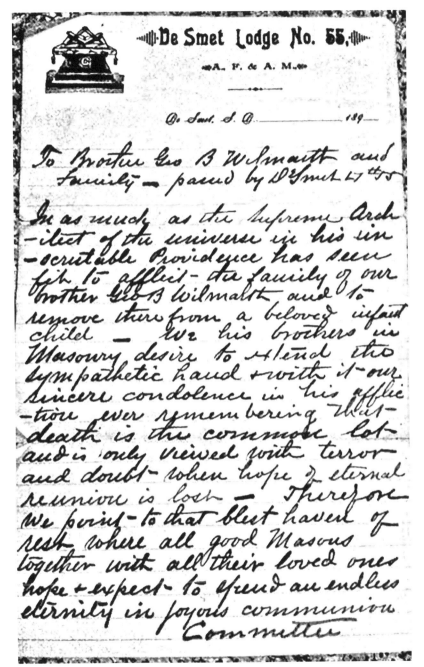

The letter of condolence from De Smet Lodge to George Wilmarth.
Courtesy Peggy Ward.

George and Maggie Masters are not mentioned in the *Little House* books, but scholars of Laura Ingalls Wilders know them from her unpublished autobiography as the young couple who stayed with the Ingallses during the hard winter of 1880-81. The picture Laura painted of George during that winter is not flattering, but in reality, he became an upright man and contributing member of society. After a time working for the railroad, George worked for lumber yards in De Smet, and served four years as the town's postmaster. In the late 1890s, he tried to enlist in the Army to fight in the Spanish American War, but was denied for physical health reasons. Not deterred, he joined the National Guard, and attained the rank of Captain. Such service is not surprising when one considers that he had joined the Masonic Lodge in De Smet. George was obviously a "good man" at his core, and the fraternity helped him develop into a "better man." He was initiated in the first degree on September 15, 1884, passed to the second degree on October 6, 1884, and raised to the third degree on November 17, 1884. George held several offices, including Worshipful Master of the Lodge in 1889 and the first Worthy Patron of Bethlehem Chapter #13, Order of the Eastern Star, a position he held through 1892. His wife, Maggie, was a charter member with him in the De Smet Chapter of the Eastern Star, and held the charter office of 'Esther.' George and Maggie moved from De Smet after the turn of the century.[42]

George's brother Jesse was also an active member of the De Smet Lodge. He served in several offices in the blue Lodge, including Secretary, Junior Warden, Senior Warden, and Master. He received his 50-year membership pin on March 7, 1938, and despite his advanced age, continued to attend meetings through 1938. Jesse and his wife were charter members of Bethlehem Chapter #13, and he was the first Sentinel of the Chapter. A few years later, in 1894, Jesse was appointed Grand Sentinel for the State Grand Chapter of the Order. The Sentinel of a Chapter acts in a similar capacity as a Tyler in the Lodge, making sure that the door to the

Chapter room is secure from the outside; the Grand Sentinel is appointed to the State level rather than the local level.

Laura wrote in *These Happy Golden Years* about teaching at the Brewster School. In reality, she taught at the Bouchie School, but she changed the names of the school and her pupils there to protect their identities, because her time there was so unpleasant. This was her first teaching position. Her students, whom she named as Clarence, Tommy, and Ruby in her book, are believed to have really been eighteen-year-old Isaac and his half-siblings, Clarence, who would have been about twelve years old at the time, and Fannie, then about ten years old. The Bouchies had a troubled home life, to say the least. A year after Laura taught them, Isaac and his stepmother, Elizabeth, were in an argument which became physical. According to court testimony, Elizabeth threw a bone at Isaac, but missed; incensed, she demanded that Clarence get something – anything – and "knock Isaac's head off." Clarence – only about twelve years old at the time of the incident – picked up the bone and threw it at Isaac, hitting him in the face. The bone cut Isaac's cheek, and he contracted tetanus. He died less than two weeks later from the disease. Clarence and Elizabeth were both convicted of manslaughter; Elizabeth was fined instead of being sent to jail because she was pregnant. Clarence was sentenced to six months in jail, but he got out early for good behavior. Upon adulthood, he moved to Chicago and worked for the railroad, and a few years later moved to the Ft. Edward area of New York where he continued his work with the railroad, and also worked as a firefighter.

Clarence was very active in the Masonic Lodge there, as well as the Odd Fellows and the Brotherhood of Locomotive Engineers. He was well respected in the community. When he was killed in a shooting accident in 1902, it was reported that more than 800 Masons, as well as several hundred other people, went to view his body while it lay in state in the Masonic Lodge. He was given a ritualistic Masonic funeral (see an example in Appendix A) in New York, after which his body was shipped to De Smet for burial. Men of De Smet Lodge #55 performed Masonic rites at his interment on August 31, 1902.[43]

Minutes from Clarence Bouchie's Masonic burial service in De Smet.

In *Little Town on the Prairie*, Laura wrote that her father Charles attended a meeting of the county commissioners to organize the county, which was held at the Whiting homestead; Charles brought the family's cat home from the meeting.[44] At that meeting, appointments were made until the offices could be filled by election; Charles was appointed as a Constable, and W. E. Whiting as County Clerk. At another meeting held at the Ingalls home, appointments were made of a Mr. J. Smith as Sheriff, Charles Ingalls and Mr. Gibson as Justices of the Peace, and W. E. Whiting as County Registrar of Deeds.[45] James Smith was a charter member of the Lodge, and served as Secretary its first year. Wilton E. Whiting was also a charter member of De Smet Lodge, serving as Senior Warden that first year. The Whiting and Ingalls families were connected through marriage – Laura's double cousins Ella and Alice married Lee and Arthur Whiting, respectively.

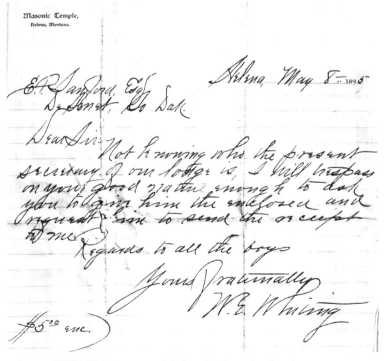

Letter Will Whiting sent with his De Smet Lodge dues payment.

During the 1880s and into 1890, Almanzo's brother Royal operated a feed store and later a general store. He was not content with these enterprises, however, and decided to move back to Spring Valley, where his parents still lived. He opened a variety store there just before Christmas in 1891. He was still a bachelor at that point, and his mother began to send him on errands to the widow Electra Hutchinson's. Her ploy worked, and in March, 1893, Royal and Electra were married. Electra had four children, and she and Royal had three of their own. Only one survived to adulthood, their daughter Angelina Bernice. Bernice grew up to marry George Granger in 1929. He was a Rochester, Minnesota attorney who later became a well-known judge. He was also a Freemason. Royal retired in the early 1920s, and died in 1925. He is buried in Spring Valley.[46]

Royal Wilder.

When Royal first left De Smet to explore the idea of moving to Spring Valley, Charles minded the store for him while he was gone. Once Royal left for good, Charles saw an opportunity to fill the vacancy, and he opened his own store, Ingalls & Company, in 1892. The other stores in town already had the loyalty of their customers, however, so after a year, Charles closed the store front and instead took his goods by wagon to outlying farms, where the residents were unable to get to town often. In this way he was able to add to the meager living he made from carpentry and other odd jobs.

New Goods Just Arrived!

A large number of New Articles just opened, among them you will find Hosiery for men, women and children; Suspenders for men and boys; Tinware at one-half ordinary prices; Harness, Halters, Fly Nets, Water Pails, Milk Pans, Cups, Dippers, etc.; School Supplies.

TEN-CENT COUNTER !

Toilet Soap, Needles, Thread Pins, Buttons, Scissors, Brushes, Paper, Envelopes, Pens, Pencils, Table Linen, and many other useful articles at very LOW PRICES. **INGALLS & CO.**

An advertisement from Charles's store.

Through the 1880s, Grace was still living at home and attending the local school at De Smet. She, like Carrie, was involved in activities with other youth in town, particularly with the church's Young People's League. Later, Grace attended Redfield College, some 80 miles away. After college, she, as so many women of her family had, became a teacher for a short while, and taught at Lincoln School near Manchester. There, she met Nathan Dow, a farmer, and they were married at her parents' home on October 16, 1901. They lived on his family farm in Manchester, and Grace became involved in local organizations such as the Ladies' Aid Society and the Manchester Extension Club, a group whose aim was to "maintain the highest ideal of home life." She occasionally wrote local-interest articles for local newspapers (the *De Smet News* and the *Huronite*) – another tradition among the Ingalls girls.[47]

In Florida, Almanzo and Laura were not faring well. The climate may have helped Almanzo, but Rose broke out in a heat rash and Laura could not tolerate the heat and humidity – or the attitude of the locals, who she felt treated her with contempt because she was a "Yankee." She was leery enough of her neighbors to make a habit of carrying a concealed pistol everywhere she went. Nor had the couple been able to earn a living. So in August, 1892, after less than a year, they left Florida and went back to De Smet, South Dakota, to be near Laura's family until they could plan out their next move.[48]

The Wilders arrived back in De Smet about a month after Charles and Mary returned from a trip to Chicago for surgery on Mary's face, to ease the pain of neuralgia.[49] Almanzo and Laura purchased a house in town. They enrolled Rose in school, even though she was below the age of enrollment, and after school she went to her grandparent's house where Caroline and Mary looked after her until Laura or Almanzo picked her up in the evening. For the next two years, Laura worked twelve hours a day, six days a week, for the town's dressmaker, and Almanzo worked odd jobs around town: carpentering, painting, clerking in stores.[50] They saved every penny they could, but even so, Laura paid the $2 initiation fee to join Bethlehem #13, the local Eastern Star Chapter.

Laura's petition for membership was received on November 9, 1893. It was recommended by Mary Sanford (her old friend Mary Power) and Mr. Seelye. Her petition was read in the meeting that evening, and the investigating committee was appointed, being Helen Remmington, Emma Gipson, and Mr. Richardson. On November 13, the committee

From the minutes of the meeting at which Laura petitioned to join.

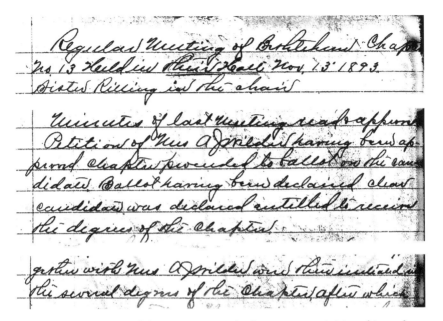

From the minutes of the meeting at which Laura was initiated into the Order of the Eastern Star.

reported favorably, and the Chapter voted to accept her into membership. This was obviously expected, for Laura, along with two other petitioners, were "found waiting" in the hall, and the decision was made to initiate them that night. The Worthy Matron and Worthy Patron who presided at the meeting were Chloe Fuller and C. L. Dawley. Carrie was Treasurer in 1893, so even though she was an officer at this meeting, she did not take part in initiating her sister. Caroline was not an officer but was undoubtedly at the meeting as well.

At the very next meeting, November 27, 1893 a petition was read from Charles Ingalls. He had been recommended to the Chapter by Mrs. Owen and Mr. Fuller. Edwin Sanford had recommended Charles, but then crossed out his recommendation. That was because he was not yet a member of the Order of the Eastern Star himself, and therefore was not authorized to recommend someone else. Edwin joined the Order four months later. After Charles's petition was read in meeting, a committee was assigned to investigate him. The committee members were Mary Sanford, Emma Gipson, and Mr. Richardson. Upon a favorable report at the next meeting and receiving the vote, Charles was initiated into the Order on December 11, 1893.

Petition for Degrees.

Nov 22nd 189 3

To the Worthy Matron, Officers and Members of Bethlehem Chapter

No. *19.*, Order of the Eastern Star:

The undersigned respectfully petitions to receive the degrees of the

Order of the Eastern Star, and become a member of your Chapter. If

accepted he pledges *himself* to a cheerful obedience to the laws of the

Order.

(Signed) *C. P. Ingalls* age 57

Residence *De Smet*

Recommended by *H. of Owen* of *Bethlehem chapter* &

of *DeSmet* Lodge, A. F. & A. M. of *DeSmet S.D.*

C. S. G. Fuller

Approved, *Mary Sanford*

Emma Gipson } Com.

R. H. Richardson

Charles's petition to join the Order of the Eastern Star.

At that same meeting, two of his daughters were elected into offices for the year of 1894: Laura as 'Adah,' and Carrie as Treasurer for another year.

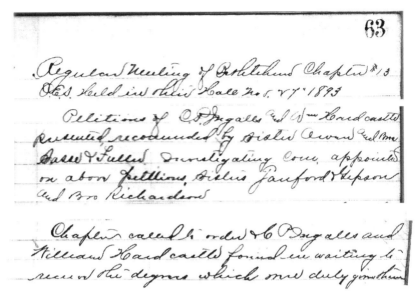

From the minutes of the meetings at which Charles petitioned to join and at which he was initiated into the Order.

From the minutes of the meeting at which Laura was installed into her first office in the Order of the Eastern Star, that of 'Adah.'
Carrie was re-installed as Treasurer at this meeting.

Charles was installed as Treasurer of the Masonic Lodge one week later, his second year in that position.

Report of the C. P. Ingalls, Treas. of DeSmet Lodge
No 55 A. F. & A. M. for the year ending Dec. 17, '94.
Receipts

Balance on hand from last report	55	32
Dec. 12. 93. Rec'd from Sec'y	50	00
Jan 16 - 94 "	15	75
Mar 5 - 94 "	15	00
Apr. 2 - 94 "	5	00
May 7 - 94 "	48	50
" 23. " "	15	25
June 18 - 94 "	10	00
" 18 - " "	6	50
July 2 " "	19	00
" 23 " "	36	00
Nov. 5 " "	8	75
Dec 5 " "	7	50
Total receipts	292	57

Vouchers herewith.

Total Receipt $292.57
    " Disbursed   163.95
Bal. on hand - $128.62

Respectfully Submitted.
C. P. Ingalls

A page from one of Charles's report as Treasurer of the Lodge.

Report of the Treasurer of the
Eastern Star Lodge to May 22, 1893.

Carrie Ingalls, Treasurer

Report of Treasurer from November
13th 1893, to December 10th 1894.
Carrie C Ingalls, Treasurer.

Receipts		Disbursements	
November 13th 1893	16.50	Jan. 22nd, 1894	1.75
January 31st 1894	11.75	Jany 22nd "	.60
February 25th	6.00	Jany 22nd "	1.52
April 24 "	2.18	Jany 24th "	1.25
April 24th	4.50	Feb. 11th	1.05
May 28th	2.25	Jan. 25th	12.50
Sept. 24th	1.75	April 24th	13.50
Sept. 24th	5.25	June 8th	6.70
Nov. 13	3.00	June 8th	6.25
December 10th	9.25	Aug. 13th	6.28
	62.40		53.35

Total amount received. Total
$62.40
53.35
9.05

Balance from last report
$6.68
Total amount on hand
$15.73

While Charles was Treasurer of the Lodge, Carrie served as Treasurer of the local Eastern Star Chapter.

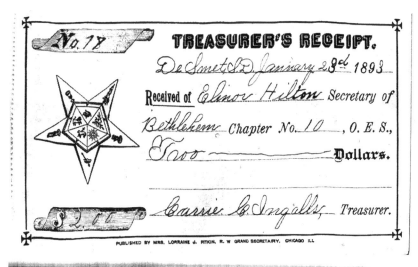

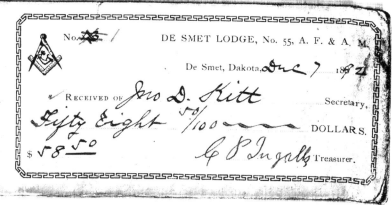

Receipts of Carrie and Charles. Although Charles's is dated 1892, he was not yet the official Treasurer until the installation on December 21 of that year; however, he began his duties early as a Pro Tem officer.

Laura served on investigating committees, and approved a new candidate in May, 1894. She did not fulfill her term in the station of 'Adah,' however. That summer, she and Almanzo were on the move again, for the final time. They were headed to Missouri. Laura had turned in her demit from the Chapter on July 9, 1894 – just about a week before they left town on July 17, 1894 – but it wasn't recorded until it was read at the next meeting on July 23.

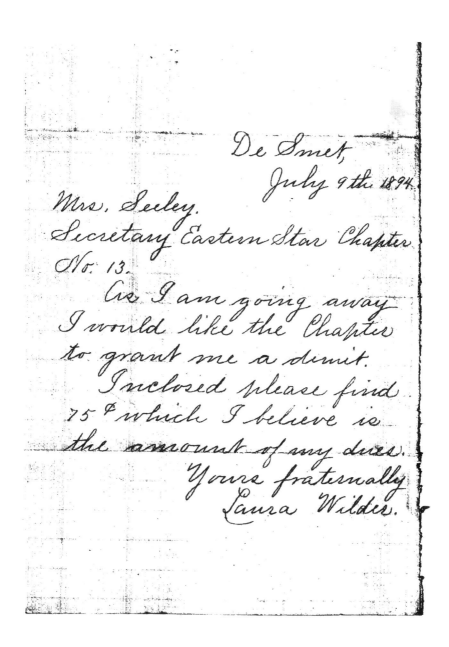

De Smet,
July 9th. 1894.

Mrs. Seeley.
Secretary Eastern Star Chapter
No. 13.
　　　As I am going away
I would like the Chapter
to grant me a demit.
　　　Inclosed please find
75¢ which I believe is
the amount of my dues.
　　　　　Yours fraternally
　　　　　Laura Wilder.

Laura's request for a demit from Bethlehem #13.
She was planning ahead; having a demit would allow her join another
Chapter in the future.

Before Laura left for Missouri, her family gathered for a photograph.
From left, Caroline, Carrie, Laura, Charles, Grace, and Mary.
At this time, Charles was a Master Mason and Treasurer of the Lodge.
Notice his Masonic pin on his vest.
Charles, Caroline, Laura, and Carrie were all members of
Bethlehem #13, Order of the Eastern Star, serving in various offices.
Courtesy South Dakota State Historical Society.

Carrie continued as an active member, working her way through most of the offices. She served Bethlehem Chapter #13 as Warder in 1895, Electa in 1896, Associate Conductress in 1897 and 1898, Conductress in 1900, Associate Matron in 1902, and Worthy Matron in 1903. Throughout these years, she also performed special duties. Some of these included serving on investigating committees of petitioners and acting as installing officer at the installation of other officers. She was used in an example of how to properly initiate a candidate, and was even appointed to contact "those members who have been so conspicuous in our meetings of late, by their absence" and encourage them to attend the meetings, informing them that "their presence is necessary to make our Chapter a success."

Carrie was elected Worthy Matron for the year 1903.

Charles, though never holding office in the Eastern Star Chapter, was active in various ways. He recommended candidates, and was frequently appointed to investigating committees. As a Master Mason, Charles also served the Lodge as he was able, including as an officer. After serving as Tyler in 1888 and 1889 and Junior Deacon in 1890 - 1892, he was elected Treasurer for 1893 and 1894. After holding the office of Tyler again in 1895, he served three years (1896-8) as Junior Warden, then was elected to the office of Senior Warden for 1899. He was installed into that office on December 18, 1898.

Minutes of the meeting at which Charles was installed as Senior Warden.

In 1900, Charles was the Junior Stewart, and then Tyler again in 1901 and 1902. The sword Charles used as Tyler was provided by George Wilmarth, a local merchant who had joined the Lodge shortly before Charles. It is unknown where Wilmarth obtained the sword, but he loaned it to the Lodge for several years. Eventually the Lodge requested to purchase the sword, but received the answer that it was not for sale; instead, the sword was given to the Lodge soon afterward. De Smet Lodge still possesses this sword; you can see Geo. B. Wilmarth's name engraved on the blade.

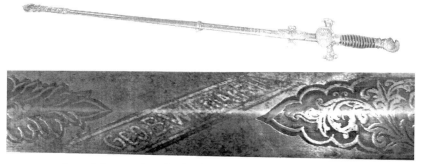

Sword shown sheathed, above, and blade detail, below.

Aside from his duties as an officer, Charles actively participated in the Lodge in other ways. He was one of three members responsible for the repair of the Lodge furnishings in 1895-6. He often acted on investigating committees for new petitioners, and sometimes filled in as an officer Pro Tem when needed. His service came to an end with his death on June 8, 1902. He died of heart disease at the age of 66 years. His obituary in the June 12, 1902 issue of the *De Smet News and Leader* read:

> *A Pioneer Gone.*
> *The people of De Smet were pained Sunday afternoon to learn of the death of Mr. C. P. Ingalls, who died at 3 p.m. of that day after a lingering illness of several weeks. Heart trouble was the cause of his death.*
> *Funeral services were held at the Congregational*

Church Tuesday forenoon, largely attended by the many friends of the deceased and of the family. After the church services were concluded, the Masonic fraternity who were in attendance in body took charge of the funeral and the remains were placed in their last resting place with solemn funeral rite of that organization.

Charles P. Ingalls was born in the state of New York sixty years ago. His life was that of the pioneer from his boyhood. At the age of 12 years he moved with his parents to Illinois, thence, a few years later, to Wisconsin, and thence to Minnesota. It was while living in Wisconsin that he married the estimable lady who is now his widow. In 1879 he brought his family to what is now De Smet. He was the first to build a dwelling in this locality, the house that now stands on the rear end of the Bank of De Smet lot is the building. In his home were held the first religious services. He was prominent in the work of organizing the Congregational church in this city, of which he was a faithful and consistent member at the time of his death. He was also a member in good standing of the Masonic order and of O. E. S.

As a citizen he was held in high esteem, being honest and upright in his dealings and associations with his fellows. As a friend and neighbor he was always kind and courteous and as a husband and father he was faithful and loving. And what better can be said of any man? Some few accomplish great things in life's short span; they control the destinies of nations, or hold in their hand, as it were, the wealth of the world, but the great many tread the common walks of life and to them falls the work of making

*the world better. He who does this work well is
the truly great man. Such was he who has lately
been called to the Great Beyond. Charles P.
Ingalls did his life's work well and the world is
better for his having lived in it.*

*There remain to mourn his death a wife and
four daughters, Mrs. Laura Wilder, Mrs. Grace
Dow, and Misses Carrie and Mary Ingalls. To
the bereaved is extended the heartfelt sympathy
of all in this community.*

As mentioned in the obituary, the Lodge conducted
a Masonic funeral service for Charles; the minutes of the
specially-called meeting read as follows:

*Special communication of De Smet Lodge
No. 55 held in their hall Tuesday morning,
June 10 A.D. 1902 A.L. 5902*

*Present: Leland Griffin, W[orshipful] M[aster],
F. W. Wright, S[enior] W[arden], I. L. Olson,
J[unior] W[arden], E. P. Sanford, Treas,
C. S. G. Fuller, Sec'y; C. L. Dawly* (sic), *S[enior]
D[eacon], O. A. Taylor, J[unior] D[eacon],
H. J. Hamilton, Tyler P[ro] T[em]*

*Lodge opened in the third degree in Masonry for
the purpose of convoying the remains of our late
Bro. C. P. Ingalls to their last resting place.*

Bearers were: Bros. Dawly (sic), *Sasse, Woodbury,
Gipson, Ferguson, Richardson.*

Bro. Fuller acting Chaplain.

*Several brethren from Lake Preston joined us
making in all 23.*

*Lodge repaired to the house of Bro. Ingalls &
escorted the remains to the church. W. M. Hall
preached the usual sermon & the service of
Masonic burial was rendered.*

*At the grave the usual services of our Order were
repeated & the accasia* (sic) *planted at the head*

236

De Smet Special communication of DeSmet
Lodge no 55 held in their hall
Tuesday morning June 10 A N 1902
A L 5902

Present
Leland Griffin W.M.
I. W. Wright Sec I L Olson J.W.
E. P. Sanford Treas C S. G. Fuller Sec
C L Dawley S D O a Taylor J D
H. J. Hamilton Tyler P.T.

Lodge opened on the third degree in
masonry for the purpose of
conveying the remains of
our late Bro C P Ingalls to
their last resting place

Bearers were Bros Dawley Sass
woodbury Gepson Ferguson Richards

Bro Fuller acting chaplain

Several Brethren from Lake Preston
joined us making in all 23

Lodge repaired to the house of Bro
Ingalls & escorted the remains
to the church Rev H all preacht
the usual sermon & the service
of masonic burial was
rendered

At the grave the usual
services of our order were
repeated + the acacia placed
at the head of the grave

Minutes from the meeting called for Charles's funeral service.

of the grave, a token that he shall rise again, ready to greet us as one by one we enter the Grand Lodge on high.

After the services at the grave, the Lodge reformed in the Lodge room where it was closed in due form.

Attest, C. S. G. Fuller, Sec'y

Notice that H. J. Hamilton filled the office of "Tyler P[ro] T[em]." That was Charles's office at the time of his death.

What are the "usual services of our Order" that were "repeated" at the gravesite? There is some variation, as each Grand Lodge promulgates the details of its own rituals, and these are occasionally revised. However, there is much similarity due to the ancient traditions. There is almost always a sprig of acacia, an evergreen symbol of immortality, mentioned in the above minutes.

Another feature of Masonic funerals is the presence of the square and compasses, which are carried on the Bible to the gravesite. De Smet Lodge #55 somehow lost the compasses taken to Charles's burial; the July 7, 1902 minutes note that the Secretary was instructed to purchase new compasses to replace those lost at the funeral of Brother Charles Ingalls. (The square currently used in De Smet Masonic Lodge does not match the compasses used, though both appear to be well-aged. Could it be that the square, like Wilmarth's sword, is still the original square, and the compasses are the replacement purchased after Charles's funeral?)

Unless family intervenes – their wishes are always respected – Masons are buried with the white lambskin apron they received upon being initiated into the Craft. The apron is laid over the closed casket before burial. It is extremely unlikely that there was objection from Charles's family, so it seems certain that he was buried with his apron. Appendix A contains more details in the instructions for a typical Masonic funeral such as Charles Ingalls had.

De Smet Lodge paid for Charles's funeral and his headstone; records indicate that they also helped with medical expenses. The minutes of the November 17, 1902 meeting show that the statement of expenses of the Lodge "through the sickness, death and burial of Bro. C. P. Ingalls" came to $72, and this amount was ordered to be paid.

Headstone of Charles Ingalls, provided by De Smet Lodge #55.

This is but one example the Masonic Lodge and Eastern Star members living up to their ideals of charity and brotherhood, with regard to the Ingalls family. Charles worked hard, but never made more than enough to barely get by; after his death, things were even tighter for the remaining family. The Lodge gave a monetary gift of $15 to Mary Ingalls in 1910. Mary had not applied to the Lodge for relief; records indicate that C. L.

Order drawn for $15 as charitable aid to Mary.

Top, a member of the Lodge brings the financial situation of Mary Ingalls to the attention of the Lodge;
bottom, the brothers vote to extend needed financial relief to her.

Dawley realized there was a need, and he brought the matter before the Lodge, which approved the donation. The receipt is made out to Mrs. Mary Ingalls, leading to the question of whether there was another Mary Ingalls that could have been the recipient of this aid. For example, Laura's cousin Peter Ingalls had married a Mary – nee' McGowin – and so she was a Mrs. Mary Ingalls. However, Peter met and married that Mary in Florida, where they were still living at the time of this receipt. Examination of all records and evidence leads to the conclusion that the "Mrs." was a mistake, and the money was indeed given to *Miss* Mary Ingalls. Other assistance was provided as well. Furthermore, after 1893, neither Charles nor Caroline were required to pay any dues; the Lodge and Chapter accorded them the title of honorary member and paid their dues for them for the remainder of their lives.

Carrie continued to pay her own dues. She worked various jobs from the time she was a teenager. These included clerking in several local stores, working in the post office, and as a school teacher, where she was remembered as being stricter than the other teachers. What she excelled at, however, was the newspaper business. She began working for the De Smet *Leader* at age nineteen, and continued sporadically through the next five years, learning all aspects of the business.[51]

Carrie's health was never strong. Laura remembered her as being frail, unable to recover from the hard winter as she should have.[52] Carrie suffered from migraines, asthma, and allergies, and she sought alleviation by traveling to other climates, searching for one in which her symptoms would be relieved. She visited relatives in Minnesota, Wisconsin, and Missouri in the early part of the century, then spent time in Boulder, Colorado, followed by a stay in Wyoming. Whether her health was at all improved by these adventures is uncertain. She was back in South Dakota by 1907, when she took a claim outside Philip, Topbar Township, in Haakon County. Carrie's fortitude was demonstrated when she built a very small shanty, about 10' square, and lived in it six months as required by the laws. Thereafter, she took a job in the nearby town of Arlington, working for the newspaper. She caught the attention of E. L. Senn, a major newspaper man – and Freemason – of South Dakota. He hired Carrie, and she established and managed several papers for him all around the area.[53]

Senn was known for two things. First was the fact that he made a very good living by running the required legal notices of homesteads and mines.[54] Those notices were the basis of his newspapers. Homesteaders – and miners – were required to run the names of witnesses who would testify that the filer had completed the required improvements to receive the patent. At five dollars per run, and a required minimum five runs per homestead or mine, the money added up.[55] Second was the fact that he insisted his employees be Republican prohibitionists. Carrie was certainly a prohibitionist, as her activity in the Good Templar's Lodge attests, but she, like the rest of her family, was a Democrat. Evidently, her work was excellent enough for Senn to allow her an exception, as she was the manager of the paper by 1909. Being absent from the town of De Smet, she did not hold any offices in the Eastern Star Chapter after she served as Worthy Matron in 1903, and the Chapter granted her demit on December 8, 1913, when she transferred her membership to the Mt. Aetna Chapter in Keystone, South Dakota.

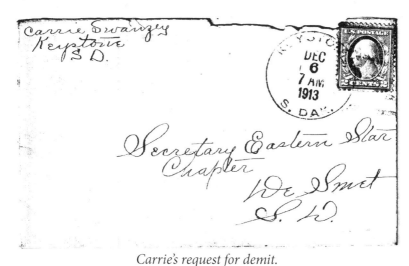

Keystone SD
Dec. 4th 1913
Sec. Star Chapter
Dear Friend
Find inclosed P.O. order
for $3.00 for dues.
Will you please send me
demit I want to join
Mount Etna Chapter here
at Keystone
Yours Truly
Carrie Ingalls Swanzey
Keystone
S.D.

Carrie Swanzey
Keystone
S.D.

Secretary Eastern Star
Chapter
De Smet
S.D.

Carrie's request for demit.

167

Keystone

I built my soul a home.
~ J. Gutzon Borglum, sculptor, Freemason

Working for Senn, Carrie was transferred to Roseland in 1910 and then to Keystone in 1911, to establish or manage newspapers for Senn in those towns. She did not work for him much longer, however; in Keystone, Carrie met and soon married David N. Swanzey.

Marriage license of Carrie and David.

169

David was born in St. Louis around April 18, 1860. Records differ regarding the year of his birth, giving it as anywhere between 1854 and 1861. When calculating his age from the date various censuses were taken and the marriage license from his first marriage, it appears most likely that he was born between 1859 and 1861, making him about 10 years older than Carrie. This matches his Masonic record, which is the source of the birth date given above.

David moved to Illinois in the late 1870s, where he worked in a store. He met his first wife Elizabeth there; they were married in Henderson County, Illinois on October 25, 1899, but made their home in Keystone, where David was already residing by that time. He had come to the area the first time about 1883 to scout for a mica mine for the Round Oak Stove Company, the manufacturing company for which he worked.[1]

David N. Swanzey.

After spending some time in the area, he decided to relocate to Keystone. Upon settling there, David went to work as the Keystone depot agent for the CB&Q (Chicago, Burlington &

Quincy) Railroad. His interest in area mining did not diminish, however, and he purchased several mines, taking advantage of the General Mining Act of 1872, which allowed patents on claim mines for only $5 per acre (i.e., the law allowed men to claim a mine on public lands, work it for at least six months, and then purchase the land for $5 an acre, receiving title and thereby making it private, as opposed to public, land). David's interest in acquiring mines gave him an intense curiosity about the local geology, to which he gave concentrated study and soon became an acknowledged area expert.[2]

About 1884, a young attorney from New York visited several times to preview the area and, if deemed a wise investment, secure options in a tin mine. According to friends of David Swanzey, the attorney was guided about the area by David and another man, William Challis. The attorney was eager to learn the names of all the area landmarks. One day, while standing under a particular hill, he asked its name. The peak had been known locally by several names, including Sugarloaf Mountain, Cougar Mountain, and Keystone Cliffs, but having no official name, David told the attorney, "We'll name it after you!" Thus was Mount Rushmore christened, for Charles Rushmore was the attorney's name. The attorney Charles Rushmore himself wrote a letter when construction on the monument began, confirming the account; it may be viewed at the Mount Rushmore Museum.

Keystone itself was named for the first mine in the area, the Keystone mine. As masons (and Masons) know, a keystone is a wedge-shaped stone at the top, center of an arch, which supports the entire structure. Mining was indeed the central activity around which Keystone and the surrounding area was built. The industry grew quickly for a number of years, with an influx of men to Keystone and surrounding areas to work the mines. In the late 1890s and early 1900s the population of Keystone had swelled to around 3000.[3]

This number included many Freemasons working in area mines, but there was as yet no Masonic Lodge. Members had to travel on horseback over rough terrain to "full moon Lodges." These were Lodges that met when the moon was full, allowing light for the men to find their way at night. David was one of those who rode monthly to Hermosa, where he joined the Fraternity when he was initiated as an Entered Apprentice Mason on May 10, 1890. David was passed to the second degree of Fellowcraft on June 7, 1890, and raised to the third degree of Master Mason on July 5 of that year.

With Battle River Lodge at Hermosa several miles away, and the population growing rapidly, it was determined that a Masonic Lodge was needed in Keystone.[4] The request for a chartered Lodge at Keystone was presented to the Grand Lodge of South Dakota in the fall of 1896. After a short delay, during which the Lodge was required to find a building in which to meet, the charter for Mt. Aetna Lodge #128 A. F. & A. M. in Keystone was granted on June 9, 1897.[5]

Charter members of Mt. Aetna Lodge; David is listed at #13.

172

Why was the Lodge not named after Mount Rushmore? Remember that, although of course the mountain was there, the national monument did not yet exist. The most noteworthy feature in town at that time was mining, and in particular the Holy Terror Mine, which was located at the base of Mount Aetna. The Holy Terror was discovered by William Franklin, who, when not working, was often found in the local saloon. The story goes that when he had been out too long, his wife would come find him, grab his arm, and drag him home behind her. As he was led out, Franklin winked and remarked to his fellow bar patrons, "Ain't she a holy terror?" When he discovered the new mine, he tried to appease his wife by telling her it would be named after her. She was surprised when she later found that Franklin had called it not the Jenny, but the Holy Terror. The mine became the largest employer of the region, and was one of the top gold producers of the nation during the years of 1894 to 1903. The men of the local Masonic Lodge did not want to call themselves the Holy Terror Lodge, and chose instead to name the Lodge after that host mount of the men's livelihood.[6]

The Holy Terror Mine.
Courtesy Robert Hayes.

The Lodge had purchased a small building on First Street in which to meet. They met on the second floor and leased out the ground floor. The first meeting was held on June 26, 1896, at which officers for the new Lodge were installed, with Spencer Palmer as the Worshipful Master. There were sixteen charter members, among them David Swanzey. David also had the honor of being installed as Senior Warden. He transferred his membership from Battle River Lodge at Hermosa to Mt. Aetna Lodge at Keystone on June 9, 1897, the same day it was chartered.[7]

Original home of Mt. Aetna Lodge - the building in center on left.
Courtesy Robert Hayes.

The Lodge in Keystone grew steadily for a number of years, due to the mining industry which continued to expand. Meetings were held the third Saturday in each month, and David could be counted on to be there. David served the Mt. Aetna Lodge as Worshipful Master in 1904 and 1905. It is the prevailing custom in Masonry for the Senior Warden to serve as Master the next year. This is not always the case, however, and for some reason David did not follow the usual pattern, having a gap of several years between his year as Senior

The charter officers of Mt. Aetna #128 A. F. & A. M. David, as Senior Warden, is second from right in front row (with the white boutonnière). Courtesy Charles Childs.

Warden and his term as Worshipful Master of the Lodge. He held other offices during that time, such as Secretary in 1902.

In addition to acting as Master of the Lodge in 1905, David took on another role: according to his certificate, on the 20th of January he became a "Master of the Royal Secret of the 32nd Degree of the Ancient and Accepted Scottish Rite."

David's certificate of the Scottish Rite. Courtesy Charles Childs.

The Ancient and Accepted Scottish Rite of Freemasonry is commonly called, simply, Scottish Rite. A Rite is a prescribed form for a ritual or ceremony – in this case, the additional degrees bestowed by the organization. There are 33 degrees in the Scottish Rite. The first three of these are the Entered Apprentice, Fellowcraft, and Master Mason degrees received in the blue Lodge; the following 30 build upon these. The organization is headed by Councils, and is divided into jurisdictions called Valleys, each with four Scottish Rite divisions. The first division, the Lodge of Perfection, confers the 4th – 14th degrees. The Chapter of Rose Croix confers degrees 15 – 18. The 19th – 30th degrees are conferred by the Council of Kadosh. The Consistory confers the 31st and 32nd degrees. The final 33rd degree is a special degree not conferred by a subordinate body, but by the Supreme Council itself. Few men achieve this degree, as members must have belonged to the Scottish Rite for a prescribed amount of time, and must be elected by others for their major contributions to Masonry or society.

All degrees of the Scottish Rite are often conferred in a "marathon" of meetings, say over a weekend or every evening for a week. These days, Masons travel to one central, designated meeting place; in the days before automobiles when travel was more difficult, it was more often the case that someone authorized to bestow all the degrees traveled to the various Lodges, and conferred those degrees to any Masons there who desired to receive them.

David remained in this organization until 1914, but demitted at that time. No reason is noted for the demit; it may have been financial, or perhaps there simply weren't enough men active in the group to keep it going, especially with war breaking out and many young men leaving to serve their country.

After his time as Master of Mt. Aetna Lodge, David was elected Secretary in 1906, an office he held for an amazing thirty-three years, until his death.

In 1899, the wives of some of the Lodge members wished to organize a Chapter under the Order of the Eastern Star. It was reported that David Swanzey was one of the driving forces behind the movement to get the Chapter established, and on June 14, 1899, the Mt. Aetna Chapter of the Order of the Eastern Star received its charter.

The institutional meeting was held on June 7. As folks arrived at the Masonic Lodge, many of them were surprised to discover that only seventeen individuals could be charter members. The first seventeen to arrive were chosen as the charter members. This was a disappointment to those who arrived too late to be among the chosen, including David Swanzey. After the meeting was closed, the members and guests retired to the McDonald Hotel for a celebratory banquet, at which speeches, music and dinner were enjoyed.[8]

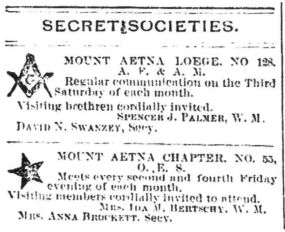

From the Keystone Miner, May 7, 1902.

In the early 1900s, calamities struck the town. First, the Holy Terror mine was forced to close in 1903, after a series of fires, fatal accidents, and floods. Most of the miners who had depended on the Holy Terror for their families' livelihood were forced to leave the area. Then, in May, 1908, a fire broke out downtown in Bacon's Hall, and the half of the town on the east side of Main Street was burned to the ground.

About that same time, in the Swanzey family, Elizabeth died in 1908 or 1909, leaving David a widower with two young children: a daughter, Mary, about four years old, and a son, Harold, around two years old. How David provided care for them while working at the depot and also overseeing his mining operations – which required much time away from home – is not known, but it seems probable that he had help from some folks in town, likely fellow Eastern Stars.

Although the Holy Terror had not successfully reopened, other mines in the area were being worked, and new ones were staked all the time. Every mine claimed had to be publicized, as well as any dispute regarding a claim. Carrie's boss, E. L. Senn, was ready to take advantage of the mine claim ads, so he sent Carrie to run the *Keystone Recorder*.[9] She worked for him only a few more months, and retired from the newspaper business when she married David on August 1, 1912.

The announcement in the *Rapid City Journal* read:

> *In Rapid City, Thursday, August 1, 1912, David N. Swanzey, of Keystone, and Miss Carrie Ingalls of De Smet, Rev. W. H. Sparling officiating.*
>
> *There are many Rapid City people who will be much surprised to read that Dave Swanzey has taken unto himself a wife. Mr. Swanzey has lived a good many years in the Hills and is known to everybody around Keystone and Hill City, and to all the old timers in Rapid City. He is very much a gentleman and the lady is fortunate in being chosen as his bride.*
>
> *The bride is an accomplished young lady, being at one time the manager of the Keystone Recorder and later was in charge of the Hill City Star. She has been living with her mother at De Smet for a few months, and came from there here except that she stopped on her way at Philip, near which place she has a claim. Mr. Swanzey met her here and they went immediately to the Episcopal*

church and were married. They left last evening
for Hot Springs, where they will spend a few
days before going to Keystone to live. They will
go immediately to housekeeping.

Carrie was forty-two years old when she married; she would have been considered a spinster, but she now had a husband and two children to care for. She never had children of her own, but raised Mary and Harold Swanzey.

Carrie with Mary and Harold shortly after her marriage.

In addition to caring for her newly acquired family, Carrie became very active in the community, and the Mt. Aetna Chapter of the Order of the Eastern Star in particular.

The exact date that she first attended this Chapter is not known, as those records have been lost to fire. We know that Carrie's demit from the Bethlehem Chapter in De Smet was read on December 8, 1913, so she evidently did not transfer her membership until she was ready to serve as an officer in Keystone, it being a requirement that officers of a Chapter must be members of that Chapter. The first written record we have of Carrie in the Chapter at Keystone is the Grand Chapter of South Dakota file, which shows that "Carrie I. Swanzey" was installed as the incoming year's 'Esther' of Mt. Aetna Chapter on December 26, 1913 – just about five months after her marriage and a couple of weeks after she demitted from the De Smet Chapter.

Carrie's first office in Keystone was as 'Esther.'

180

After her year as 'Esther,' Carrie served Mt. Aetna
Chapter as Worthy Matron in both 1915 and 1916, having
been installed on December 11, 1914. Interestingly, David did
not act as Worthy Patron alongside her; instead, their good
friend – and a leading member of the City of Keystone, in
addition to being a pillar of the Lodge and Eastern Star – John
Snowie acted in that capacity.

Carrie had another Star duty those years, as well: she
was commissioned by the Worthy Grand Matron of South
Dakota to serve as Grand Representative to Texas. A Grand
Representative is charged with representing her state's Grand
Chapter to another jurisdiction – in this case, Dakota to
Texas. The Grand Representatives of the two states generally

The next year, Carrie was Worthy Matron.

correspond with one another, sharing items of interest or import from their respective states. They may compare ideas and happenings, to see what is having a beneficial effect and what could be improved. A Grand Representative may assist a member in finding a Chapter in a new jurisdiction, transferring membership, and other such efforts. Their goal is to promote harmony and uniformity between the various Grand Chapters, further the success of each, strengthen the ties of fellowship, and create interest in the Order. Being selected as a Grand Representative shows not only that a great number of Stars had confidence in Carrie's ability, but also that they considered her to be an outstandingly helpful and friendly person. It is noted in the Grand Chapter records that her appointment was made toward the end of 1915 and was to be effective from January 1, 1916 to December 31, 1919.

Grand Representatives of Other Grand Chapters Near South Dakota.

STATE	NAME	ADDRESS	DATE			EXPIRES		
			Day	Month	Year	Day	Month	Year
michigan	Mrs. Ethel Bundy	Lake Andes	1	Jan	1916	1	Jan	1919
Texas	Mrs. Carrie Swanzey	Keystone	1	Jan	1916	31	Dec	1919

Grand Chapter records show Carrie's appointment as Grand Representative to Texas.

Carrie held an office in the Chapter every year for the next decade. She served as Conductress in 1917, Secretary in 1918 and 1919, Conductress again in 1920, and Secretary 1921-24. The Chapter met on the second and fourth Fridays of each month, and Carrie could almost always be found in her seat.

In 1917, another fire raged through Keystone. This one destroyed the west side of town, including the Lodge building. The meetings of the Lodge and Eastern Star were moved into the basement of the Methodist Church for the next 4 years, until the next big fire on Thanksgiving Day in 1921 burned it down, too. From 1922 to 1927 they met in another basement, that of the Congregational Church, of which Carrie was an active member. In 1927 the Lodge and Eastern Star moved to the upper story of the Schoolhouse, where they met for the next 40 years. It seems unusual to think now of groups like the Freemasons and Eastern Star having a meeting room in a public school building, but it was really hearkening back to the beginning, when Masons regularly built the public school buildings in their efforts to promulgate education for all, and then met within those buildings themselves.[10]

The Lodge met in the upstairs room of the schoolhouse for many years. The building now houses the Keystone Area Historical Museum.

Through all these years, the brothers and sisters of Mt. Aetna Lodge and Mt. Aetna Chapter kept their spirits high, carrying on the work of the fraternity. They held special observances of Christmas and Easter, and patriotic gatherings on President's Day. During war years, members worked with the Red Cross, gathering donations of clothing and making bandages. The Eastern Star Chapter started a War Prisoner Fund to which they donated regularly, and also purchased war bonds, as did the Lodge. Charitable aid was given as needed.

In 1926, Carrie and David welcomed Mary Ingalls into their home. After Charles's death in 1902, Caroline and Mary had continued to live in the house he had built on Third Street. They took in boarders to receive a bit of income. Additionally, Mary tied horsefly nets and did fancy work, which she sold. She also played the organ at the Congregational Church each Sunday. She and Caroline spent the evenings reading or doing needlework. Mary had her own library of Braille and raised-print books. Although they were a help to each other, neither was in good health, and Caroline became frailer as she aged. Grace and her husband Nate, who had been living in Manchester, went to live with and help care for them.[11]

Caroline died on April 20, 1924 at the age of 84. The April 25 issue of *The De Smet News* carried her obituary:

> *Mrs. C. P. Ingalls, Pioneer of County, Dies at 84*
>
> *Kingsbury County lost one of its pioneer women in the death of Mrs. C. P. Ingalls at her home here Sunday. She and her husband came to this locality in 1879 and lived in a claim shanty on the north shore of Silver Lake before there was a De Smet.*
>
> *The death was unexpected and followed an illness of but a short time, altho [sic] Mrs. Ingalls has been feeble all winter.*
>
> *Caroline Quiner was born December 12, 1839, at Milwaukee, Wis., and died at five o'clock p.m. Easter Sunday, April 20, 1924, at the age of 84. She was married to Charles Ingalls of Milwaukee Feb. 1, 1860, whose death occurred June 8, 1902. Five children were born to this union. Mary Ingalls of De Smet; Laura Wilder of Mansfield, Mo; Caroline Swanzey of Keystone, S.D.; Frederick Ingalls, who died in infancy, and Grace Dow of De Smet.*
>
> *The family moved to De Smet in 1879 where they have since resided. In 1880 Mr. and Mrs.*

Ingalls helped organize the Congregational Church at De Smet and were faithful members of the organization to the end of their lives. Mrs. Ingalls was also an early member of the Eastern Star chapter of De Smet.

Besides the four daughters the deceased is survived by three sisters, and one granddaughter, Rose Wilder Lane.

Mrs. Ingalls was a good mother, a good neighbor, and a good friend. The last few years she has been unable to get around to see people very much or to attend church, but her interest has been with her neighbors, friends, and church. It was a pleasure to go and visit her as she was always interested, bright and happy.

There is no record that Caroline received an Eastern Star service, probably because the fraternal members of her family were not there; Charles had already died, and Laura and Carrie lived elsewhere. The relatives who remained in De Smet – Mary and Grace and Grace's husband Nate – were not

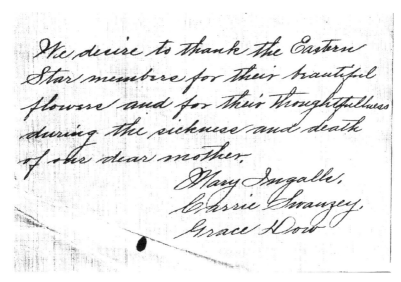

It is believed that Grace penned this note.

members of the fraternity. The notes of the Chapter do make reference to Mary, Grace and Carrie thanking the Chapter for the "flowers and kindness" given to the family; records show that the Chapter had spent $8.55 on flowers.

After Caroline's death, Grace and Nate remained in the home with Mary to help care for her. Then, in 1926, Grace and Nate moved back to his family farm in Manchester, and Mary went to stay with Carrie in Keystone. Mary was preparing to return to De Smet in 1927 when she suffered a stroke, and became invalid. She remained in Keystone, and Carrie cared for her until her death on October 20, 1928. She was 63 years old. Carrie took Mary's remains to De Smet for burial, and as she inherited the Ingalls home on Third St, she made arrangements for its continued rental.[12]

Despite her family obligations, caring for her step-children in early years and her sister in later years, Carrie was always active the community. Much of her service was devoted to the Order of the Eastern Star and to her church.

The Congregational Church to which Carrie belonged still meets in Keystone. Courtesy Lois Halley.

Carrie was not only a member of the Congregational Church, she also served as its clerk for many years. In those early days, the minister's salary was paid by parishioners' pledges, and as part of Carrie's duty, she went every month on rounds to their homes to collect. Her friend Winnie Hesnard often accompanied her. Carrie was also active in the Ladies' Aid Society, helping with dinners, bazaars, and other events. When the church building itself was in need of restoration, Carrie was a driving force in getting it done. She also helped establish the church's library, as reading and education were as important to her as they were to the rest of the Ingalls family.[13]

Nor was the church the sole recipient of Carrie's efforts. She was also a member of the Keystone Extension Club, and was active in it as well. She had a particular interest in the Club's reading program, helping with it a great deal. Widely read herself, she truly embraced the idea of promoting education, in harmony with the ideals of Freemasonry.[14]

David Swanzey, far right, with other miners in front of the depot.
Courtesy Robert Hayes.

David remained busy with his job for the railroad and his mining dreams. Always looking for the next big strike, he continued to venture upon new mining operations, but he never found the big vein he was searching for.

Carrie continued to hold office each year in the Mt. Aetna Chapter of the Order of the Eastern Star, and beginning in 1925, David also held office in the Chapter. In 1925, Carrie acted as 'Esther' while David was Warder. Carrie served as Associate Conductress in 1926; David was Secretary that year.

The 1928 return of Mt. Aetna Chapter shows that David was Worthy Patron in 1927 and Chaplain in 1928, when Carrie was Electa.

188

David was Worthy Patron in 1927, as evidenced by the 1928 notes that he, in that position, installed the incoming officers; however, the records for 1927 are missing, so it is unknown what office Carrie held.

Carrie acted as 'Electa' and David as Chaplain in 1928. In 1929, 'Adah' was the role that Carrie took. David served the Chapter as Worthy Patron that year, and also for 1930, when Carrie became Secretary. Carrie remained Secretary for the next seven years; during those years David held the office of Associate Patron in 1931 and 1932, Worthy Patron

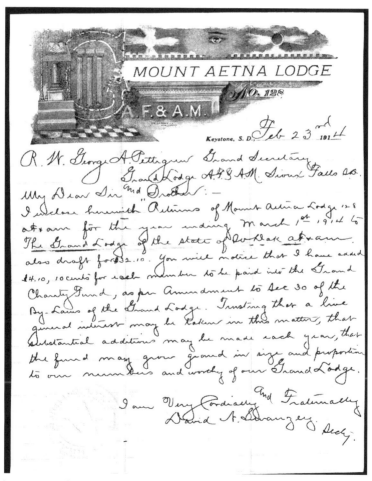

A letter David wrote to the Grand Lodge as Secretary of his blue Lodge.

again for 1933 and 1934, Associate Patron in 1935 and 1936, and Sentinel in 1937. Remember that David was also elected Secretary of the Lodge for all of those years, from 1906 until 1938.

David was re-elected to the office of Sentinel in the Eastern Star Chapter for 1938, but did not complete the term as he died on April 9 of that year. The minutes of the meeting for David's funeral, held on Monday, April 11, 1938, read as follows (some names are illegible):

> *A Lodge of M[aster] M[asons] was declared open for the special purpose of conducting funeral service for Brother D. N. Swanzey. The Master had appointed Bro. A. I. Johnson as Marshal and the order of the service was lined out. Acting as bearer of the three great lights – H. B--- of Battle River Lodge; Brother R--- as Chaplain assisting Rev. Pipes of Rapid City. Pall bearers appointed by the Master were as follows: Brothers Ben Rush, Ralph Peabody, Gus L--, Basil Canfield, Theodore Hesnard and Pete S--.*
>
> *Assisting the Master we were honored by the presence of our Grand Master Brother H. Chapman of Sioux Falls. Present also were the district deputy grand Master Manning of Center.*
>
> *In the line of march honoring the memory of our deceased brother were brethren from Hill City including Brother Crouch, Master of Hill City Lodge. Present from Custer Lodge were brothers Broyles, Manning; brothers from Battle River lodge included brothers S--- and Hesnard who assisted as pall bearers. Brethren from Rapid City included Brothers Wilson, master of Rapid City Lodge, Lampert, Poznarsky and others.*
>
> *The funeral procession was formed and the lodge moved to the Congregational Church where the religious services were under the*

*directions of Rev. Pipe of Rapid City. Following
the religious services, the Masonic services were
duly conducted by Bro. T. A. Blewett. The line of
procession was then carried to the cemetery where
the services of committal were duly carried out.*

*The Masonic obituary of Brother D. N. Swanzey
is given below.*

The minutes of the meeting called for David's funeral service.

The number of dignitaries that attended David's funeral is noteworthy. It is a testament to David's standing within Freemasonry that the Grand Master of South Dakota was present, along with the District Deputy and three Worshipful Masters (his own Lodge's and two others). Brothers from several Lodges of the area, in addition to his own, were also in attendance.

A Masonic obituary is what is written in the records of the local Lodge and also sent to the Grand Lodge under whose jurisdiction the Lodge falls. It gives a brief outline of the deceased's Masonic affiliation. Masonic obituaries are not generally made public, but may sometimes be obtained by descendants from either the local Lodge or Grand Lodge.

OBITUARY REMARKS

David's Masonic obituary written by Mt. Aetna Lodge.

The Mt. Aetna Chapter of the Order of the Eastern Star also wrote a Masonic obituary:

Brother David N. Swanzey was a charter member

*and assisted in organizing Mt. Aetna Lodge
No. 28 A. F. & A. M. and was instrumental in
organizing Mt. Aetna Chapter No. 55, OES. A
faithful conscientious worker in both orders.
A past master and long time secretary of the
Masonic Lodge and served as Worthy Patron of
Mt. Aetna Chapter for many years. Buried with
Masonic honors.*

The notes in the Grand Chapter's records indicate that in
addition to the Masonic funeral David received, the Eastern
Star also performed a memorial service for him.

David's public obituary read:

*David N. Swanzey is Buried at Keystone: Rites
for David N. Swanzey, 83, Keystone Resident for
more than 50 years, were held from the Keystone
church Monday afternoon. Burial was at Keystone.
The Rev. J. E. Pipes, Episcopal minister, Rapid
City, officiated. Survivors include his widow and
one son, Harold Swanzey, living at Keystone;
a daughter, Mrs. Monroe Harris, Mystic, and
several grandchildren. Born in St. Louis, Mo,
April 18, 1854, Swanzey came to the Black Hills
in 1884 as a representative of an eastern stove
company. He was engaged in securing a mica
deposit to be used in manufacturing isinglass,
at that time a feature of almost every stove.
He became interested in mining generally and
settled near the present site of Keystone. Swanzey
owned at least six mines in the Keystone vicinity.
One of which he later sold to the late Thomas A.
Edison. He was the founder of the Big Hit Mines
located in upper Keystone. For 18 years he was
the agent for the CB&Q Railroad in Keystone.
Swanzey was involved with the Masonic Lodge
and Eastern Star Chapters and was a Charter
Member of the Masonic Lodge.*

The creation of Mount Rushmore had an impact on Carrie and her family, and on the local Masonic Lodge and Eastern Star Chapter.[15] The idea for the monument at Mt. Rushmore began with Doane Robinson, who was at various times a farmer, an attorney, and South Dakota's State Historian. He was also a Freemason. Robinson wanted to bring tourism to the state, and thought that having famous figures sculpted into some of the unusual geologic formations would create a unique attraction. At least, that's the official story. Residents who lived in the area at the time say that the owners of the Holy Terror were preparing to open the mine again – after four previously unsuccessful attempts – and they wanted to find some way to attract men who could work the rock in the mine, so they'd be there and ready when it opened. Maybe both stories have some truth to them. In any case, Robinson's original idea was to base the figures in the Needles, but when he brought in the sculptor, that idea was nixed, as the formations were not deemed strong enough. The sculptor, Gutzon Borglum, another Freemason, liked the southeast face of Mount Rushmore, and it was his idea to sculpt the four Presidents to depict the creation and expansion of the nation. Robinson gained approval from the State early in 1925, and a dedication was held at the mount on October 1st of that year. The ladies of the town, including Carrie, helped host the influx of visitors for the event.[16]

The idea of Mt. Rushmore had an inspired start, but as yet no funding. With the help of Robinson's friend in the U.S. Senate and brother in the Lodge, Peter Norbeck – who, incidentally, was a very good friend of Carrie's former boss, E. L. Senn – the monument soon received federal backing, and the work began in 1927.[17] Over the next decade and a half or so, more than 400 men made their way to Keystone to work on Mt. Rushmore. New life was breathed into the local economy, which had fallen dramatically since the closing of the Holy Terror mine in 1903. Many of the incoming workers were Masons who attended the local Lodge, and were befriended by David Swanzey. Some of them were family men whose wives visited or joined the Mt. Aetna Chapter of the Easter Star, and were known by Carrie. According to old Lodge members, Borglum himself visited Mt. Aetna Lodge on occasion. Among those who attended regularly were two of Borglum's assistants, Ivan Housar and W. S. Tallman. Tallman even served a term as Master of Mt. Aetna Lodge.[18]

The sculptor ("master mason" in every sense of the word) Gutzon Borglum died near the end of the project, but his son Lincoln Borglum – another Freemason – took over until the project ran out of money and work stopped. The monument was originally envisioned and planned as to-the-waist figures, not merely the faces that we have today. Lincoln Borglum had begun work on the monument in 1933 as an unpaid laborer, and worked his way up the chain of command until he was the final authority, serving not only as head of the sculpting but also being appointed the first superintendent of the National Memorial. He later moved to Texas and built several religious edifices before his death in 1986.[19]

Mount Rushmore.

As good as the idea for Mt. Rushmore was, and as talented as Gutzon and Lincoln Borglum were, the monument still would not have come to fruition without the efforts of another Freemason, John Boland. Past Master of Mt. Aetna Lodge (in 1913) and Mayor of Rapid City in 1924 when Gutzon Borglum first visited the area, Boland was named president of the executive committee ordered by President Coolidge for the Mount Rushmore National Memorial Commission. He was the executive director of the project and controlled its finances. During the Depression years, this was no easy task, but Boland managed to keep the project going until the main part, the heads of all four planned Presidents, was complete.[20]

Another of the workers on Mt. Rushmore was David's son, Harold Swanzey. He worked on the mountain intermittently between 1927 and 1934, earning between thirty-five and fifty cents per hour as a "laborer." He is listed on the wall of workers at the monument.

Harold Swanzey.

Harold was born December 20, 1907, so he was five years old when his father married Carrie Ingalls. He and his older sister, Mary, were raised by Carrie. Carrie is remembered as planning and hosting many parties, Sunday School picnics, and other activities for the young folks, and by most accounts had a good relationship with them, particularly with Harold. Carrie had a special sympathy for him, as he was a sickly child, just as she herself had been. He was also hard of hearing. Harold was sometimes called "Davie" because he resembled his father so much; he was also called "Red" because of his flaming hair.[21]

Harold was beginning to follow his father's steps in the Craft. He petitioned Mt. Aetna Lodge in February of 1939. Upon being investigated, reported on favorably, and passing the vote, he was initiated as an Entered Apprentice on March 18 of that year. The next month, on April 11, 1939, Harold was passed to the second degree of Fellowcraft.

Harold's Masonic record.

Carrie was proud of his decision to join, but heartache soon followed. Just five days later, on April 16, 1939, Harold and his friend and brother in the Lodge, Theodore Hesnard (who had been a pallbearer at David's funeral almost exactly a year before), were traveling in a 1932 Ford Roadster, and, failing to make a curve, went airborne off the side of the road, crashing head-on into a tree. Both young men were killed. Carrie was devastated. Harold did not receive a Masonic funeral, as only

Master Masons were accorded that honor.

Harold's sister, Mary Swanzey, attended a private school in Sioux Falls. She later became Mrs. M. Monroe Harris, and, following in Carrie's steps, she joined the Order of the Eastern Star, as did her daughter, Betty, and other descendants.

After the deaths of David and Harold, Carrie maintained her interest in the community. In fact, the words most used to describe her by those who knew her in these later years were "neighborly" and "interested."[22] She continued to actively participate in the organizations closest to her heart – her church and the Eastern Star. She is said to have never missed a meeting, except for the week David died. She also continued to hold an office in the Chapter every year. The year of David's death, 1938, she was serving as Secretary for the Chapter, and she held that office the following two years as well. In 1941, she began filling the station of various Star points: 'Adah' in 1941, 'Martha' in 1942, 'Adah' in 1943, 'Ruth' in 1944 and 1945, and 'Adah' again in 1946.

Carrie also had additional duties in the Order. She was appointed Chapter historian by the Worthy Matron several years, and she fulfilled this duty by writing an accurate account of the history of the Chapter, from its beginning through the happenings in those years. She wrote a history of Rob Morris, the founder of the Order of the Eastern Star, which she delivered at the October, 1943 meeting. Moreover, she was also called upon to present a separate program on each of the Star points, telling about the history, symbolism, and meaning of each. Carrie was certainly qualified to do this, having acted in the capacity of each of these offices throughout the years. She prepared these programs herself and presented them to the Chapter throughout 1943 and 1944. The Chapter evidently greatly enjoyed Carrie's presentations: the records show that it was "by the request of the Worthy Matron and the entire Chapter" that Carrie presented "an original short story" in November of 1944. She again presented an original story at the annual Eastern Star School of Instruction on

From Carrie's history of Mt. Aetna Chapter.

January 26, 1945. A School of Instruction is where members learn or review the secret work, the rituals and degrees, and other works of the Order. It is unknown whether this was the same story or a new one, as, unfortunately, no details about the stories themselves are given. We can see some of Carrie's style in the history of Mt. Aetna Chapter that she wrote for the Grand Chapter of South Dakota. For the October 9, 1942 meeting, she began, "Chapter was opened after a considerable delay due to a swarming multitude of wasps who had taken over the Chapter room. After a blitz gunning attack by the brothers and sweeping up operations by the sisters, it was possible to hold Chapter." The next month she stated, "The chill fall air subdued the wasps to a quiet existence."

On June 1, 1946, Carrie celebrated 55 years as a member of the Order of the Eastern Star. In recognition of this fact, on May 24, 1946, the Mt. Aetna Chapter held a special observation for Carrie. She was given the honor of being conducted to the east, and after a review of her years in the Order, she was lead through the Chapter room in a floral ceremony, at the end of which she was presented with a gold 50-year membership pin and a certificate from the Chapter. She was reported to be very moved by the tribute, and remarked that she had "always lived for Eastern Star."

 key was conducted to the east and W.M. marie munson presented her with oister Carrie Swanzey with a 50 year membership certificate in the u.E.S. Sister Swanzey was then conducted through the Labyrinth in a beautiful floral ceremony and then reconducted to the east again where our w.P. Gerald Munson presented Sister Swanzey with a beautiful,gold, 50 year u.E.S. pin. Sister Swanzey almost over come with emotion thanked the chapter for the pin and the tribute paid her.

un June 6th a special meeting was called at 2 r.M. at the uongo . Church for the purpose of attending our late oister Swanzey's funeral. The regular eastern otar funeral service was conducted , preceded by a short service by the nev. Carl Loocke. oister Swanzey passed away very suddenly on June 2nd and after the services in neystone, the remains were shipped to ve Smet, 3.vak. for burial there. eastern Star services were held at ve Smet on June 7th. Quite a number of nillCity Chapter members attended the services here in neystone.

Top, Carrie, front center, with her sisters in Mt. Aetna Chapter the night she received her 50-year pin. Courtesy Lois Halley.
Bottom, the Grand Chapter record of that event, and of her death.

Only nine days later, on June 2, 1946, Carrie died unexpectedly from a complication of diabetes, at the age of 75. Services were held in Keystone at the Congregational Church on the afternoon of June 6. After the regular service, an Eastern Star service was given by the Mt. Aetna Chapter. Carrie's remains were then sent to De Smet to be buried with her parents and her sister Mary. In De Smet, the Bethlehem Chapter held an Eastern Star service at her interment, so Carrie actually had two Eastern Star funeral services.

At the meeting following her death, on June 14, the charter of the Chapter was draped in black in Carrie's honor, as is customary in the Order upon the death of members, and she was given a memorial tribute. Mt. Aetna Chapter voted in October of that year (1946) to set up a permanent display in honor of Carrie, in which they would display her 50-year certificate and pin alongside a photo of Carrie with the Chapter officers taken the night they were presented.

Although her death was sudden, Carrie had been prepared. There was found a sealed letter to one of her friends with instructions and final wishes, which were carried out. She also had a will. Upon David's death, Carrie had inherited most of his estate, consisting primarily of four mining operations, each of which may have included several individual mines, but which were not then in production. She also still owned the 160-acre homestead outside Philip that she had claimed back in 1907.[23] She provided for their disposal and her estate to be handled as summarized below.

After declaring this to be her last will and testament, Carrie first directs any debts to be paid. She then instructs her executor – later named as Walter G. Miser, a Rapid City attorney and judge – to place "suitable markers" at the graves of David, his first wife, and their son Harold in Keystone, and at her own grave in De Smet. This provision is a clue to the mystery of her husband's burial marker. David Swanzey's gravestone has the dates 1856-1939. The gravestone of his first wife says 1876-1908, although according to records she was born in March of 1872 and died June 3, 1909. These discrepancies make more sense in light of the fact that both stones were made years after their deaths, in accordance with Carrie's will.

There is also a mystery regarding the gravestones of Carrie's family in De Smet. Some have wondered why her father's headstone is an old, original stone, but the rest of the stones in the family plot in De Smet are similar, newer stones. As late as 1944, there was no marker for the grave of Laura and Almanzo's son, and probably not for that of Caroline or Mary either. When Laura sent a contribution to the cemetery association that year for upkeep on her deceased son's grave, the workers there could not find it. It is not known whether there had never been any markers other than Charles's in the Ingalls plot, or the markers had deteriorated. From Carrie's will and probate records, we see that her marker was placed in the 1940s. It is believed that Rose placed the remaining stones for Caroline, Mary, and Laura's infant son later, and had them made to match Carrie's. In any case, they did receive "suitable markers" at last.

In her will, Carrie next requests the Masonic Lodge in Mt. Aetna to make the final arrangements regarding her services and remains, and the Lodge and Chapter in De Smet, "which were so good to my father and mother," to arrange for her burial there. In consideration for making these arrangements, Carrie arranged that a payment of $300 be made to Mt. Aetna Lodge and $200 to De Smet Lodge. Presumably, Mt. Aetna Lodge received the larger amount since they had to arrange the transport of her remains.

Carrie next mentions her sisters: to Laura, she left no material bequest, as she felt that the "character" of her estate made it "more a burden than a benefit." Carrie wasn't flush with cash; her estate was real estate and mines, not all of which were clear in either boundary or title. It probably would have been a headache to deal with, and Carrie may also have realized that Laura received enough income from the farm and her books that she was not needful of a bequest. To Grace, Carrie left the house in De Smet and a stipend of $600/year. However, Grace had preceded Carrie in death, and Carrie had already sold the house a couple of years earlier, so these two items had no effect. The will was made on April 10, 1940, after her sister Mary had died, and so no mention of her was made.

Carrie then directs her executor to clear titles and mark boundaries to all real estate and mines. She authorizes payment from the income of their operation to do this. The mines were not operating at the time of her death, but the executor was still able to clear titles.

To her step-daughter, Mary Swanzey Harris, Carrie left only $100, since Mary was already set to inherit a portion of her father's estate after Carrie's death. Harold, having already died when the will was made, was not mentioned.

Finally, Carrie directed her executor to sell the Big Hit Group of mines. One fourth of the proceeds was to be paid to the executor, with the balance, in addition to the remainder of her estate, to be given to the Mt. Aetna Masonic Lodge.

An affidavit was filed later, stating that Carrie did not leave anything to the Mt. Aetna Eastern Star Chapter because the Masons would "always have a place for the Eastern Stars and take care of them," and that it was better to have one organization in charge to the benefit of both.

In particular, Carrie wanted the Lodge to find a new building. They were still meeting on the second floor of the old school house building, and there were several elderly members for whom the stairs were a hardship. She felt a one-story building would be better suited to the physical condition and needs of the members.

The property that Carrie left Mt. Aetna Lodge consisted of four mining groups and two unpatented mining claims, for a combined 15 mines covering about 165 acres, and the Topbar Township homestead claim of 160 acres. The Lodge was able to lease the mines to the large Homestake Mining Company for $2,000/year, negotiable every five years.[24] They sold the homestead claim and with the proceeds did purchase a single-story Lodge building, which served them well for many years. True to their word and their mission, they also took care of the Mt. Aetna Chapter of the Eastern Star. Unfortunately, the membership of the Lodge and Chapter dwindled through the years, and eventually the Mt. Aetna Lodge and Chapter merged with the Battle River Lodge and Chapter at Hermosa. The building that had been purchased with Carrie's money was sold, and became a restaurant. Carrie's 50-year pin and certificate, along with the photo taken at their presentation, had been displayed at the Chapter until it merged, when they were given to friends according to her last wishes. A copy of the photo was donated to the Keystone Historical Museum, where it may still be viewed.

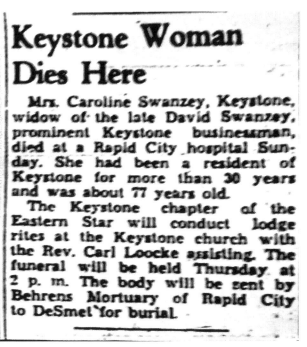

Keystone Woman Dies Here

Mrs. Caroline Swanzey, Keystone, widow of the late David Swanzey, prominent Keystone businessman, died at a Rapid City hospital Sunday. She had been a resident of Keystone for more than 30 years and was about 77 years old.

The Keystone chapter of the Eastern Star will conduct lodge rites at the Keystone church with the Rev. Carl Loocke assisting. The funeral will be held Thursday at 2 p. m. The body will be sent by Behrens Mortuary of Rapid City to DeSmet for burial.

From the Rapid City Journal.

LAST WILL

OF

CAROLINE I. SWANZEY

I, Caroline I. Swanzey, of Keystone, South Dakota, do hereby make, publish and declare this, my Last Will, hereby revoking all former wills:

First: I direct that my just debts and funeral expenses be paid as soon after my decease as may conveniently be done.

Second: I direct that my executor, hereinafter named, place suitable markers at the graves of my deceased husband, David N. Swanzey, of his first wife, and of his deceased son, Harold D. Swanzey, at the cemetery in Keystone, South Dakota, and at my grave at DeSmet, South Dakota.

Third: It is my hope that Mount Aetna Lodge No. 128 A.F.& A.M., of Keystone, South Dakota, of which my deceased husband was a member, will take charge of all local arrangements for my burial, and that the Masonic Lodge at DeSmet, South Dakota, and Bethlehem Chapter No. 13 O.E.S., of which I was a member, and which were so good to my father and mother, will attend to my burial in the Ingalls family lot at DeSmet, South Dakota. I therefore give to Mount Aetna Lodge No. 128 A.F. & A.M. the sum of Three Hundred and no/100 ($300.00) Dollars, and to Bethlehem Chapter No. 13 O.E.S. at DeSmet, South Dakota, the sum of Two hundred and no/100 ($200.00) Dollars.

Fourth: To my dear sister, Laura (Mrs. A.J.) Wilder, of Mansfield, Missouri, I give no material bequest, because the character and extent of the residue of my estate may be such as to make any bequest to her more of a burden than a benefit.

Fifth: To my sister, Grace Dow, of Manchester, South Dakota, I give my former home in DeSmet to have and to hold the same to her during the term of her natural life, and after her death to the Trustees of the Masonic Lodge at DeSmet, South Dakota to have and to hold the same absolutely and forever.

First page of Carrie's will.
Carrie was always called by her nickname to differentiate her from her mother, so few documents use her given name of Caroline; her will and obituary are among those that do.

To Whom It May Concern:

We were close friends of Carrie Ingalls Swanzey for many years. She often reminded us that "Masons take care of the Stars".

Several of us were present when her will was read. A question arose as to why the Eastern Star Chapter was not mentioned. Judge Walter Miser, her lawyer, explained that she had discussed that but felt it was better to have the Masonic Lodge as beneficiary because "they would always have a place for the Eastern Stars and take care of them". He said they felt it would be better for one organization to be in charge of business related to the estate to benefit both.

Dated: Nov. 12, 1990

A.I. Johnson

Willmeta Johnson

Subscribed and sworn before me this __13__ day of __Nov__ 1990

My commission expires __July 27__, 1990

Notary Public

Affidavit regarding Carrie's will.

Mansfield

Love and service, with a belief in the future and expectation of better things in the tomorrow of the world, is a good working philosophy...For there is no turning back nor standing still; we must go forward, into the future, generation after generation toward the accomplishment of the ends that have been set for the human race.
~ Laura Ingalls Wilder, author, member of the Order of the Eastern Star

After they returned to De Smet from Florida, the Wilders read literature advertising Missouri as "The Land of Big Red Apples," prosperous and easy to farm. For Almanzo and Laura, who had endured several years of drought, hail, dust storms, and just about every other occurrence of nature that could ruin a crop – or a person's spirit – this was irresistible. At the ages of 37 and 27, respectively, and with a seven-year-old daughter, Almanzo and Laura loaded up the wagon and set out on July 17, 1894, to start a new chapter of their lives. Their friends Frank and Emma Cooley, along with their sons, Paul and George, caravaned with them. The trip was a typical one for that time and place – hot or rainy by turns, little food and no comforts. Almanzo sold asbestos fire mats, or, more often, bartered them for milk or other items they needed, to keep them going. Laura kept a journal of the trip. Part of it was printed in the local De Smet newspaper, and the entirety of it was posthumously published as a book titled *On the Way Home*.[1]

All along the way, they met others who were also searching for a better life. Many of them were leaving the drought-ridden Dakotas behind and heading east, as were the Wilders and Cooleys. Others were coming from that direction, and it must have been disheartening for the young couples to hear of others' misfortunes in the land to which they were bound.[2]

Advertisements like this one enticed Almanzo and Laura to Missouri.

After six weeks of travel, they arrived at Mansfield, in Wright County, Missouri, on August 30, 1894. The town had been established in 1881 around the railroad, and was flourishing by the time the Wilders arrived. Laura noted in her journal that it was a town with a population of about three to four hundred, and there already existed everything they could want, including two churches (Methodist and Presbyterian, though; not Congregational), a school, two general stores, two drug stores, a department store, a livery stable and blacksmith, and of course the depot. There was also a bank, a doctor and a dentist, and, a little out of town, a flour mill. A Masonic Lodge, an Odd Fellows Lodge, and the Women's Temperance Union

An early photo of Mansfield, Missouri.

were well established by then as well, and an opera house – the sign of civilization in that era – was located upstairs above the department store. The area population relied on grain farming, lumber, and livestock for their livelihood.[3]

The first thing Almanzo did in Mansfield was begin the search for a home, looking at the first possibility that very day. That one did not suit their needs, but he found a prospective site a few days later, and took Laura to see it. She fell in love with it. Not only did it have water (in the form of a spring) and wood (in the form of trees), it had fruit – or would. The property had several hundred apple trees, two hundred of which had been planted on the only four acres of cleared land. There was also a cabin on the property. It was very small and dilapidated, without even a window, but they could live in it until they could erect a home; they were used to living in little houses, after all. The farm was ideally located, outside of town but close enough for Rose to walk to school. Almanzo had some reservations about the appropriateness of the property for farming, due to its many rocks and ridges, but Laura "took a violent fancy" to it and insisted it was the only place she wanted, so they put down their only cash, a hoarded $100 bill, as payment, making a note for the remaining $300 of the sales price.[4]

They named the farm Rocky Ridge, and began the intensely laborious process of turning it into a working farm with a nice farmhouse. It was back-breaking work, especially for a small, crippled man and a small woman (Almanzo was less than 5' 6" tall, and Laura was short of 5'), but they persisted. That first fall and winter, they cleared half the land, with Laura working the cross-cut saw across from Almanzo. They used the wood to fence the property and build a small barn and henhouse, trading work with neighbors when a helping hand was needed. The rest of the wood they sold in town for seventy-five cents a load. The next spring they were able to put in a crop and plant a garden, along with more apple trees. Almanzo was able to add a room onto the cabin. Even Rose helped with the family finances; she helped plant both garden and crops, and gathered berries to sell in town for a dime a gallon.[5]

During that first year, they realized that the little cabin was not situated quite right, and in 1896, they moved the room addition Almanzo had built to a more desirable location nearby, and added a room to it. The old cabin became a barn. The family earned money by continuing to sell cord wood that they cut from their property, and selling eggs from Laura's hens and fresh produce from the garden. Laura once remarked that they all felt rich when they were finally able to afford a calf and a pig. Then Laura was able to sell butter, too, at ten cents a pound.[6]

At the end of 1897, a sad event worked to improve the lot of the Wilders. Their friend Frank Cooley died. He had owned a hauling business, and Almanzo was able to purchase Frank's wagon from his widow and take over the business. As agent for the Waters Pierce Oil Company, he delivered kerosene and other products to area farms, providing a new source of income. Since Almanzo now needed to be in town much of the time, and the farm was not yet producing, the Wilder family moved into a house in town. By subletting a room to a clerk at the local bank, Mr. N. J. Craig, they were able to bring in some money to help pay the rent on the home. In addition,

Laura served meals to local railroad workers, something she had become practiced at in her young days working in hotels. They relaxed with books in the evenings.[7]

During the summer of 1898, Almanzo's parents came to visit, along with his oldest sister. They were on their way to Louisiana, where others of Almanzo's siblings, Eliza Jane and Perley, lived, to join them. The elder Wilders gave their son a tremendous gift – the deed to the small home in town he was renting. Almanzo was now able to use his entire income toward the farm, and they continued improvements, purchasing an additional six acres that year, and 40 more acres in 1899.[8]

In the early summer of 1902, Laura received word that her father, Charles, was gravely ill. He had been ill several months, and the family knew he would not live much longer. Laura took a train to De Smet and arrived in time for a last farewell before Charles died on June 2. It was also the last time she ever saw her mother, or her sister Mary.

A few months later, the Wilders received a pivotal visit from Almanzo's sister, Eliza Jane, and her son. It was obvious to the veteran teacher that Rose was far too advanced for the small school in Mansfield. In fact, Rose considered the other students, as well as the instructor, "stupid," and had stopped attending the school. While it might seem out of character for Laura to allow her daughter to drop out of school, she knew that school only provides an education if one is learning there, and Rose was not. So when Eliza Jane requested that Rose be allowed to accompany her back to Crawley, Louisiana, to complete her schooling in the larger, more advanced schools there, Almanzo and Laura let her go, even though they did not think very highly of Eliza Jane. Rose was happy to go, as she was never content with farm work or small town life. She did very well in her last years of school, and graduated in 1904. Although she did not have the opportunity to obtain a higher education, her own natural talent was honed enough at the school in Louisiana that when, a few years later, she pursued her dream of writing, she was almost instantly successful.

First, though, she had the immediate need of making a living, and she took telegraphy training from a friend at the Mansfield railroad depot. She was soon working for Western Union in Kansas City, and then Indiana and San Francisco. It was there that Rose met Claire Gillette Lane, whom she married in 1909.[9]

The Wilders' farm became gradually more prosperous as the years ticked by. In 1905, they were able to realize a profit from a small land deal. The previous year they had purchased three town lots, and by selling them at a higher price, they supplemented their income. They used the proceeds to purchase twelve more acres of farm land.[10]

The work was endless, but they took time off for a little fun now and then, too. They enjoyed their favorite pastimes of riding horses and spending pleasant evenings reading. They also followed the example of their Puritan forebears and, as they had been taught, observed the Sabbath on Sundays. Without a Congregational Church, the Wilders chose the Methodist Church as their house of worship. They never officially joined the church, but were faithful in attendance and participated in its activities; William Anderson notes that they were at the dedication of the new church building in December, 1899, and that Laura organized the church's first bazaar.[11]

Church was not the only opportunity they had to meet with others; a new Chapter of the Order of the Eastern Star was organized in Mansfield in 1897, and Laura was a part of it. She had demitted properly from Bethlehem Chapter in De Smet on July 23, 1894, before moving to Missouri, so she was in good standing in the Order. She had to be approved by the new Chapter to join, however, so she could not be a charter member. Still, she was present at the first meeting on May 15, 1897, when Mansfield Chapter No. 76, Order of the Eastern Star, was instituted and constituted. In fact, she was appointed to an office, that of the Star point 'Esther,' at that first meeting, before she was even officially admitted to the Chapter. She paid the $1 dues, and her petition for affiliation was read on

May 21. An investigating committee was appointed, composed of Sisters McNaul and McKey and Brother McKey. At the next meeting, on June 4, the committee reported favorably, and a ballot was taken. The result was that Laura was admitted to the Chapter.

That first year, Laura was not an officer, since her membership was not finalized until after the offices had been filled. However, she frequently filled in as Pro Tem officer when the regular officer was absent. The first few meetings, she was appointed to the station of 'Esther.' Thereafter, she often acted as Secretary Pro Tem; more of that year's minutes were taken by Laura than by the official Secretary – which must be why Laura was elected to that office the following year of 1898.

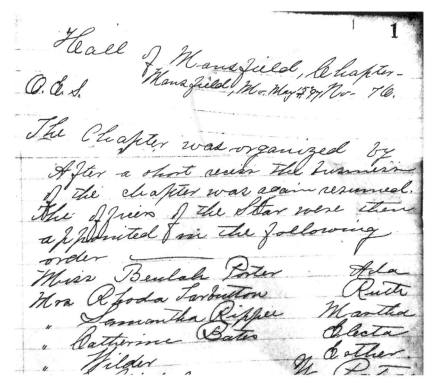

From the minutes of the first meeting.
Laura was appointed to the office of 'Esther' for that meeting.

*At the second meeting, Laura's petition was received. She was again
appointed to the station of 'Esther.'*

*At the third meeting, Laura's petition was approved and she was voted
into membership. Immediately thereafter, Laura was appointed to the
investigating committee of Emma Cooley, her friend from De Smet.*

214

Emma Cooley, Laura's friend who had come from De Smet with Laura's family, also joined the Chapter in 1897. Soon, Mr. Craig, the banker who had boarded with the Wilders in town, also joined. He, and later his wife, remained lifelong friends of the Wilders. In all, Laura and Almanzo were credited with bringing twenty people into the Order through the years.

Laura held the office of Associate Matron in 1899, and Conductress in 1900. Another duty she had in 1900 was acting on the committee for a play, "Female Masonry," that the Chapter put on for an entertainment. It was reported that the committee on entertainment received this play, which was a parody of "side degrees." Laura and the others on the committee assigned parts to members, held rehearsal, and presented the program. No further details are given, so we do not know whether Laura herself played a part.

From the minutes.

It wasn't long after Laura helped establish the Mansfield Chapter of the Eastern Star that Almanzo joined the Mansfield Masonic Lodge. He was initiated as an Entered Apprentice on July 27, 1898, passed to the second degree of Fellowcraft on August 31, 1898, and raised to the sublime third degree of Master Mason on December 21, 1898. Almanzo maintained his membership in the Masonic Lodge his entire life, attending meetings on the Wednesday evening on or before the full moon each month. He held office three years, serving as Tyler in 1901, 1903, and 1905.

Masonry in Missouri was almost a hundred years old by then. The first Lodge in the Louisiana Purchase – of which the land that became the state of Missouri was a part – was chartered in November, 1804, under the jurisdiction of the Grand Lodge of Pennsylvania. That same Grand Lodge warranted the second Lodge in September, 1808, with famous explorer Meriwether Lewis as Master of the Lodge. William Clark joined his fellow explorer in the Lodge the next year. By 1821, the year Missouri entered statehood, there were at least six Lodges within its boundaries, and a Grand Lodge was formed. It was seventy years later that the Lodge in Mansfield was chartered, on October 15, 1891.[12]

The Grand Lodge of Missouri returns show when Almanzo was initiated, passed, and raised in Mansfield Lodge.

216

☞ SEND DUES WITH RETURNS. ☜

RETURNS

TO THE

Grand Lodge of Missouri,

FOR THE YEAR ENDING

July 31st, A. D., 1 *901*

BY

Mansfield Lodge, No. *543*

Held at Town of *Mansfield*

Post-Office Address, *Mansfield*

County of *Wright* *Mo*

OFFICERS.

L. B. Anson W. M.

O. D. Paterson S. W.

R. M. Rogers J. W.

H. C. Jones Treasurer.

S. J. Hoover Secretary.

E. C. Anson S. D.

S. N. McNaul J. D.

P. W. Newton S. Steward.

L. O. Neider J. Steward.

A. J. Wilder Tyler.

TIME OF REGULAR MEETING.

Wednesday night on or before Each full moon

TIME OF ANNUAL ELECTION.

Last meeting in Dec

DATE OF CHARTER,

Oct 15 — 1891

WOODWARD & TIERNAN PRINTING CO., ST. LOUIS

Almanzo held his first office in the Lodge, that of Tyler, in 1901.

Laura had the honor of serving the Mansfield Chapter of the Eastern Star as Worthy Matron in 1902. As part of her duties as Worthy Matron, Laura called a special meeting on April 23, at which the Chapter hosted the Worthy Grand Matron of Missouri. Laura also attended the session of the Grand Chapter held at Sedalia in late October. She reported on the meeting to her Chapter at their November 7 meeting.

81

December 6, 1901
Mansfield Chapter No. 76 met in regular session in Masonic Hall.
Officers present Sister Kate Boles Associate Matron
Sister Lenore Jones Conductress
Sister Laura Wilder Ada
Sister Nettie McNaul Esther
Total number present ten.
After the opening the Chapter elected the following officers for the ensuing year.
Worthy Matron   Laura E. Wilder
Worthy Patron   W. E. Jones
Associate Matron   Martha Clark
Secretary   Lenore B. Jones
Conductress   Nettie McNaul
Treasurer   Brother McNaul
Associate Cond.   Laura Young
There being no further business before the Chapter it was closed in regular order
                   Laura E. Wilder
                   Secretary pro. tem.

Minutes from the meeting at which Laura was elected Worthy Matron for the year 1902.
Notice that although Laura's office was the station of 'Ada' (sic), she also filled in as Secretary Pro Tem for this meeting – one of many meetings she did this.

Almanzo petitioned the Chapter for membership the first month Laura was Worthy Matron. At the reading of his petition on January 17, Laura assigned Brothers Young and McNaul and Sister Jones as a committee to investigate him. The committee gave their favorable report on February 7, and the Chapter voted to accept him into membership that evening. Almanzo was initiated into the Order of the Eastern Star on February 21, 1902. He and Laura now attended the meetings together twice each month, on the first and third Fridays.

Above and below, from the minutes of the meetings at which Almanzo petitioned and joined the Order.
Notice how Laura signed the minutes as the Worthy Matron.

219

These were not the first mentions of Almanzo in the minutes of Mansfield Chapter, however. The first was on February 3, 1899, when a bill from A. J. Wilder was presented. The bill was for fifty-five cents, which was the amount he had spent on lumber to construct a table for a banquet that the Stars held for the Masons. Incidentally, Laura and the other members who attended this meeting were braving the elements to be there. Just a few days later, February 11, 1899, Mansfield recorded their coldest temperature in history, twenty-six degrees below zero, in what came to be known as "The Great Blizzard of 1899."

From the minutes.

He was mentioned later as a "profane" who gave testimony – by committee, since, as a non-member, he could not be present in a meeting – in a trial against a woman who was accused of making libelous remarks against another sister in the Chapter. Laura and Almanzo were listed as witnesses to the remarks. The trial was not recorded, as was the one in which Charles and Royal had testified years earlier in De Smet, so we do not know whether the Wilders recalled hearing the alleged slander, but the resulting sentence of "not guilty" is noted.

Once initiated, Almanzo was regular in his attendance, and even frequently held office. A craftsman, he hand-made items that the Chapter needed, such as the table mentioned above and at other times furnishings were needed. He also made emblems, staffs, and flower stands for the Chapter. The minutes of August 1, 1902 record the thanks of the Chapter for some of these items. Almanzo also continued his attendance at the Lodge, and he and Laura were present at the banquet held for St. John's Day that year.

Courtesy Laura Ingalls Wilder Home Association, Mansfield, MO.

Almanzo supplied items the Chapter needed.

As one can well imagine, Almanzo's name was difficult for some of the members. He mostly went by "A. J.," or just his last name, Wilder. It seems some of the Masons and Stars weren't quite sure what his name really was. He is listed in the records sometimes correctly as A. J. or Almanzo, but sometimes also incorrectly, as Alonzo, Asiah, and even Andrew. I searched the records from the chartering of the Lodge to be sure some or all of these weren't referring to someone else, but there was no other Wilder in Mansfield Lodge or Chapter. All references to a Wilder are meant to indicate Laura or, as in these cases, Almanzo.

A couple of instances where Almanzo's name was noted incorrectly. The Secretary of the Lodge would have been the one who filled out the forms; evidently, he did not know A. J.'s name.

Laura was again elected to the office of Worthy Matron in 1903. She appointed Almanzo to the office of Sentinel for the year. Laura became the first Worthy Matron from Mansfield to attend the Grand Chapter's School of Instruction, which was held at Seymour in June of that year. Laura reported to the Chapter afterward that it was pleasant, but she did not learn anything new regarding the work. This is not surprising; Laura had been raised memorizing scriptures and readings with her sisters, so she was well trained in such mental exercises. Laura again hosted the Worthy Grand Matron of Missouri at a meeting, and she had the privilege of introducing Carrie to her Chapter during Carrie's visit in September of that year. Carrie was Worthy Matron of Bethlehem Chapter #13 in De Smet, so Mansfield Chapter hosted two Ingalls sisters as Matrons at the same time that night, although of course only Laura acted as Worthy Matron. Carrie's visit extended to the following meeting two weeks later.

From the minutes.

Also in this term, Laura attended the meeting of the Grand Chapter of Missouri in the fall of 1903. At the end of her second year as Worthy Matron, the Chapter gave Laura a special gift. The minutes record the event:

Bro. Thirkield made an eloquent speech on behalf of the Chapter, presenting the Past Matron Laura E. Wilder with a beautiful Past Matron jewel. Sister Wilder being completely taken by surprise was unable fitly to express her thanks for the gift but requested that it might be entered in the minutes that she feels amply repaid for the efforts she has made on behalf of the Chapter by the love and appreciation shown her by its members.

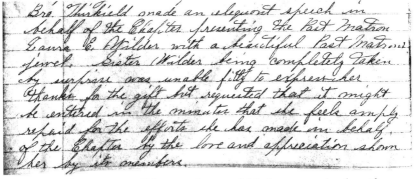

From the minutes of the meeting at which Laura received a gift.

The Chapter had paid $5 for the pin, a grand token of appreciation.

Although it has been believed that Laura was Worthy Matron in 1904, she was actually Secretary that year. The mistake comes from a notice in the January 22, 1904 issue of the *Mansfield Mail*. It lists the meeting times of the Chapter and has the information, "Laura Wilder, W. M." However, it seems the paper was just running the usual announcement that they had for the past year, and no one had given them the correct names for the new year yet. The minutes clearly show Laura elected as Secretary for that year, and later issues of the *Mail* that year do list the correct Worthy Matron and Patron, and Laura as Secretary. In addition to that office, Laura was on the social committee, responsible for planning refreshments and entertaining pastimes for the Chapter to enjoy together.

Laura's greatest honor in the Order of the Eastern Star came in the summer of 1904, when she was selected as District Deputy Grand Lecturer for the Grand Chapter's 1904-05 year (although the local chapters were still holding office per calendar year, the business and fraternal years at the state level ran August 1 – July 31). Her appointment to this office proves Laura's mastery of the work. As District Deputy Grand Lecturer, she was responsible for visiting all the Chapters in her district to oversee and review their work, ensuring that the rituals and other works were being done correctly. After visiting each Chapter (and remember, this was still in the days of horse and buggy), Laura then gave a report of their standing to the Worthy Grand Matron and other attendees at the state's Grand Chapter meeting, which was held in St. Louis on September 28-30, 1905.

FORTY-SIXTH DISTRICT.

Mansfield, Mo., September 25, 1905.

Mrs. Linda J. Sears,
  Worthy Grand Matron.

Dear Sister: I realize with regret that my report is not as complete as it should be, and had fully intended to do better, but we are told that good intentions make excellent paving-stones.

Mansfield and Hartville Chapters are in good condition and take great interest in the work of the Order.

A strong friendship exists between these Chapters and visits are often exchanged which are a great help in keeping up the interest.

Mountain Grove Chapter, I understand, is in good condition.

I am sorry to report that Friendship Chapter of Ava has given up its Charter. Thanking you for the honor conferred upon me in my appointment, I am,

Fraternally yours,

LAURA E. WILDER,
D. D. G. L., Forty-sixth District.

Laura's report to the Grand Chapter as District Deputy Grand Lecturer. Printed in the Proceedings of the Thirty-first Annual Meeting of the Grand Chapter, Order of the Eastern Star, State of Missouri, 1905.

The brevity of her report is typical. With Chapters from the entire state reporting, as well as the business of the Grand Chapter itself being conducted, no doubt everyone appreciated speakers who were not long winded. While she was District Deputy Grand Lecturer, Laura and her Chapter again hosted the Worthy Grand Matron of Missouri.

Laura kept the office of Secretary of her Chapter for 1905, as well as serving on the visitation committee. The persons on this committee regularly visited ill or homebound members and kept them company. Almanzo held the office of Warder that year.

Laura remained highly involved in the Eastern Star the following year. Her office for 1906 was the Star point of 'Martha,' and she also served on three committees. The entertainment committee was the one she probably enjoyed most, as she always loved a good party. She was also on the auditing committee, and the committee that sent much needed supplies to the Masonic Home, a home operated by the Grand Lodge and Grand Chapter for widows and orphans. In June, the Order's School of Instruction was held in Mansfield, and Laura almost certainly attended. She also again attended the session of the Grand Chapter, which was held in Kansas City that year, the last weekend of September. The pin she obtained at that meeting is currently on display at the Laura Ingalls Wilder Home in Mansfield.

Laura was not the only Wilder who actively participated in the Order. Almanzo used his woodworking skills in crafting items needed by the Chapter. He frequently served as an officer, and he served on various committees. He, like Laura, was often appointed to investigating committees, to meet petitioners and make inquiries regarding them, in determination of their suitability for the Order. Occasionally, he was selected to help draft Resolutions of Respect, a statement written upon the death of a member. The Resolutions declare what the deceased had meant to the Chapter, lingering on the positive effect and contributions made by the individual, and how much the

While Laura was in Kansas City for the Eastern Star meeting, she took time to visit Rose, who was living there at the time and working as a telegrapher. She also had her photograph taken.
Courtesy Laura Ingalls Wilder Home Association, Mansfield, MO.

Laura's pin from the Eastern Star meeting.
Courtesy Laura Ingalls Wilder Home Association, Mansfield, MO.

Chapter will miss the decedent. The Resolutions are written in the minutes, and a copy is given to close family members; if the deceased person was well known in the community, the Resolutions of Respect may also be published in the local paper.

Known throughout his life as a quiet man, Almanzo evidently felt comfortable in the Chapter: the minutes of the meeting of March 1, 1917, indicate that Almanzo provided the entertainment during the social hour that evening. It would be very interesting to know what sort of entertainment he provided, but, unfortunately, the minutes give no indication as to what he actually did. Almanzo was not a musician, and was generally known to be a man of very few words. However, some who knew him say that once he opened up, he had a terrific sense of humor, so perhaps he regaled the members with his best jokes, funny stories, and riddles.[13]

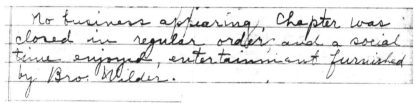

From the minutes.

Almanzo was appointed Warder, and Laura filled the station of 'Electa' in 1907. In 1908, Laura served as Associate Matron; she then moved into the east as Worthy Matron again in 1909. Almanzo held the office of Treasurer in 1908, but it appears that Laura did much of this work. One of the things accomplished was the purchase of a ledger, in which to keep the history of payments, as well as affiliation information, of each member. Almanzo was re-elected Treasurer for 1909, but he evidently declined the office, as another person was installed in that position and Almanzo served as Pro Tem Warder when needed.

In reviewing the minutes of the meetings of Mansfield Chapter, it appears that Laura was a bit pedantic about the rituals and works of the Order. She often instructed the members on the proper method and protocol of Chapter business, such as elections and other such procedures. When she became Worthy Matron for the third time, in 1909, she immediately began having reviews of the degrees and work of the Order in the meetings, even calling special meetings to practice – something she had done in her previous terms as well – since she felt the Chapter needed more practice to perform them correctly. Upon her installation, Laura appointed her committees for the year, and the paper reported that she held a tea for the social committee in March. No doubt they planned many pleasant evenings for the Chapter.

From the minutes.

Laura and Almanzo have finished eating a light supper.[14] After clearing the table, Laura dresses in her Star dress; at her option, the Worthy Matron may request a particular color or even style of dress for her officers. Laura always wears a hat and gloves when she goes to town, but tonight she takes care to select a hat that is easily removed. Almanzo dons a suit, then hitches up the buggy. When Laura comes out, he helps her into the buggy and tucks a dust blanket over her lap for the short ride to town. His swift Morgan horse has them at the meeting hall in short order.

The meeting is held in the upstairs room of the Lodge building. In the anteroom, Almanzo leaves his hat and Laura lays aside her hat, gloves, and shawl. Hats are not worn in the Chapter room, as they stand (symbolically) between the wearer and God above. Gloves and wraps are not customarily permitted, as they "come between" the warm, friendly contact with which members should greet one another.

The layout of the room is similar to its layout for a Lodge meeting, but has some additions. Arranged around the room are the five chairs of the Star Points. Behind each of these chairs is a pedestal, with the emblem of the office placed upon it. The altar is in the center of the room, with a closed Bible upon it. The Charter of the Chapter has been set out near the Secretary's seat. In the corner is the signet of the Eastern Star, the five-pointed star, colored according to the degrees, and with the symbol of each station illustrated within its respective point.

Laura proceeds to the east, because she is Worthy Matron this year. She takes her jewel – the emblematic Star with a gavel in the center, representing her position of authority – from her chair and places it around her neck, then steps back out to the anteroom. Most of the other officers are lined up there also, including Almanzo, who has placed the jewel of his office, that

The Mansfield Masonic Lodge and Eastern Star Chapter met for many years in the upstairs rooms of this building, today the Weaver Inn.

231

of Sentinel, over his collar. The Worthy Patron is in the east; he raps the gavel and instructs, "All who are not members of the Order of the Eastern Star will retire."

He then directs the Associate Conductress to invite the Worthy Matron and other officers to enter the Chapter room.

The Associate Conductress relays the invitation and the officers enter in designated order. Laura has chosen the songs she wishes played during her year, and may have selected or designed a special "march" into and out of the chapter room, just for fun. The officers march to their stations, and the Conductress escorts Laura to the east, where she calls the meeting to order, saying, "The officers will take their respective stations and prepare for the active duties of the Chapter."

Laura directs that the door to the Chapter be secured, and that no interruption be permitted while they are engaged in the ritual of opening the Chapter. After the doors have been secured by the Warder and Sentinel using ritual knocks, Laura calls on each officer in turn to give the duty of their station and the badge of their office. The Star Point officers also explain their badges, reminding the members of the virtues personified by the heroines. For example, 'Esther' explains, "My badge is the crown and scepter within the triangle, an emblem of royalty and power. In the exercise of authority we should be governed by justice and unselfish loyalty to the welfare of others. It was by the practice of these virtues that Esther was able to save her people from extermination." Thus the lessons of the degree are reinforced at every meeting. After each explanation, the Star Point in that station gives the secret sign of her degree, and the Chapter responds with the appropriate secret word or phrase.

Next, Laura directs that the Conductress attend at the altar. At the rap of Laura's gavel, every member stands and faces the altar in a respectful attitude while the Conductress approaches the altar and opens the Bible to the specified scripture. They remain standing in a reverent attitude as the Chaplain gives the invocation.

Now Laura may call for an opening ode. As much as she enjoyed singing and music, she surely had one at each meeting. The ode is followed by the Pledge of Allegiance to the flag.

"I now declare Mansfield Chapter, Number 76, Order of the Eastern Star, duly opened for the transaction of business. Sister Warder, you will so inform the Sentinel," Laura says.

As in the Lodge, there is a secret signal knock to indicate the securing and the opening of the doors. While the Chapter is being ritually opened and closed, no one may enter or leave. The knock this time lets the Sentinel know that the meeting has been opened, and any latecomers may now be admitted, after the proper procedure with the Warder to open the door.

As Worthy Matron, Laura presides over the business of the Chapter. The agenda contains the usual business of organizational meetings: special introductions, reading of the previous meeting's minutes, reports from the Secretary regarding correspondence received, a financial report from the Treasurer, announcements, and so forth. New petitions for membership are appointed to a committee for investigation; after hearing the committee's report at the following meeting, balloting for membership is held. In Laura's days as Worthy Matron, the Chapter was new and growing. There was an initiation at almost every meeting, and other business of beginning a Chapter was also needed. Things such as purchasing jewels and ledgers and arranging for janitorial work were taken care of in the business portion of the meetings, in addition to regular practices of the work and explanations of it. Charitable work was also handled. During one of Laura's tenures at Worthy Matron, she oversaw completion of quilts the members made and sent to the Masonic Home in St. Louis.

On motion it was decided to have a meeting on Friday afternoon and evening for the purpose of finishing two quilts commenced some time ago for the Masonic Home.

From the minutes.

She also made sure the Chapter sent items for the children in the Home at Christmas. Food, clothing, and other items were regularly sent to the Masonic Home. Local individuals needing assistance were cared for, sometimes by members performing necessary work for them, and other times by the Chapter purchasing items that they needed. In the war years, members of the Chapter made bandages and underclothing to donate to the Red Cross. The minutes of the Chapter are full of examples of its members practicing the ideals of Freemasonry.

The business of Chapters today almost always involves discussion of some type regarding scholarships, either discussing their guidelines, organizing fundraisers for them, voting on recipients, or other such deliberations. Additional charitable work is also handled.

When all business is complete, there is usually a program. Special programs are optional, but given Laura's thirst for knowledge and her way of creating opportunities to learn whenever she could, it seems logical that she would take full advantage of the opportunity presented here. The program may be on any topic of interest, and would likely have a moral to it. In fact, minutes of the Mansfield Chapter show that Laura herself frequently gave a "talk" (often described as a "pretty" or "nice" talk which was "beneficial") to the Chapter. The elocution training she had received in Burr Oak served her well during these talks, as it had when she was Lecturer. People who heard her speak said she was "a delightful talker"

Laura made sure everything was done correctly in the Chapter.

who would "keep you spellbound."[15] The program time of a meeting might also be used to practice the secret work or rituals of the Order, as Laura often did in her years as Worthy Matron. Sometimes, the programs are strictly for fun: a skit or musical presentation might be given.

After the program, Laura asks the Associate Matron, "Do you know of any further business to come before the Chapter at this time?"

Upon being informed that there is not, she then directs the Warder, "You will inform the Sentinel that we are about to close the Chapter, and direct him to permit no interruption while we are thus engaged."

Once the Warder and Sentinel have secured the door, Laura calls for the closing ode, followed by the benediction. Then, again, "Sister Conductress, you will attend at the altar."

After the Bible is closed, Laura says, "Sisters and Brothers, we go forth into the world not knowing what trials may await us in the journey of life. Let us not be dismayed, for our Heavenly Father has promised to strengthen and uphold us by the right hand of His power. Farewell."

The Chapter responds, "Farewell."

Laura declares the meeting closed, and the Warder informs the Sentinel, so that the door is unsecured and opened.

Refreshments are generally served after the meeting, providing time for friendly visitation. As charitable work is almost always undertaken, the satisfying feeling that comes with helping others adds to the overall joviality.

There were no unusual happenings in the Chapter in the year of 1909, until the very last meeting of the year. On December 31, the new officers for 1910 were installed by Laura. She was often the Installing Officer through the years, both in her own Chapter and surrounding ones, as her command of the work made her especially eloquent. Following the installation ceremony on this night, the Chaplain held a watch meeting, having been directed to do so by Laura, as Worthy Matron, at the previous meeting. Watch meetings, also called watch night services, were first held by John Wesley, founder of the Methodist Church. (The Wilders were attending the Methodist Church in Mansfield. Many of the other Chapter members were also Methodists.) The meetings generally included singing hymns, prayer, scripture reading, uplifting conversation, and reflection on the old year and resolutions for the new. The purpose of these meetings was to provide an alternative to the drunken parties often held on New Year's Eve. It is not common for Chapters to hold watch meetings, but since the installation was held on New Year's Eve, it seems they wanted to be sure the party afterward adhered to the principles of the Order. This installation was Laura's last act as Worthy Matron, although she remained active in the Chapter. She was soon caught up in moving, and a new venture – writing for farm journals.

From the minutes of Laura's last meeting as Worthy Matron.

It is uncertain exactly when Laura and Almanzo moved back to Rocky Ridge Farm, but it was at least by June of 1910, when they sold the little house in town. Rose returned to Rocky Ridge about the same time her parents did. She had suffered a difficult pregnancy and stillbirth of her son in November of 1909, and went home to her parents' to recuperate.[16]

By now Rocky Ridge had become a self-sustaining farm, if not a very prosperous one. The Wilders had a productive apple orchard, and shipped loads of fruit by train to cities such as Memphis, Kansas City, and other destinations. In addition to fruit and other crops, Almanzo raised a few cattle and other livestock. Laura was known as an expert poultry keeper. She was so recognized in this field that she was often invited to speak on the subject – more instances she was thankful for her elocution training. She was quoted extensively for an article titled "Poultry Raising as an Occupation for Women" in the September 13, 1910 issue of *The American Food Journal*. This paper was published in Chicago, which is about 500 miles from Mansfield – quite a distance for word of Laura's chicken mastery to travel. The essence of her remarks in this paper was repeated through the years: chickens are easy to come by, easy to raise, and, by selling eggs, chicks, and hens in a strategic manner, a decent livelihood could be had from an ordinary flock. Laura wrote a few columns for the *St. Louis Star* and the *Missouri State Farmer* on the subject; this was the beginning of her literary career. She spoke on poultry raising at various agricultural meetings in the area. Being unable to attend one such meeting, she wrote out her speech and sent it along for someone else to read at the meeting. The editor of the *Missouri Ruralist* journal heard the speech. He was so impressed that he asked Laura to contribute articles to the *Ruralist.* Her first article for that journal appeared in February, 1911. She wrote only a few articles a year at first, but gradually she wrote more, until she was a regular columnist. Eventually, she even became editor of the "Home" section. Her columns were sometimes picked up by other papers, and her articles appeared in such papers as the Coffeyville (Kansas) *Daily Journal*, North Platte's *Semi-Weekly Tribune* and the *St. Louis Globe-Democrat.* In June, 1919, an article in *McCall's* titled "Whom Will You Marry?" carried the byline of Laura Ingalls

Wilder – the first time she used this name in publication. She also had articles appear in *Country Gentleman* and the *Youth's Companion*, the paper which had brought such joy to her own household when she was a girl.[17]

Laura's writings revolved around home life on a farm and in a small town, but usually had larger lessons. The point of the story is often promotion of a virtue such as integrity, honesty, charity, or the value of education – the same virtues that were continually reinforced in her life both at church and in the Eastern Star. As John Miller writes, "Mostly she advised readers about how to enjoy life more fully and how to become better people rather than instruct them about how to become better farmers or homemakers...Hard work, honesty, thrift, and self help were, not surprisingly, central themes."[18]

As she began to write more frequently, Laura became less active in her social organizations for a time. She continued to regularly attend meetings of the Eastern Star, but did not hold an office from 1910 until 1915. These years were especially busy for Laura on the farm, another reason for her declined participation in various clubs.

During those years of 1911-1914, Almanzo hired help to complete the little farm house, and transform it into Laura's dream home. They designed the home themselves, with Laura taking the leading role, and included several special customizations. One of these was the lower height of the counters, making them easier for the short couple to work on. Laura was also very appreciative of the 'pass-through' that Almanzo built in the wall between the kitchen and dining room, as it saved her many steps a day. The farmhouse at Rocky Ridge was the first home in the area to have running water, thanks to an ingenious method Almanzo engineered to route water from the spring behind the house, into the kitchen. He even piped the water directly into the cook stove, for hot water on demand long before electricity came to the area. The description of this system was the basis of one of Laura's first articles for the *Missouri Ruralist*. Titled "So We Moved the

Spring," it appeared in the April 20, 1916 issue.

The kitchen was not the only room with special designs. The parlor featured window seats beneath extra large windows. Laura called the windows her ever-changing pictures, and refused to cover them with curtains. The walls in the parlor were paneled with hand-planed oak from the farm; the ceiling beams and stairs were also handcrafted from Rocky Ridge oak. This was all done by Almanzo and Laura with hired help, as there was no mill in Mansfield.

Another customization in the home was the little library. Like all members of her family, Laura was always an avid reader. Rose described one detail Laura wanted in her dream house: "And in the parlor there would be a bookcase, no, *two* bookcases, big bookcases full of books, and a hanging lamp to read them by, on winter evenings by the fireplace."[19] She got her wish, and more: there were actually several bookcases, which Almanzo built into walls in one corner of the parlor, creating a walk-in library.

Laura also got her wish regarding the fireplace. Laura insisted on the fireplace being constructed of three large boulders – one for each side, and one across the top – instead of several smaller stones. Although at first he was against the idea as too impractical and difficult, Almanzo eventually gave in. His own contribution to the fireplace was on the outside: he put a row of fossils found on the farm around the chimney at eye level.

Of course, all this work took several years, a little at a time as they could afford it. Several mentions in the local newspaper, the *Mansfield Mirror*, throughout 1913 and 1914 report on the progress of the work, and on August 6, 1914, it announced that the "Wilders have their new house finished." Laura and Almanzo must have been so happy when that announcement

> Mr. Wilders have their new house finished. It improves the looks of the place immeasurably.

The completed Rocky Ridge Farm home.

could be made! They furnished the home with pieces from the catalog, complemented by several pieces of furniture that Almanzo crafted himself in his woodworking shop.

Even with all his work on Rocky Ridge Farm, Almanzo did his part in the community, as so many good Masons do. Some of his activities in the community, as well as the workings on Rocky Ridge Farm, are known from snippets in the *Mansfield Mirror*. A few of the interesting facts we learn include that he was on the highway committee that planned the new highway in 1913. That fall, he volunteered to serve as superintendent of cattle, sheep, swine, and goats at the 1913 County Fair. This position was not a judge, but more of an organizer, who received and placed entries and such work as that. He also won first place in two divisions at the county fair, one for his millet and the other for a steer. Almanzo's corn crop was noteworthy; he brought into the paper's office a stalk of corn eight feet tall.[20]

The following year, he again won two divisions at the County Fair, one for a Durham cow said to give fifty pounds of milk a day, and the other for a Brown Leghorn. One wonders

> Best Pen Brown Leghorns:
> First, $1; second, 50c.
> First, A. J. Wilder
> Second, Mrs. J. M. Hensley

From the October 22, 1914 issue of the Mansfield Mirror.

if the Leghorn was really Laura's, since she was the poultry expert. She was a superintendent of poultry that year, as she was several years (1914, 1915, and 1917, at least), and perhaps she either could not or did not wish to enter a division which she oversaw. Or, perhaps the chicken really was Almanzo's. A few years later, in 1918, both Laura and Almanzo are listed – but listed separately – as each donating a Leghorn rooster, among other items, to the Red Cross auction. Laura donated a Leghorn rooster and 15 eggs; Almanzo donated a Leghorn rooster, two hens, and a bushel of potatoes. Did Almanzo have his own chickens? Or did Laura let Almanzo donate some of her flock?[21]

Almanzo found a new crop in 1915, when he planted Sudan grass and was able to harvest eight-foot-tall hay only 61 days later. His Sudan won second place in its division at the Fair in 1916. He volunteered his farm to host the agriculture class from the local school as they studied legumes, alfalfa, clover, and apples, and acted as superintendent of horses and mules for the Agricultural Fair in both 1916 and 1917. In 1917, Almanzo again got mentioned for his corn, this time because he was growing "patriotic corn" with red, white, and blue kernels. This was particularly appealing since the U.S. had recently entered World War I.[22]

Almanzo would have been proud to show his family around Rocky Ridge. He got the opportunity when his brother, Perley, visited in 1918. On the other hand, he must have been heartbroken when, in 1919, hunters killed one of his horses. His name immediately appeared on "No Hunting" lists, letting hunters know that they were not allowed on his property. A similar event had happened in 1916, when one of his sows was shot. It was a matter of pride with Almanzo that he never allowed hunters. In one article on his apple orchard, he tells

MISSOURI RURALIST

WITH WHICH IS COMBINED THE BREEDERS SPECIAL
A WEEKLY JOURNAL FOR MISSOURI FARMERS AND BREEDERS

Vol. IX. Whole No. 503   Saturday, June 1, 1912   Price $1.00 Per Year

FROM this 12 year old apple tree in the Ozark country of Missouri were gathered at one time five barrels of No. 1, and three barrels of No. 2 apples. They were highly colored and of most excellent flavor. This tree is a sample of the trees on the hundred-acre orchard farm of A. J. Wilder, who is shown standing at the side of the tree. After a fruitless struggle on the plains of Dakota, Mr. Wilder came to Missouri, settling at Mansfield. He purchased 40 acres of undeveloped land by going in debt for it and went to work. Mother Nature rewarded his well meant if not well directed efforts—he knew nothing of orcharding at the time. Mr. Wilder has since added another 60 acres. He is out of debt, his land has more than doubled in value and his orchard is regarded by nurserymen and apple buyers as one of the best in the Ozark country.

Almanzo's apple orchard made the front cover. The article carries the byline of A. J. Wilder, but many believe that Laura wrote it.

how he did not have to spray his trees for many years, because the quail kept the bug infestations down. Once the quail diminished due to the hunting of them on neighboring farms, he had to begin spraying.[23]

In 1921, Almanzo grew wheat with heads over seven inches long, and won first place for his Timothy Grass, Orchard Grass, and two-year-old horse. He was also mentioned as being well versed in growing strawberries in the area, for newcomers to inquire about that industry. The Chamber of Commerce held a town-wide sale in the spring of 1921, and Almanzo was one of the three committee members who organized the event. The following spring, Almanzo was busy with Governor of Orleans, a pure-bred Morgan horse he brought in from a U.S. Army Remount Service farm. Almanzo always had a special fondness for Morgans, and he hoped to improve the quality of the local horse stock, to the benefit of area farmers. He still had time to tend his apple orchard, though, and his Pippins won second place in that year's Fair. The year 1926 found him again superintending the horse and mule division of the Fair. He was a charter member of the Bermuda Onion Growers Association in 1927.[24]

The Government Stallion

"Governor of Orleans" is expected to arrive April 21st, and will stand this season at my farm, one mile east of Mansfield.

This stallion is a thorough-bred Morgan from the government Horse Farm at Middleburg, Vermont and is sent here for the purpose of raising horses for the U. S. army. Fee $10.00 number of mares limited. If you want service see me at once.

A. J. WILDER.

From the April 20, 1922 issue of the Mansfield Mirror.

On trips into Mansfield, Almanzo often visited with men at the pool house, and was known about town as man who looked stern and was quiet, but really a lot of fun. People who knew Almanzo described him as "a cut up," "witty," and with "a great humor."[25]

Almanzo continued to enlarge and improve the farm as he was able. Eventually, Rocky Ridge Farm encompassed approximately 185 acres. With the exception of a couple of treed lots which they kept for wood and lumber, the farm was cleared and cultivated in crops or as pasture for the livestock. Almanzo was busy with his orchard, sheep and goats, hogs, cattle, and horses, in addition to the wheat and grass crops. Laura's specialty always remained the poultry.

Always busy, Laura also found time to work in the community. She was named Vice President of the 16th District of the Missouri Home Development Association, and organized several local branches in her area. She used her position toward the betterment of all farm women, making needed changes in her district. One very practical need was in the local trading centers. Women who accompanied their farmer husbands to these places had no facilities to use while there. This discouraged their attendance, and thus, their participation in the business. Laura always felt that a farm was a joint venture with a husband and wife working as partners, and to encourage the women to be active in it, she worked to establish public ladies' restrooms in the trading centers.[26]

The September 7, 1916 issue of the *Mansfield Mirror* mentions that a local man of the town purchased two acres of land in Keystone from Mrs. D. N. Swanzey – Laura's sister Carrie. It seems likely that Laura connected the purchaser and the seller, hopefully to the advantage of each.[27]

While her parents were busy on the farm and in the community of Mansfield, Rose was busy beginning her own illustrious career. After her recuperating stay at Rocky Ridge, she and her husband traveled extensively, working various jobs. Among other enterprises, Rose became one of the first female real estate agents in California, but she also did much freelance writing. This lead to an offer in 1915 that marked a milestone for Rose and, by extension, her mother: she was hired by the *San Francisco Bulletin*. It was soon after her new employment here that Laura took a trip to visit her. Rose paid Laura's travel expenses, and gave her parents enough cash to cover the money Laura would have made if she'd remained home, and to hire help for Almanzo while she was gone. Laura was 48 years old when she made this trip, which lasted about two months. The letters Laura wrote home to Almanzo were published after her death as the book *West From Home*. During her stay, 28-year-old Rose helped Laura learn to write in such a way so as to reach a wider audience than she did with her poultry and home articles. They visited the Panama-Pacific International Exposition (also known as the San Francisco World's Fair), and Laura was able to write some articles from her experiences there. These articles, aided by the training she had received from Rose, helped Laura achieve a goal of more regular contributions to the *Missouri Ruralist* and a wider readership. Simultaneously, while with the *Bulletin*, Rose began writing serial stories that ran over several issues. Her talent gained her immediate recognition, and it wasn't long before Rose had her own byline. She grew apart from her husband, and they divorced in 1918. That same year, she stopped working at the *Bulletin* to write freelance. Her first book, *Henry Ford's Own Story,* was published in 1918. Others followed in quick succession, and Rose was a well-known author in just a couple of years. She was commissioned to write the biography of Herbert Hoover, which was published in 1920 as *The Making of Herbert Hoover*; then the Red Cross hired her to go to Europe and report on postwar conditions. She traveled the European continent, and her writings became known the world over.[28]

In 1917, Laura opened a new chapter in her life when she took a job with the local Farm Loan Association. She was a founding member of the Association, and was voted into the

Mansfield National Farm Loan Association

Makes Federal Government Loans
at 5 1-2 per cent interest on 34 yrs.
time, with privilege of paying sooner if desired. For particulars inquire

John W. Brentlinger, Pres.
Mrs. A. J. Wilder, Secy.

From the 9-21-22 issue of the Mansfield Mirror.

A receipt made by Laura as Secretary of the National Farm Loan Association. From the collection of Eric Dodson, courtesy Mansfield Area Historical Society & Museum, Inc.

office of Secretary-Treasurer the first year. She held that position for ten years, and made over a million dollars worth of loans to local farm families. This was in keeping with her philosophy, and Masonic philosophy, of bettering life for all.[29]

Laura remarked in *These Happy Golden Years*, "Everything is simple when you are alone, or at home, but as soon as you meet other people you are in difficulties." For someone who had been shy and uncomfortable around others as a girl, Laura found in her adult years that she really very much enjoyed the company of others, and she found plenty of time to socialize. As one might expect from Laura, even her social life was not merely social, but had a higher aim. It began with the Ladies' Aid Society at church, with the purpose of serving others. It is unknown exactly when Laura joined, but it was most likely very soon after arriving in Mansfield. Although she and Almanzo remained active and regular in attendance at the Methodist Church, Laura's activity in the Ladies' Aid Society became more sporadic through the years. In 1913, the Mansfield newspaper mentioned that the Society was happy to have Mrs. Wilder at a meeting in May, the first she had attended in a year.[30]

The local chapter of the American Red Cross – founded by Clara Barton, another member of the Order of the Eastern Star – also had service to others as their priority. During World War I, citizens everywhere showed their patriotic colors, and the citizens of Mansfield, including the Wilders, were no different. Laura devoted several columns to various aspects of it, primarily life on the home front. While not able to contribute a great deal financially to charitable efforts, the Wilders donated what they could. Charitable relief involves service as well as money, and Laura and Almanzo were busy in such work. "Bessie" joined the Red Cross in August, 1917, at the second meeting of the group. The ladies of the Red Cross regularly met to make undershirts, bandages, and similar items to send to hospitals near the front. Sometimes the meetings were held at the Masonic Lodge. In addition, they held regular fundraisers and benefits in the form of dinners and auctions. Laura was usually on one of the committees of these functions. At the end the war, Mansfield held a Homecoming for all the "boys" returning from service, the largest gathering the town had seen. Once again, Laura was one of the active participants, this time working on the refreshment committee. The patriotism evinced by the citizens of Mansfield was a pride in their country's fight against tyranny, not the superiority of nationalism. When the war came to an end, they found ways to send aid to individuals in those countries that had been more directly affected by the war.[31]

RED CROSS FORMED

Mansfield Organization Is Perfected Saturday Afternoon

The Mansfield Red Cross organization was perfected at a meeting held in the park Saturday afternoon. Speeches were made by Dr. R. M. Rogers, J. Lon Dennis, C. A. Stephens and Mrs. W. M. Divan. The work of organizing was done by Dr. R. M. Rogers, who proved himself to be not only a good speech-maker but a splendid organizer as well.

The officers elected were
Dr. R. M. Rogers, Chairman.
C. A Stephens, Vice-Chairman,
Geo. B. Freeman, Secretary.
J. E. Craig, Treasurer.

The members to date, besides the charter members named last week are Mrs. C. L. Beach, C C. Hensley, J. Lon Dennis, Mrs. Bessie Wilder, Mrs. J. W. Roberts, Mrs. Clara Duckworth, G. E. Tombleson, C. A. Stephens,

From the August 2, 1917 issue of the Mansfield Mirror.

Even after the war, Laura's patriotism did not wane, and she remained very involved in politics. She acted as Chairman of the Democratic Women's group in 1919, an organization that worked toward improvement of society for everyone through political means. She attended a meeting of the 16th congressional district in Rolla in August of that year.

The Board of Governors of the Mansfield Chamber of Commerce appointed Laura to the committee on Agriculture Farming and Produce in 1921. In 1925, she even made a run for the position of Collector of Pleasant Valley Township. Her bases for running were her history of community service and her work with the Farm Loan Association. Laura lost the election by a wide margin, and that was the end of her political career. Although she did not run for any further offices, she always retained her interest in politics. The substantial time and effort that both Laura and Almanzo devoted to various

Democratic Women Meet

Pursuant to call, the Democratic ladies of Pleasant Valley township met Aug. 12 in the directors' room of the Bank of Mansfield. Dr. W. M. Hamilton, committeeman of Pleasant Valley township, presiding. Mrs. A J. Wilder was elected temporary chairman and Mrs. Blanche Anderson secretary. The following permanent officers were elected: Mrs. A. J. Wilder, chairman; Miss Maude Reynolds, secretary Mrs. A. J. Wilder was elected township committeeman to attend the township meeting to be held at Hartville Aug. 19. A vote of thanks was extended to G.W. Freeman for the use of the directors' room. There were several ladies present. After discussing topics of the day' the meeting was adjourned.—Miss Maude Reynolds, Secy.

From the August 14, 1919 issue of the Mansfield Mirror.

community activities is entirely in harmony with their values as people of faith, and as members of the Masonic fraternity.[32]

Laura helped organize a literary society in the neighboring town of Hartville. Named the Athenians, after the Greek town of Athens, whose citizens promoted intellectualism, the ladies group met monthly to discuss literary topics. They held reviews of books, musical compositions, and dramatic presentations. A primary object of the Athenians was a county library system, a goal Laura felt was entirely laudable. They worked many years before accomplishing the goal. Laura served in various offices of the group through the years. She remained active with this group at least into the 1940s, and generally hosted a meeting at her home each summer.[33]

Other groups that Laura was involved with at various times were the Interesting Hour club, the Friday Study club, and the Justamere Club. These clubs all dealt with current events or other topics of interest. Of these, Laura seemed to be most active in the Justamere club, another group she had helped organize. It was established in June, 1919, and Laura was elected as its first Secretary. The official song of the club was written by Laura. Entitled "We Are All Good Friends," it was set to music by Jean Jacques Marquis Du Chatelard Chateau, a friend of Rose's who had visited Mansfield the previous fall. Laura served as the group's President in 1921, and was usually mentioned among attendees or hosts. When Rose was in Mansfield, Laura sometimes persuaded her to join in the meetings, and Rose occasionally even provided the program and entertainment, delighting the group with stories of her travels and adventures. Laura's active participation in so many social groups shows that she was a respected and well-liked individual in the community. Those who remembered her indicated that, although she was somewhat

The regular monthly meeting of the Justamere Club was held Tuesday afternoon with Mrs. G. W. Miller as hostess. Refreshments were served to the following members—Mesdames N. J. Craig, J. E. Craig, D. H. Kay, G. W. Freeman, J. A Fuson, W. A. Black, A. J. Wilder, M. E. West and G.W.Miller and Miss Maude Reynolds, and two visitors, Mrs. C.C.Newton and E A. Sisk Mrs. Newton assisted the hostess in serving.

"We Are All Good Friends" was adopted as the club song. This is an original composition by Mrs. A. J. Wilder, and was set to music by M. Jean Jacques Marquis of Du Chatelard Chateau on Lake Geneva, Switzerlend, who visited at the Wilder home last fall. The composition was played and sung for the first time at this club meeting by Mrs. J. E Craig.

From the April 15, 1920 issue of the Mansfield Mirror.

prim and proper, she was also friendly and modest, and never spoke ill of anyone.[34]

There were other fun times, too. The local paper often noted visits made or received by the Wilders, usually on Sunday afternoon. In 1920, Laura threw a birthday party for Rose – even though Rose was in Europe. Other than the guest of honor, it had all the things parties normally have: food, music, fellowship. Photos of Rose placed around the room constituted the decoration. The main event of the evening was writing letters to Rose, which Laura packaged together and sent to her daughter. Another time, Laura showed her patriotism by hosting a party for George Washington's birthday, complete with Americana decorations and party favors.[35] Through the years, there were many more mentions in the paper of other gatherings and parties hosted by the Wilders.

Through all of this – home building, farm work, writing for farm papers, community service, working at the Farm Loan Association, political involvement, and social activities – Laura and Almanzo remained involved in the Eastern Star. Although neither held office in the early 1910s, they remained regular in attendance and occasionally filled an office Pro Tem when

Eighteen members of the Eastern Star went to Seymour Monday to put on the degree work for the Seymour O. E. S. that night. At 5 o'clock bountiful refreshments were served. Those in the party were Mesdames J. B. Freeman, H. B. Paul, M. E. West, N. J. Craig, G. S. Burney, H. E. Newton, J A. Hylton, J. D. Reynolds, W. B. Hitchcock, J. E. Seymour, F.H. Riley, W. B. Fullington, A. J. Wilder, Elizabeth Coday, J. A. Fuson, Miss Maude Reynolds, J.A.Hylton W.B.Hitchcock.

From the November 25, 1915 issue of the Mansfield Mirror.

needed. In 1915, they again began holding offices, and Laura was part of a group that went to the neighboring town of Seymour to perform the degree work for the Chapter there. Also that year, Laura filled the office 'Adah.' She was Associate Matron the next three years, and Chaplain in 1919. Almanzo served as Sentinel in 1917 and 1918; then it was ten years before he held another office in the Chapter.

The Wilders surprised the Chapter in January, 1917 with an Eastern Star party: completely unexpectedly, the meeting was moved to Rocky Ridge Farm, where Laura had prepared refreshments served in the design of the Star emblem. They all enjoyed a social time, and Laura played music on the Victrola that she and Almanzo had received from Rose for Christmas – the impetus for the party.[36]

DAY, JANUARY 11, 1917

An Enjoyable Occasion.

One of the most enjoyable affairs of the season took place Friday night. Mansfield Chapter, Order of the Eastern Star, while in session in their hall were surprised by an invitation to adjourn to the home of A.J. Wilder and wife. The usual order of things was reversed, the party being surprised instead of the hosts, for the invitation was a complete surprise to the chapter members, who had expected only the regular meeting. Three cars conveyed the merry crowd to Rocky Ridge Farm, where the oak-paneled, oak beamed living room was alight from the fire in the large fireplace and the glow of rose shaded lamps from the dining room. Delicious and unique refreshments were served during the evening. The table decorations were in the Star colors, the centerpiece being the regular Star emblem of the order in the correct colors. The edibles served on each plate were also in the proper colors and design of the Star. After lunch the guests gathered in the firelight and listened to the wonderful violin music of Kreisler and Esman, selections from well-known operas, Victor Herbert's orchestra and Hawaiian stringed instruments. The music was furnished by a Victrola, the Christmas gift of Rose Wilder Lane of San Francisco, daughter of the hosts. With music and conversation the time passed without a dull moment and the guests departed, regretting that the evening had been too short.

The Mansfield Mirror reported on the surprise Christmas party Laura and Almanzo gave for the Chapter.

A Bulletin from the Comforts Committee
Navy League of the U.S. was read and a
motion was made by Sister Wilder that we
take up this work, which was carried by
vote of the Chapter, and the Secy instructed
to write for further information & instruction.
Sister Mary West, W.M. + Sister Wilder a.M.
instructed the new members in the secret
work of the Order

124

Dec. 1st 1916

Mansfield Chapter No. 76 met on the
above date in regular session, being
opened in due form, with the following
officers in their stations

Worthy Matron	Sister Ella Craig
Worthy Patron	Bro. Wilder
Associate Matron	Sister Jessie Fuson
Treasurer	" Emma Hitchcock
Secretary	" Wilder
Adah	" Alice Freeman
Martha	" Gertrude Riley
Organist	" Daisy Carnell

Members present, Bros. Fuson + Craig
Being the regular meeting for the election
of officers, the following were elected by
paper ballot.

Worthy Matron	Sister Mary West
Worthy Patron, unanimous	Bro. Horace Paul
Associate Matron	Sister Wilder
Secretary	" Irene Paul
Treasurer	" Hitchcock
Conductress	" Burney
Associate Conductress	" Gertrude Riley

No further business appearing, Chapter was
closed in regular order.

Laura E. Wilder
Secy Pro Tem

Examples of Laura's and Almanzo's continued activities in the Chapter. Top, Laura led the Chapter in charitable work and review of the ritual work. Bottom, Laura was in the office of 'Adah,' but she also filled in as Secretary Pro Tem. Almanzo acted as the Worthy Patron Pro Tem.

253

On the evening of April 4, 1919, it was Laura who received the surprise. That night, she and Mary West, the only two women to serve three years as Worthy Matron in Mansfield, "were presented by the Marshal [such presentation is a show of honor], and as a token of the appreciation of the Chapter for their untiring services as Worthy Matron each for three years, the Worthy Patron presented each one with a book, gifts from the Chapter."

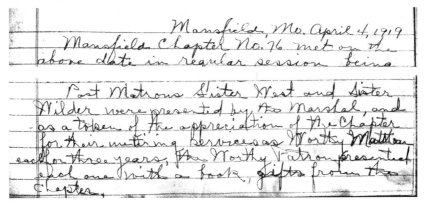

From the minutes.

A "surprising" feature of the regular meeting of the Eastern Star Friday night was the surprise given in honor of Mesdames Mary E. West and A. J. Wilder, both of whom enjoy the distinction of having served the chapter for three years as worthy matron, a distinction enjoyed by no other member of the local chapter. On behalf of the chapter, Worthy Patron, W. A. Black presented each of them with a gift, following which refreshments were served and a general good time enjoyed.

From the April 10, 1919 issue of the Mansfield Mirror.

This antique plate is from the Mansfield Chapter of the Order of the Eastern Star. Although Laura did not own the plate, she most likely enjoyed refreshments served from it. From the Eric Dodson Collection, courtesy Mansfield Area Historical Society.

Laura continued to hold office regularly, as 'Ruth' in 1921 and 1922, Marshal in 1923, and 'Martha' in 1925. In April, 1925, Laura attended an Eastern Star School of Instruction.[37] Rose drove Laura and some other ladies to the town of Seymour for the meeting. Rose was not able to participate in the School, since she wasn't a member, but there was plenty of time for visiting.

There were two other significant events in Laura's life in these years. Rose had returned to Mansfield for Christmas in 1923, and remained for several months. She attempted to make life easier for her parents throughout this time. One of her first moves toward this goal was to give them a special gift: a Buick. Almanzo and Laura now officially left the horse and buggy days behind, as Rose taught each of them to drive.[38]

Soon, Rose would be returning to Europe and Albania, but before that, she planned some time with her mother: she and her good friend and fellow author, Helen Boylston, took Laura to California. In addition to being able to spend time with her daughter, the trip provided Laura with a break from her many duties, which was desperately needed: Laura wrote to her aunt Martha Carpenter in June, 1925 that she was recovering from a serious illness, "very near to nervous

Mansfield Chapter No 76.
Order of the Eastern Star.
Friday evening, Dec 5th 1924.
At a regular meeting held on the above date, the following officers were in their places:
Sister Ella Swan ——— Worthy Matron
" Bessie Wilder ——— Marshal Pro. Tem.

Sister Reed and Sister Wilder examined our new members Sister and Bro Livingston, in open chapter, which we all enjoyed and which gave much credit to the members in their proficiency.
Election of officers for the ensuing year, was next in order, with Sisters Reed and Wilder as tellers.

Almanzo and Laura continued to serve the Chapter for many years. Laura did not hold an office in 1924, but she filled in as a Pro Tem as necessary, and performed other duties. At this meeting, she examined new members and took a leading role in the installation of new officers.

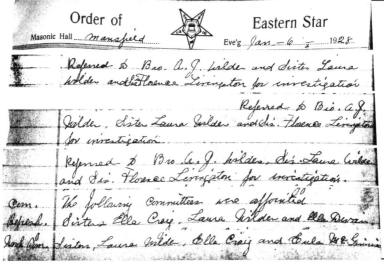

The month before his seventy-first birthday, Almanzo was still active. He was referred to three investigating committees at this meeting. Laura (almost sixty-one) was assigned to the same committees, in addition to the refreshment and work committees.

prostration." This is severe fatigue, and no wonder, with all that Laura had been doing: caring for a home and helping on the farm, writing articles, working at the Farm Loan, political involvement, all the social clubs and activities, and dealing with Rose. Although Laura and Rose loved one another, Rose's modern ways, heedless of others' opinions, clashed with her mother's more traditional values.[39]

After returning from the trip, Laura resumed her activity in the Chapter. In 1926, when she held the office of 'Electa,' she attended the District Meeting in the nearby community of Mountain Grove. Laura was Chaplain in 1927. The year 1928 saw Almanzo in office again – he served as Warder, while Laura served as Conductress. Her final office was as Chaplain, in 1929, 1930, and 1931. Almanzo served as Sentinel in 1931.

This was the end of the Wilders' time in the Order of the Eastern Star; they each asked for and received a demit on December 14, 1931. They had been members in the Order for about forty years. Almanzo maintained his membership in the Lodge, however, and remained in good standing as a Master Mason until his death.

The last offices held by Laura and Almanzo were for the year 1931 – she as Chaplain, and he as Sentinel.

It is likely that their finances had some part in their decision to demit. The depression was bearing down on them, and they needed to cut every possible expense.

Another event that may have contributed to the Wilder's demission from the Order at that time was the change of focus in Laura's life. Most of Laura's social activities diminished greatly for the next few years. The Wilders had begun to slow down. Laura stopped writing articles for the *Missouri Ruralist*; she had only two articles published in 1925, both for *Country Gentleman.* She also stopped working for the Farm Loan Association, and even stopped raising poultry. After the end of the war, the demand for farm produce decreased, and prices went up; the poultry industry was no longer profitable on a small scale such as Laura had. Instead, Laura spent much time with Rose, who was guiding her through the process of writing books about her childhood and adolescence.[40]

Rose and Helen were in Paris and Albania from 1926 to 1928. In 1928, Rose moved back to Mansfield, this time for an extended stay. She saw how hard her parents worked, and worried that it was too much for them at their advancing ages. Again, she searched for ways to ease their burden, and again her solution was extravagant: she built them a house.

The rock house.

From a plan in the Sears Roebuck catalog, but with special custom designs added by Rose based on homes she had seen in Europe, Rose had a smaller, more modern home built over the hill from the existing farmhouse. The idea was that the new home, called "the rock house," as Rose had it sided with native fieldstone, would take less maintenance and upkeep. Also, having modern plumbing and electricity throughout – the first house in the area to have it, at considerable added expense to Rose – everyday chores like cooking were simplified. No longer did Almanzo need to chop wood and Laura build a fire in the stove just to prepare dinner. Almanzo and Laura moved into the rock house Christmas week, while Rose remained in the farmhouse.

With the farmhouse to herself, Rose entertained a continual procession of friends at Rocky Ridge. She had connections with a wide variety of persons, and Laura was often at the farmhouse visiting with them. Many of these friends were writers, such as Dorothy Thompson, Sinclair Lewis, Genevieve Parkhurst, and Catharine Brody, and they often worked while at Rocky Ridge. There can be little doubt that seeing all this literary activity influenced Laura to think about her own writing.

Another inspiration may have been the 50th anniversary of the founding of De Smet, South Dakota. The town was having an Old Settler's Day in celebration, and invited everyone they could find who had been there in 1880 to attend, or send memories to the paper. Although Laura was not able to attend the commemoration, this may have helped her realize that people would be interested in the stories she had from her girlhood. At the very least, memories of the old days with her family must have been stirred – as they were for Carrie and Grace, both of whom were among those who submitted reminisces. (This marked a literary beginning for Grace; she began to regularly contribute items of local interest to the paper, adding yet another writer to the family.) Laura did not send an article for this event, submitting a poem instead. Perhaps she did not want to give away the stories she hoped to later use in her book.[41]

It was soon after this that Laura gave Rose a copy of *Pioneer Girl*, her autobiography covering her girlhood years from age five to her marriage. Rose edited the manuscript and sent it to her own agent, pitching it as a magazine serial. At the same time, she took a few stories from the beginning of the manuscript and pitched them as a picture book, which Rose thought could be titled *When Grandma Was a Little Girl*. She gave copies of this to some of her friends in the industry as well. Although no one was interested in purchasing either format, one of the friends sent it to Marion Fiery, who worked in the juvenile department at publishing company Alfred A. Knopf. Fiery saw potential in the work, but suggested that it be expanded to a young reader's book, instead of a picture book. With Rose's expert guidance, Laura expanded these stories into a portrait of a year of pioneer life in Wisconsin. Rose again edited the manuscript for her mother and sent it to Fiery. Knopf accepted the book, but then, in an unexpected turn of events, they decided to close their juvenile department before the book was published. Acting once more on Fiery's suggestion, Rose and Laura placed the book with Harper & Brothers, who accepted it and gave it the title of *Little House in the Big Woods*.[42]

While waiting for this book to be published, in 1931, Laura and Almanzo made a trip to South Dakota. They visited Carrie and Grace before stopping in De Smet for the second Old Settler's Day on the way back. It was on this trip that Laura and Grace sorted through the things left in the old Ingalls home on Third Street after the deaths of Caroline and Mary. After their return to Mansfield, Laura wrote the first draft of her second book, this one based on her husband's boyhood. Rose continued to tutor Laura on structure and other aspects of writing. Laura gave the manuscript of *Farmer Boy* to Rose for editing even before the first book was published.[43]

Laura was 65 years old when her first book, *Little House in the Big Woods,* was released in April, 1932. The book was an instant success. It was recognized by the Junior Literary Guild and favorably reviewed by publications as prestigious as the *New York Times*.[44] Not only did critics rave, but more importantly, children – and indeed, whole families – loved it. The stories of family togetherness touched readers, and the adults recognized a larger message: for generations past, people had lived by their own wits and hard work, and they could do the same, even during those depressed times.

Farmer Boy told the story of a year in Almanzo's childhood. When it was published in 1932, it was also well received by the public and critics alike. This same year, Rose wrote *Let the Hurricane Roar*, her own telling of the settling of the Dakotas. A work of fiction, it nevertheless drew from the stories Rose had heard of her grandparents' experiences. Rose's book was written for an adult audience, and became a bestseller.

Laura was already working on her third book. This one, called *Little House on the Prairie* upon publication, was different. Since the first two books were primarily family anecdotes, Laura was able to use only her or Almanzo's memory (with geographic details supplied by Rose); this third book, however, encompassed a broader environment and historical events which required research. Rose helped in the research as she continued to advise her mother on the writing. Published in 1935, this book was also praised, although it later stirred controversy due to its portrayal of Native Americans and the attitudes of the white settlers who displaced them.

Just before *Little House on the Prairie* was released, Rose received an offer to write a history of Missouri. Needing the finances, and wishing to leave Mansfield, where she never felt at home, Rose accepted, and moved to Columbia near the State Historical Society to do research. This signaled a change for Laura and her writing. Now she no longer had her writing mentor close at hand. The instruction Rose gave for Laura's fourth book, *On the Banks of Plum Creek,* was done through the mail, as it would be for all the future books. This system worked well; *Plum Creek*, released in 1937, was the first of Laura's books to be named a Newberry Honor book. Each book that followed received the same honor. The country was still struggling through the throes of the Depression, and the hardships endured – and triumphed over – by the Ingalls family in this novel reminded readers that there had always been challenges and difficult times, but with determination and hard work, you could work your way through them, and find satisfaction in simple, everyday pleasures. This emphasis on self-reliance and joy in simple living appealed to the innate need for security of readers living in an insecure time.[45]

The year held another honor for Laura: she was invited to speak at a book fair in Detroit. A good friend, Silas Seal, agreed to drive her and Almanzo to the event. In her presentation, Laura told her listeners that she wanted to preserve the stories she had heard growing up, and let the newer generations know "more about the beginnings of things" and the "spirit of the frontier."[46]

Now that Rose had left permanently, there was no reason for the Wilders to remain in the very modern but still unwanted rock house. Laura and Almanzo were able to move back into the farmhouse. The rock house was more modern and convenient, but the farmhouse was Laura's dream home, and it was where she wanted to be.

Laura continued with her writing. She and Almanzo made two more trips to South Dakota – one in 1938 and again in 1939 – with visits to Carrie, Grace, and Old Settler's Day in De Smet, and Laura used these trips to refresh her memory of her girlhood days and the founding of the town where the remainder of the series was set.[47]

Her next book was titled *By the Shores of Silver Lake*. With this book, Rose and Laura clashed over the vision of the series as a whole. Rose still saw it as a "juvenile," entirely for younger readers. Laura, however, was already receiving loads of fan mail, from readers wanting more; she knew that readers following along the series were growing up themselves, and that for their interest in the books to remain, they must be able to relate to a maturing "Laura" in the forthcoming books. When *Silver Lake* was published in 1939, it sold well, despite the fact that much of the material in this book overlapped Rose's latest adult fiction, *Free Land,* which had been released the previous year.[48]

Laura's *The Long Winter* was published in 1940, followed by *Little Town on the Prairie* in 1941 and *These Happy Golden Years*, the final book of the series, in 1943. Throughout the series, the same themes recurred. In and of itself, any one scene in Laura's books might seem an insignificant example of her values, but each scene is just one moment in a lifetime of living by those principles. Reading through the series, each value becomes clear, so that while they may be presented subtly at times, readers cannot help but come away with the realization of what they are. The themes recur in the fictionalized books because they were important to the real Laura and her family. Self-reliance was primary, made possible by the strength of support from family. Home was a place where everyone helped one another, working to the good of all. Faith gave them courage in facing difficulties, as well as comfort when times were hard. Religious training was provided to the Ingalls girls from birth. Education was strongly promoted, with schooling to be taken advantage of whenever possible. Learning was not limited to the schoolroom, however, and the Ingallses believed in helping themselves to knowledge by any means possible. Patriotism was emphasized as the basis of freedom and independence, and the good of community advanced above that of the individual. Laura and her sister are continually reminded that one should place others before self. This is shown in Laura's reaction when her father talks to her about becoming a schoolteacher, in *By the Shores of Silver Lake*:

> *"Another thing, Laura," said Pa. "You know Ma was a teacher, and her mother before her. Ma's heart is set on one of you girls teaching school, and I guess it will have to be you. So you see you must have your schooling.*

> *Laura's heart jerked, and then she seemed to feel it falling, far, far down. She did not say anything. She knew that Pa and Ma, and Mary too, had thought that Mary would be a teacher. Now Mary couldn't teach, and– "Oh, I won't! I won't!" Laura thought. "I don't want to! I can't." Then she said to herself, "You must."*
>
> *She could not disappoint Ma. She must do as Pa said. So she had to be a school teacher when she grew up.*[49]

This scene not only illustrates the ideal of selflessness, but also demonstrates familial devotion, obedience to authority, and the courage and self-discipline of fortitude, in addition to the advancement of education. All of these principles, which provide the basis of the *Little House* books, were the values Laura and her family lived by, which they learned at home and in church – and in the fraternity of Freemasonry, which works to reinforce these values in members' lives.

With the completion of *These Happy Golden Years*, Laura set down her pencil and retired. The accolades continued, however. Laura's books continued to be recognized, winning prizes such as the Harry Hartman Award, the Hobby-Horse Award, and the *New York Herald Tribune* Book Festival prize.

The *Little House* books constitute an important body of literary work, being the first books for children that described all aspects of the American Frontier. It was also the first series to "grow up" along with its readers. The author of the books was rightly lauded as a significant children's author. In 1948, the city of Detroit named a branch of its public library after Laura; in 1950, a library in Pomona, California named a room in her honor. The work of the Athenians finally paid off, and Wright County established a county library in 1951; the Mansfield branch was appropriately named for Laura. Perhaps her most distinguished acclaim occurred in 1954, when the American Library Association created the Laura Ingalls Wilder Award, and named her its first recipient. The award was created to honor authors or illustrators whose books, published in the United States, have made, over a period of years, a substantial and lasting contribution to literature for children. What meant more to Laura than all these, however, were the letters of appreciation from young readers, who told her how much the books meant to them.[50]

The Little House books got new illustrations by Garth Williams in 1953. These are the most well-known editions.

Despite Laura's growing fame, she and Almanzo lived simply on Rocky Ridge Farm, as they had always done. Things were slower and quieter now, as were the Wilders. They sold the rock house and other parts of the farm, so that farm work was lessened. However, they retained a life interest in the farmhouse, so that they could stay in their dream home for the remainder of their lives. Laura explained that they had an enjoyable routine, which for Almanzo consisted of caring for his few goats, gardening, and working in his wood shop; for Laura, days were spent in housework, cooking and baking, and daily walks with her dog that included a stop at the mailbox. Evenings were spent quietly reading, listening to the radio, or playing a game such as cribbage. They spent time with their friends, and attended church and social events when their health allowed. In 1943, the Methodist Church held a special dinner for the Wilders in celebration of their 58th wedding anniversary. In 1946, Laura attended a meeting of Methodist and Presbyterian ladies. There, she met Irene Lichty, who was later instrumental in establishing the Laura Ingalls Wilder Home and Museum in Mansfield. Laura and Almanzo continued to make visits and receive guests. They received a visit from Carrie in 1944; this was the final time any of Laura's Ingalls family members were together. Laura and Carrie were both aware of the historic interest in their family generated by the *Little House* books, and they discussed the possibility of a memorial to the Ingalls family in De Smet, but evidently no action toward this was taken by them.[51]

Almanzo's health was weak through most of the 1940s, and in the summer of 1949, he suffered a heart attack. Although he seemed to improve for a time, another struck in October, and he passed away at Rocky Ridge Farm, held tightly in Laura's arms. He was 92 at his death on October 23, 1949. His obituary ran in the October 27, 1949 issue of the Mansfield Mirror.

A. J. Wilder Well Known Resident Dies Suddenly

Almanzo J. Wilder, 92, a pioneer resident of Mansfield and one of its best known residents, died at his home, Rocky Ridge farm, Sunday morning following an illness of several weeks, with only his wife, Laura Ingalls Wilder, with him at the time. Although Mr. Wilder had been seriously ill he was thought to be in an improved condition when death took him after he suffered a sudden heart attack. Mr. and Mrs. Wilder have resided since 1894 at their farm just east of the city on Highway 60. A son of James and Angeline Day Wilder, he was born in Malone, N.Y., on February 13, 1857, and with a brother went to South Dakota in 1879.

Mr. Wilder and Laura Ingalls Wilder, who has received acclaim as a writer of children's books, a native of Wisconsin, who moved with her family to South Dakota, were married on August 25, 1885, in De Smet, S.D. Nine years later they came to Missouri settling in Mansfield. They have on [sic] daughter, Rose Wilder Lane, like her mother a well known writer, who now makes her home in Danbury, Conn.

Mr. Wilder once save [sic] his snowbound town from

starving by driving 40 miles through a blizzard for wheat. He is the hero of his wife's famous series of pioneer juveniles. Mr. Wilder was a member of the Mansfield Blue Lodge of the Masons, and in earlier years was active in civic affairs of the community.

Funeral services are to be held tomorrow (Friday) at 2 p.m. at the Mansfield Methodist Church with Rev. Carleton Knight officiating.

Burial will be in the Mansfield cemetery under the direction of the Steffe Funeral Home.

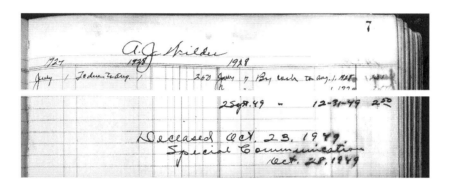

Lodge records provide the date of the Special Communication that was called for Almanzo's funeral service.

Since Almanzo had remained a life-long Mason in good standing, a Special Communication of Mansfield Lodge was called for his funeral on the 28th of October. The Lodge performed the Masonic funeral rites at his service. Although there is note of the service in the Lodge records, the actual minutes of the meeting no longer exist. Mansfield Lodge wrote Resolutions of Respect, a copy of which they provided Laura. This copy may be seen at the Laura Ingalls Wilder Home in Mansfield. As Almanzo had been a well-known and respected member of the community, the Resolutions of Respect from the Lodge were published in the November 3, 1949 issue of the *Mansfield Mirror.*

RESOLUTIONS OF RESPECT

WHEREAS, It has pleased the Supreme Architect of the Universe to call from labor to rest, our dearly beloved Brother Alamanzo J. Wilder, who died October 23rd, 1949; Therefore, be it

RESOLVED That, in the death of Bro. Wilder, his family has lost a devoted husband and father the Lodge a faithtul and useful member, and the community an upright and honored citizen.

RESOLVED, That we will ever bear in grateful remembrance the zeal and fidelity with which Bro. Wilder discharged his Masonic duties, and will try to imitate his devotion to the grand principles of our Fraternity.

RESOLVED, That we tender our heartfelt sympathy to the bereaved widow and daughter, and recommend them to the care of that God whom Bro. Wilder served, and in whom he trusted.

RESOLVED, That a copy of these Resolutions be spread upon our records, and an engrossed copy sent to the family of our deceased Brother.

Signed

Don Livingston
Don Hunter
A. M. McQuay

The Resolutions of Respect for Almanzo were printed in the Mansfield Mirror on November 3, 1949.

Laura was now left alone on the farm, but she had her good friends nearby, who kept her spirits up. Each week, she had a driver take her to town, where she did her errands: banking, shopping, a stop at the library, perhaps a visit to the hairdresser. She visited schoolchildren, and sometimes received them at her home, where she was always gracious and friendly. Each year, Laura received thousands of letters from children. They had all been touched by her writing, and wanted to make a connection with this remarkable person. She answered each one personally as long as she was able; but eventually, there were so many that she could not keep up, and a form letter was created to send in answer. She still spent time reading each evening, and her preferred genre was westerns, no doubt remembering with pleasure the times about which she read.[52]

The world was saddened when news came of Laura's death on February 10, 1957, at the age of 90. Even the *New York Times* ran her obituary:

> *Mrs. Laura Ingalls Wilder, author of the "Little House" series of children's books, died yesterday at her farm near here after a long illness. Her age was 90.*
>
> *Wrote First Book at 65*
>
> *Mrs. Wilder wrote her first book in 1932 at the age of 65. At the insistence of her daughter, Rose Wilder Lane, herself a novelist, Mrs. Wilder recalled her early days as a child of a pioneer family in the "Little House in the Big Woods."*
>
> *The story told of the Wisconsin farm where she was born and from which her family set out in a covered wagon for Indian Territory. Their adventures were described in the "Little House on the Prairie."*
>
> *A schoolteacher at the age of 15, she became a housewife three years later upon her marriage to Almanzo J. Wilder in 1885. He died in 1949 at the age of 92.*
>
> *After the birth of their daughter, the Wilders moved from Smet, S.D., to Florida. They later went to the Ozarks. She became famous there for her books and for her gingerbread.*
>
> *Mrs. Wilder was for twelve years editor of The Missouri Ruralist. She also had been poultry editor of The St. Louis Star and a writer of magazine articles before becoming an author of*

books.

Her books include "The Long Winter," "On the Banks of Plum Creek," "By the Shores of Silver Lake," "Farmer Boy," a story of her husband's childhood, and "These Happy Golden Years."

Mrs. Wilder's books have been translated into three languages. In 1949 a library in Mansfield was dedicated in her honor.

The Children's Library Association established the Laura Ingalls Wilder award in 1954 for a lasting contribution to literature for children. Mrs. Wilder was the first recipient of the medal.

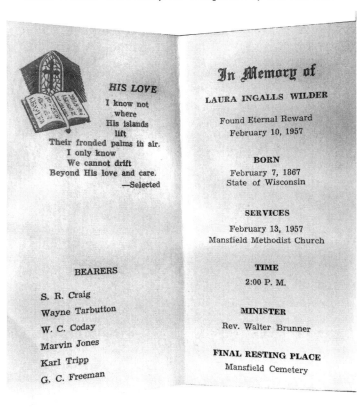

HIS LOVE

I know not
where
His islands
lift
Their fronded palms in air.
I only know
We cannot drift
Beyond His love and care.
—Selected

In Memory of

LAURA INGALLS WILDER

Found Eternal Reward
February 10, 1957

BORN

February 7, 1867
State of Wisconsin

SERVICES

February 13, 1957
Mansfield Methodist Church

BEARERS

S. R. Craig

Wayne Tarbutton

W. C. Coday

Marvin Jones

Karl Tripp

G. C. Freeman

TIME

2:00 P. M.

MINISTER

Rev. Walter Brunner

FINAL RESTING PLACE
Mansfield Cemetery

The program from Laura's funeral. From the Leah Mae Davis/Kathy Short Colletion, courtesy Mansfield Area Historical Society & Museum.

Rose handled the final arrangements, burying her mother next to her father in the Mansfield cemetery. The farm house at Rocky Ridge – Laura's dream home – she left as it was, and helped Laura's friend Irene Litchy create an Association to purchase it and turn it into a museum.

The popularity of Laura's books has never diminished. They have been translated into 45 languages and sold around 60 million copies.[53] Even after her death, her readers have wanted to know more about Laura and her family. In response to that desire, her journal of the Wilders' move from De Smet to Mansfield was published in 1962 as *On the Way Home*. It was followed by a previously unpublished manuscript of her early married years, *The First Four Years*, in 1971. The letters Laura wrote home to Almanzo when she visited San Francisco in 1915 were released as *West from Home*. Her books have inspired television shows, movies, and theatrical productions. Residents of each place Laura lived have created a memorial to her in some way. Tens of thousands of people visit these sites each year (they are listed in Appendix B), and researchers continue to pore over her writings, letters, and other extant documents to learn more about Laura, seeking to learn what has made her the endearing and enduring figure she has remained to be through the past 80 years. What more can we learn about her, and more importantly, from her?

The Ingalls family was a family of writers: Charles, Mary, Laura, Carrie, and Grace – as well as Rose – all did some public writing, whether for church bulletins, newspapers, or books. Even Caroline wrote the history of the Congregational Church in De Smet. It is unfortunate that none of them wrote of their experiences in Freemasonry and the Eastern Star, but it is not surprising, as the workings of the Lodge and Chapter are not done for show. The fact that Charles, Caroline, Laura, Almanzo, Carrie, and David all chose to join, and become active members, speaks for them regarding their feelings toward the fraternities. They undoubtedly received many of the same benefits that millions of other persons have gained and continue to experience. Such benefits include the opportunity to get to know a variety of persons across all socio-economic backgrounds, all seeking improvement of self and society; abiding friendships; and comfort in the support of the brothers and sisters. Laura and her family probably received fulfillment in the worthy community service and charitable work of the fraternity. The rituals, emphasizing morality and the search for truth, were something on which they could contemplate and reflect for inspiration or comfort. On the practical side, the rituals provided opportunity to improve their memory, and working through the offices helped develop public speaking ability and management and organizational skills. The Ingalls family placed a high value on education; the emphasis of Freemasonry on public and personal growth and education surely brought them great satisfaction. The importance Freemasonry places on work equaled the importance Laura and her family gave it. In fact, all of the values held dear by the Ingalls and Wilder families are the same values extolled by Freemasonry. We see the ideals of Masonry – such as family, faith, education, charity, courage, independence, patriotism, fortitude, and self improvement – shine through in Laura's books, as well as her earlier writings for the *Missouri Ruralist*.

Wherever they were, and whatever their circumstances, these core values remained the same and helped them through. The Masonic Lodge and Eastern Star helped the family practice these virtues, by both showing them new ways to exercise the principles, and giving them an outlet in which to do so. Yet, Masonry by itself is nothing. It takes people – individuals, like Laura and members of her family, willing to give of themselves – working in it to make it worthwhile. The fact that Charles and Caroline, Carrie and David, and Laura and Almanzo all chose to devote time, effort, and finances to the Craft helps us understand the values that made them the people we still admire and wish to emulate. Perhaps, as Laura said, reflecting on this past can educate and inspire us today.

Appendix A:
Funeral Services

Masonic Funeral Service

The following instructions were first published in 1878 by the Grand Lodge of California. It is likely that the funerals of Charles Ingalls, David Swanzey, and Almanzo Wilder differed very little. Masonic funerals in America today are still similar.

All brethren in attendance at a funeral should be decently clothed in black, with crape upon the left arm, and with white gloves and aprons.

The brethren having assembled at the Lodge-room, the Master opens the Lodge.

The service is then commenced, as follows:

Master: What man is he that liveth and shall not see death? Shall he deliver his soul from the hand of the grave?

Response: Man walketh in a vain shadow; he heapeth up riches and cannot tell who shall gather them.

Master: When he dieth he shall carry nothing away; his glory shall not descend after him.

Response: Naked came he into the world, and naked must he return.

Master: The Lord gave, and the Lord hath taken away; blessed be the name of the Lord.

Solemn music may here he introduced, after which the Master, taking the sacred roll in his hand, says:

Let us die the death of the righteous, and let our last end be like theirs.

Response: God is our God forever and ever: He will be our

guide even unto death.

The Master then records the name and age of the deceased upon the roll, and says:

Almighty Father! Into thy hands we commend the soul of our beloved brother.

Response: (*Repeated thrice, giving the Grand Honors* each time.*) The will of God is accomplished! So mote it be! Amen!

The Master then deposits the roll in the archives, and repeats the following prayer:

Most glorious God! Author of all good, and Giver of all mercy! Pour down Thy blessing upon us, we beseech Thee, and strengthen our solemn engagements with the ties of sincere affection! Endow us with fortitude and resignation in this our dark hour of sorrow; and grant that this afflicting dispensation from Thy hands may be sanctified in its results upon the hearts of those who now meet here to mourn! May the present instance of mortality remind us of our own approaching fate, and draw our attention toward Thee, the only refuge in time of need; that when the awful moment shall arrive at which we, too, must quit this transitory scene, the enlivening prospect of Thy mercy may dispel the gloom of death; and that, after our departure hence, in peace and in thy favor, we may be received into Thy everlasting kingdom, to enjoy the just reward of a virtuous and pious life. Amen!

Response: So mote it be.

Solemn music may here again be introduced during which a procession is formed. If the body be not in the Lodge room the procession will move to the house of the deceased, and thence with his remains to the place of sepulture in the following order:

The Tyler with a drawn sword; Stewards with white rods; Master Masons; Junior Deacon; Holy Writings; Senior Deacon with blue rods; Secretary and Treasurer; Junior and Senior Wardens; Past Masters; The Master; The Reverend Clergy; The Body, with the insignia placed thereon; Pall Bearers; Mourners.

Upon arriving at the place of burial the members of the Lodge will form a circle around the grave; the clergyman and officers of the Lodge will proceed to its head, and the mourners will be placed at its foot. The services will then be resumed by the Master as follows:

Once more, my brethren, have we assembled to perform the last sad and solemn duties to the dead. The mournful notes which betoken the departure of a spirit from its earthly tabernacle have again alarmed our outer door, and another has been taken to swell the numbers in that unknown land whither our fathers have gone before us. Our brother has reached the end of life. The brittle thread which bound him to earth has been severed; and the liberated spirit has winged its flight to the undiscovered world. The silver cord is loosed; the golden bowl is broken; the pitcher is broken at the fountain; and the wheel is broken at the cistern. The dust has returned to the earth, as it was; and the spirit has returned to the God who gave it. While we deplore the loss of our beloved brother, and pay this fraternal tribute to his memory, let us not forget, my brethren, that we, too, are mortal; that our bodies, now so strong and vigorous, must ere long, like his, become tenants of the narrow grave; and that our spirits too, like his, must return to the God who spake them into existence. "Man that is born of woman is of few days, and full of trouble. He cometh forth as a flower and is cut down; he fleeth also as a shadow, and continueth not." The Almighty fiat has gone forth – "Dust thou art, and unto dust shalt thou return" – and that we are all subject to that dread decree, the solemn cause of our present meeting, the daily observation of our lives, and the mournful mounds which indicate this population of the dead, furnish evidence not to be forgotten. Seeing then, my brethren, that life is so uncertain, and that all earthly pursuits are vain, let us no longer postpone the all-important concern of preparing for eternity; but let us embrace the present moment, while time and opportunity are offered, to provide against that great change when all the pomps and pleasure of this fleeting world will pall upon the sense, and the recollection of a virtuous and well spent life will yield the only comfort and consolation. Thus we shall not be hurried, unprepared, into the presence of that all-wise and powerful Judge, to whom the secrets of all hearts are known; and on the great day of reckoning we shall be ready to give a good account of our stewardship while here on earth. With becoming reverence, then, let us supplicate the

Divine Grace to insure the favor of that Eternal Being whose goodness and power knows no bounds; that, on the arrival of the momentous hour when the fading taper of human life shall faintly glimmer in the socket of existence, our Faith may remove the dark shroud, draw aside the sable curtains of the tomb, and bid Hope sustain and cheer the departing spirit. This city of the dead, my brethren, has an overwhelming emphasis in its solemn silence. It tells us of the gathering, within its embrace, of the parents' fondest hopes; of the disseverance of all earthly ties to the departed ones who gave us birth; of the darkness into which the bright prospects of the loving husband and the devoted wife have suddenly been engulphed; of the unavailing grief of the affectionate brother and the tender sister; of the dread sleep of death which here envelopes the subjects of many an early, many an instantaneous call into eternity, given in the midst of health, of gayety, and of brightest hopes. And our departed brother, where is he? All that remains of him, here on earth, is now enclosed in that narrow coffin, a lifeless mass of clay. The deep, the agonizing sorrow of those to whom he was most near and dear – the scalding tears which have been shed upon his last earthly tenement – the manly and fraternal grief of his brethren of the Mystic tie– are all by him unheeded. His every faculty has fled; the purple current which sustained his life has ceased to flow; the tongue, which was wont to give utterance to the emotions and feelings of the heart, performs no more its functions; the eyes, which so late reflected the movements of the intelligent principle within, are now closed in death; – unfitted to remain longer upon earth, we lay him reverently beneath its surface. A little, narrow spot is all that he now can fill; the clod will hide him from our view, and the places which have known him here will know him no more forever. We consign him to the grave – to the long sleep, of death; and so profound will be that sleep that the giant thread of the earthquake, even, shall not disturb it. There will he slumber until the Arch-Angel's trump shall usher in that eventful morn, when, by our Supreme Grand Master's word, he will be raised to that blissful Lodge which no time can remove, and which to those worthy of admission will remain open during the boundless ages of eternity. In that Heavenly

Sanctuary, the Mystic Light, unmingled with darkness, will reign unbroken and perpetual. There, amid the sun-beam smiles of Immutable Love, under the benignant bend of the All-seeing Eye, in that temple, not made with hands, eternal in the Heavens – there, my brethren, may Almighty God, of His infinite mercy, grant that we may finally meet, to part no more.

The following invocations are then rehearsed by the Master and responded to by the brethren.

Master: May we be true and faithful, and may we live and die in love!

Response: So mote it be!

Master: May we profess only that which is good, and may we always act in accordance with our professions!

Response: So mote it be!

Master: May the Lord bless and prosper us, and may all our good intentions be crowned with success!

Response: So mote it be!

Master: Glory be to God in the highest! On earth, peace and good will toward men!

Response: So mote it be, now, henceforth, and forevermore. Amen!

The apron is then taken from the coffin and handed to the Master; the coffin is deposited in the grave and the Master continues:

This Lamb-skin (or white apron) is an emblem of Innocence, and the peculiar badge of a Mason. It is more ancient than the Golden Fleece or Koman Eagle, and, when worthily worn, more honorable than Star or Garter, or any other order which earthly power can confer. This emblem I now deposit in the grave of our deceased brother (*drops it in the grave*). By this act we are reminded of the universal dominion of Death. The arm of Friendship cannot oppose the King of Terrors; the shield of Fraternal Love cannot protect his victim, nor can the charms of innocence avert his fatal touch. All, all must die. This grave, that coffin, and this circle of mourning friends remind us that we too are mortal, and that ere long our bodies also shall moulder into dust. How important then it is for us to know that our Redeemer liveth, and that He shall stand at the latter day upon the earth.

Taking the sprig of Acacia in his hand: This Evergreen, which once marked the temporary resting place of one illustrious in Masonic history, is an emblem of our enduring faith in the immortality of the soul. By it we are reminded that we have an immortal part within us, which shall survive the grave, and which will never, never die.

By it we are admonished that, though like our brother, whose remains now lie before us, we too shall soon be clothed in the habiliments of death, and be deposited in the silent tomb, yet, through the loving goodness of our Supreme Grand Master, we may confidently hope that, like this evergreen, our souls will hereafter flourish in eternal spring.

The brethren here move in procession around the grave, each depositing therein a sprig of evergreen. The Secretary then drops the Boll upon the coffin; and then the public Grand Honors are given.

Master: From time immemorial it has been the custom among the Fraternity of Free and Accepted Masons, at the request of a brother, to accompany his remains to the place of interment, and there to deposit them with the usual formalities of the Craft. In conformity to this usage, and in accordance with the duty which we owe to our departed brother, whose loss we now most deeply do deplore, we have assembled in the character of Masons to offer up to his memory, before the world, the last sad tribute of our affection; thereby demonstrating the sincerity of our past esteem for him, and our steady attachment to the principles of our beloved Order. The Great Creator having been pleased, in His infinite wisdom, to remove our brother from the cares and troubles of this transitory life, thus severing another link in the fraternal chain by which we are bound together – let us, who survive him, be yet more strongly cemented by the ties of union, friendship, and brotherly love ; that, during the brief space allotted to us here, we may wisely and usefully employ our time, and, in the reciprocal intercourse of kind and friendly acts, mutually promote the welfare and happiness of each other. Unto the grave we have consigned the body of our deceased brother– earth to earth, ashes to ashes, dust to dust: – there to remain until the last trump shall sound on the resurrection morn. We can trustfully leave him in the hands of a beneficent Being, who has done all things well; who is glorious in His holiness, wondrous in His power, and boundless in His goodness; and it should only be our endeavor so to improve the solemn warning now before us that, on the great day of account, we too may be found worthy to inherit the Kingdom prepared for us from the foundation of the world. To the bereaved relatives of him we mourn, who now stand heart-stricken by the heavy hand which has thus been laid upon them, we have but little of this world's consolation to present. We deeply, sincerely, and most affectionately sympathize with them in this afflicting dispensation; and we put up our most fervent prayers that "He who tempers the wind to the shorn lamb" will look down with compassion upon the widow and the fatherless, in this their hour of desolation, and will fold the benevolent arms of His love and protection around those who are thus bereft of their earthly stay.

The Master, or Chaplain, will then repeat the following prayer:

Almighty and Eternal God, in whom we live, and move, and have our being, and before whom all men must appear at the Judgment-day to render an account of their deeds while in this life – we, who are daily exposed to the flying shafts of death, and who now surround the grave of one who has fallen in our midst, do most humbly beseech Thee to impress deeply on our minds the solemnities of this day, and to grant that their remembrance may be the means of turning our thoughts from the fleeting vanities of the present world to the lasting glories of the world to come. Let us be continually reminded of the frail tenure by which we hold our earthly existence; that in the midst of life we are in death; and that however upright may have been our walk, and however square our conduct, we must all submit as victims to the great destroyer, and endure the humble level of the tomb. Grant us Thy divine assistance, O most merciful God, to redeem our mis-spent time; and in the discharge of the important duties which thou hast assigned us in the erection of our moral edifice, wilt Thou give us wisdom to direct us, strength to support us, and the beauty of holiness to adorn our labors and render them acceptable in Thy sight. And when our work on earth is done, and our bodies shall go down to mingle with their kindred dust, may our immortal souls, freed from their cumbrous clay, be received into Thy keeping, to rest forever in that spiritual house, not made with hands, eternal in the heavens. Amen!

Response: So mote it be!

The Master then approaches the head of the grave and says:
Soft and safe to you, my brother, be this earthy bed! Bright and glorious be thy rising from it! Fragrant be the cassia sprig that here shall flourish! May the earliest buds of Spring unfold their beauties o'er this your resting place, and here may the sweetness of the Summer's last rose linger longest! Though the cold blasts of Autumn may lay them in the dust, and for a time destroy the loveliness of their existence, yet the destruction is not final, and in the Spring they shall surely bloom again. So, in the bright morning of the world's resurrection, your mortal frame, now laid in the dust by the chilling blast of Death, shall spring again into newness of life, and expand in immortal beauty, in realms beyond the skies. Until then, dear brother, until then, farewell!

Benediction: The Lord bless us and keep us – the Lord make His face to shine upon us, and be gracious unto us – the Lord lift upon us the light of His countenance and give us peace.

Response: Amen! So mote it be.

Thus the services end. The procession will re-form and return to the Lodge-room and the Lodge will be closed in the customary manner.

*The public Grand Honors of Masonry are given thus: Cross the arms upon the breast, the left arm outermost, the hands being open and palms inward; then raise them above the head, the palms of the hands striking each other; and then let them fall sharply upon the thighs, the head being bowed. This will be thrice done, and, at funerals, the action will be accompanied with the following ejaculation: "The will of God is accomplished. So mote it be. Amen."

Eastern Star Funeral Service

The following was first published by the General Grand Chapter, Order of the Eastern Star in 1890. Caroline and Carrie each had a similar service; in fact, Carrie had two of them.

At the burial of a sister, the badges of the members and officers should be draped with crape. A floral five-pointed Star should be provided, having flowers of the appropriate colors for the several points. The Star officers should each have a small bouquet, or a few loose flowers of the appropriate color. A few flowers should also be provided for the Worthy Matron and Worthy Patron. The floral Star may be deposited with the casket, or be retained by the family of the deceased.

This service, although primarily designed for use at the Grave, can be performed within the Chapter room, the Church, or other appropriate place.

If a procession is formed, it will march in the following order: Marshal and Sentinel, Members, Warder and Electa, Martha and Esther, Ruth and Adah, Conductress and Associate Conductress, Secretary and Treasurer, Matron and Associate Matron, Patron and Chaplain.

During the services, the officers and members will occupy the following positions around the grave or casket:

Secretary – Treasurer – Conductress - Associate Conductress – Warder – Sentinel – Matron – Patron – Chaplain – Mourners - Members.

When all is ready, the services should commence with a short strain of solemn music, "The Lord is my Shepherd," etc. after which the Worthy Patron will say:

Sisters and Brothers, we have gathered at this solemn hour to perform those final rites which affection has prescribed for our departed sister. She, who was with us but yesterday, has been summoned hence by a messenger who cometh sooner or later for us all. How appropriately may we gather around her remains, and together pay love's tribute to her memory. She has indeed passed beyond the reach of praise, or the touch of censure. It is not, therefore, to her that we tender this our heart's saddest offering.

We are here in acknowledgment of sacred ties now severed, of memories tenderly cherished, and hearts touched with sympathy for loved ones bereaved. Our sister has finished her allotted task in the conflict of life. The chapter of her earthly sojourn is closed, but her many virtues shall not go unrecorded. For a time we have walked with her in the pilgrimage of life, and around the same altar we have learned the lessons of our Order. As she was faithful to her convictions of right, as she was obedient to the demands of honor and justice in her station; as she loved kindred and friends, and in affliction evinced a trustful faith; and as she lived in the spirit of charity and the love of truth, so shall be her reward. Remembering her many virtues, we are indeed mourners at her grave, and in the house of sorrow we would drop the tear of affectionate sympathy. Sisters, brothers, and friends, as we stand in this solemn presence we may hear the voice of this Providence speaking to us. Not long shall we wait ere we obey the inexorable decree of Death, and follow our sister. How brief and full of mystery is human life! Who can fathom its purpose, or disclose its issues. We entered life as it were but yesterday; to-day we perform our allotted task, and to-morrow we go – who knows whither? We strain our eyes in vain endeavor to scan with mortal vision the infinite shore. But, thanks to our Heavenly Father, who gives fruition to His children's hopes, He bids us look yet again. Standing beside the Broken Column, we may, with Martha's trustful faith, look beyond the shore of time, and know that our sister, though lost to mortal vision, is only waiting beyond the river to welcome us to our eternal home. "In my Father's house are many mansions; if it were not so, I would have told you, I go to prepare a place for you, that where I am there ye may be also." O, let the comforting assurance come to us, "That if our earthly house of this tabernacle were dissolved, we have a building of God, a house not made with hands, eternal in the Heavens." Instructed by this Providence, may we go from this place of mourning, and this hour of reflection, with the inspiration of a new hope, and earnest purpose. "So live, that when thy summons comes to join the innumerable caravan that moves to the pale realms of shade, where each shall take his chamber in the silent halls of death. Thou go not, like the quarry-slave at night, scourged to his dungeon, but, sustained and soothed by an unfaltering trust, approach thy grave like one who wraps the drapery of his couch about him, and lies down to pleasant dreams."

Singing of any appropriate hymn.

Worthy Patron: The examples and symbols of our Order are full of useful and impressive lessons. They speak to us in this solemn hour with unwonted significance. These floral tributes, the offering of sisterly affection, echo voices often heard from the several points of our Star; they symbolize, in the ritual of our Order, virtues which should adorn our lives. How appropriately, then, may they bear an important part in this solemn ceremonial. Sisters of our Star, you who represent the five distinguished heroines of our Order, have you anything to offer ere we leave the grave of our departed sister? Sister Adah, what is the voice and tribute from the Blue point of our emblematic Star?

Adah: Blue symbolizes fidelity, and is appropriate to Jephthah's Daughter, who, in the morning of life, surrendered to the grave the brightest of earthly hopes, that she might be faithful to her convictions of right, and preserve her father's honor. As a token of faithfulness to the memory of our sister, I deposit in her grave this tribute of faithful love. *(At the proper time each officer will drop into the grave, or place upon the casket, the flowers provided for that purpose.)*

Adah deposits her tribute, and then, addressing Ruth, says:

Sister Ruth, what is the voice and tribute from the Yellow point of our Star?

Ruth: Yellow symbolizes constancy, teaching faithful obedience to the demands of honor and justice. Ruth exemplified these virtues in humble station, and sought the society of the good and true. In token of appreciation of these virtues, I deposit in the grave of our sister this floral tribute.

Deposits her tribute, and then, addressing Esther, says:

Sister Esther, what is the voice and tribute from the White point of our Star?

Esther: White symbolizes light and purity. The heroic Queen Esther evinced the purity of her motive and love of kindred and friends, by her willingness to risk the loss of crown and life, to save her people from death. In token of sincere affection for our sister, I deposit in her grave this emblem of light and purity.

Deposits her tribute, and then, addressing Martha, says:

Sister Martha, what is the voice and tribute from the Green point of our Star?

Martha: Green is an emblem of Nature's life and beauty. The evergreen is a symbol of immortal life, and teaches us, that in the economy of God there is no death; forms change, but the spirit survives. Martha, beside the grave of her beloved brother, avowed her trustful faith and hope of immortal life. In the full assurance of our sister's entrance upon a glorious immortality, I deposit in her grave this evergreen.

Deposits her tribute, and then, addressing Electa, says:

Sister Electa, what is the voice and tribute from the Red point of our Star?

Electa: Bed symbolizes fervency and zeal. Electa represents those who have been pre-eminent in charity, and heroic in endurance of the wrongs of persecution. In token of the fervency of our affection for our sister, I deposit in her grave this tribute of love.

Deposits her tribute, and then, addressing the Worthy Matron, says:

Worthy Matron, we have spoken from the five points of our emblematic Star, but our departed sister hears us not. Is it in vain that we speak to the living?

Worthy Matron: You have spoken well, my sisters. It is not in vain that we hear the oft repeated lessons of our Star. It is true that our sister hears not with mortal ear the lessons she was wont to learn from you; but is it true that she listens not to our words of love, and sees not the beautiful tributes strewn within her grave? May not her quickened spirit, freed from its earthly tenement, yet hover around the loved ones here assembled, listen to our words, and perceive with clearer vision our every movement? She needs not to be ministered unto; but may she not now minister to us? "Are they not all ministering spirits?" saith the apostle. Love is an attribute of the soul, and imperishable. Our sister's affection ceases not;

therefore may she not now be whispering to grief -stricken hearts, "Peace be still," "Lo, I am with you always." Think not that the spirit world is distant. Our loved ones, though lost to mortal sight, may yet be with us in spiritual existence. Let their loving presence be to us a perpetual inspiration, calling us to a higher moral and spiritual life. These beautiful flowers are the highest expression of Nature's loveliness. We never tire of looking at their perfect and delicately variegated tints. From time immemorial they have been endowed with expressive language. They speak to us, "To whisper hope whene'er our faith grows dim." But these floral emblems, with all their exquisite loveliness, are but dim reflections of the glories that may be unfolded to our spiritual vision. In token of our hope that such an unfolding of spiritual life may come to us all, I scatter these flowers within the grave of our departed sister. May we cherish her memory and emulate her virtues.

Deposits her tribute, and then, addressing the Worthy Patron, says:

Worthy Patron, within the grave, hallowed by the tenderest ties of human affection, we scatter these floral emblems of Nature's loveliness, and spiritual life. May we not trust all else to the Father's loving care?

Worthy Patron: The Infinite Father's ever watchful care is nowhere more impressively taught, than by His voice speaking to us through the floral kingdom. Over the whole earth where life exists, flowers bloom in endless variety and profusion. Some open with the rising sun, and close with his setting rays. Others open to the full moon and starry firmament, and shrink before the piercing gaze of the king of day. So the Father's love goes forth by day and night, to the weakest, most humble, and obscure of His children. We are told to consider the lilies of the field, and learn the paternal love of Him, beyond whose watchful care none can stray. Not a sparrow falls without His notice. "Ye are of more value than many sparrows." In token of our trust in the all-embracing love of the Infinite Father, I deposit these emblems of His watchful care in the grave of our departed sister.

Drops the flowers, and continues as follows:

Sisters and brothers, within the city of the dead, we

consign to the bosom of mother earth all that was mortal of our departed sister. The body we leave in the grave is but the casket which held the precious jewel of life. We bear it tenderly to its resting-place, because it is the form by which we knew her in our Chapter. Peacefully let it rest in the hallowed ground where we have placed it. Her grave flowerets will bloom amid all the countless activities of Nature's life. "The murmuring brook, the bird on airy wing, And whispering pines, will hear her requiem sing." Over her the fleeting shadows will the rising sun will scatter over the chambers of the dead his gladsome rays, and tint the western sky with the glories of departing day. In the hush of night the feeble rays of countless stars, traveling centuries on their journey here, will finally rest upon her grave. We leave in this lowly bed the earthly form of our departed sister, and may the hallowing influence of this providence go with us in the remaining journey of our life, and when our earthly mission is over, and we are "beyond the smiling and the weeping" of earth, may we gather with the loved ones gone before. Let us unite in prayer.

Our Father who art in Heaven, in whom we live, and in whom are all the issues of life and death, We come to Thee, in this hour of sorrow, and ask that we may so learn the lessons of this hour, that when it shall be our turn to lay aside our mortality, that we may do it with trustful faith in Thee and hope of a glorious immortality. We pray Thee to look with tender compassion upon these Thy children, whose household has been broken by this providence. May they lie passive in the arms of Thy chastening love, and realize that there is wisdom and goodness in all Thy appointments. Sanctify this bereavement to the good of us all. May it be the means of drawing us closer to Thee, and of our loving and serving Thee forever. And as it has pleased Thee to call from the toils of earth the soul of our beloved sister, we commit her remains to the silent tomb. Earth to earth, ashes to ashes, dust to dust, hopefully looking to a joyful reunion with her, in that land where separation and death are known no more, forever. Amen.

Response: So may it ever be.

Appendix B:
Where to Learn More

There are many places of interest that you can visit to see some of the things discussed, both about the Ingalls family and Freemasonry.

Freemasonry

Most Lodges have open installation of officers, fundraisers, or other events throughout the year. You generally don't have to travel far to find a Masonic Lodge or an Eastern Star Chapter, and the folks there would be happy to show you around and answer any questions.

In addition, every state has a Grand Lodge and Grand Chapter, and these often house a museum. (I don't know about Grand Lodges/Chapters in other countries, but my guess is that they do as well.) I can't recommend them enough: the ones I have visited held items tying the local Lodges to the history of the area, and this gives a really unique perspective. In Texas, for example, among other items you can see Sam Houston's Masonic apron, and the letter written by Col. Travis at the Alamo asking for help. Copies of this letter went to Masonic Lodges in Tennessee, and that's where many of the heroes (like Davy Crockett, another Mason) came from. The Grand Lodge Museum in Columbus, Missouri holds Laura's handkerchief and gloves in an exhibit that (very appropriately) focuses on the importance of music and education in Masonry; other exhibits there highlight the contributions, achievements and artifacts of Meriwether Lewis, William Clark, and President Harry Truman – all Freemasons – among others.

The Internet is an excellent source of information – if you find reputable, trustworthy sites; there is as much misinformation as there is accurate information.

The Bibliography lists a few of the many outstanding books on the subject of Freemasonry.

The Ingalls family

The Internet and many books – such as those listed in the Bibliography – may also provide information about the Ingalls family. In addition, each place they lived has created a site at which you may learn more.

De Smet: The ultimate "Laura destination," in my opinion, has to be De Smet, South Dakota, because there are so many sites there to see. The original homestead of the Ingalls family, Ingalls Homestead, is open to the public as a hands-on living history farm. http://www.ingallshomestead.com/

The Laura Ingalls Wilder Memorial Society offers tours of the family's house in town that Charles built, the Surveyor's House that the family lived in when they first arrived in De Smet, the first School house of De Smet that Laura and her friends attended, and a replica of the Brewster school house at which Laura taught. http://www.liwms.com/

Around town, you can see the home of banker and Freemason Thomas Ruth (now the Prairie House Manor Bed and Breakfast), the building that housed the Lodge at the time Charles joined (now the Heritage House Bed and Breakfast), and the original Loftus store. The church that the family attended and the current Masonic Lodge may be seen (from the street only, in most cases). The De Smet cemetery is where Charles, Caroline, Mary, Carrie, Grace, and Laura's unnamed baby boy are buried. As a bonus, the old depot now houses a museum featuring the famous prairie artist, Freemason, and nephew of Nate and Grace Ingalls Dow, Harvey Dunn. Outside of town, there is a marker at the site of Laura and Almanzo's homestead where Rose was born. De Smet puts on a Laura Ingalls Wilder pageant each summer.

Mansfield: At Mansfield, Missouri, "where the Little

House books were written," you can tour the home that Almanzo and Laura built on their farm, Rocky Ridge. Laura's dream home is cared for by the Laura Ingalls Wilder Historic Home and Museum. This site is unique in that nothing in the home has been changed; everything has been left just as it was on Laura's last day there. Also on the property is the rock house that Rose had built for her parents, and in which they lived for a few years, including the years when Laura began writing the *Little House* books. Almanzo, Laura and Rose are buried in the town's cemetery. Mansfield also hosts a summer pageant based on Laura's life. http://www.lauraingallswilderhome.com/

While in Mansfield, be sure to stop at the Mansfield Area Historical Society on the square. They have items of Laura's and Almanzo's on display, as well as many other treasures that add context to what we know about the lives of the Wilders and other members of the community. http://www.mansfieldhistorical.org/

Keystone: The Keystone, South Dakota home that David and Carrie lived in was honored with a plaque in July, 1976, but burned to the ground in yet another fire, on August 6, 1977. However, the old School House, which housed the Mt. Aetna Lodge and Chapter for so many years while Carrie was a member, is now home to the Keystone Historical Museum, and houses several artifacts from the Lodge, Chapter, and Carrie herself. The Congregational Church that Carrie attended still exists as well. Keystone is not far from Mt. Rushmore, and is well worth the visit. http://www.keystonehistory.com/

Walnut Grove: Made famous by the television show *Little House on the Prairie*, Walnut Grove, Minnesota is home to the Laura Ingalls Wilder Museum. Its exhibits are housed in a little "town:" an 1800's style home, a school house, a chapel, a depot, and a covered wagon, among other things. A few blocks away, the English Lutheran Church houses the church bell that Charles Ingalls helped pay for (in lieu of a new pair of boots, as told in *On the Banks of Plum Creek*). Outside of town, the site of the dugout the Ingalls family lived in when they first arrived in Walnut Grove is now privately owned, but as of this writing, the owners allow visitors to visit the site and play in Plum Creek. A summer pageant is put on here as well.

http://www.walnutgrove.org/index.html

Pepin: Pepin, Wisconsin is where it all began, being the birthplace of Laura. There is a replica of the little log house as described in *Little House in the Big Woods* on the home site, and a small museum in town. http://pepinwisconsin.com/

Independence: The site of the real little house on the prairie is located about 13 miles outside of Independence, Kansas. A replica of the little house shows how the Ingalls family would have lived. The well that Charles dug, as told in *Little House on the Prairie*, is located on this property. http://www.littlehouseontheprairiemuseum.com

Burr Oak and Vinton: Two sites in Iowa represent different phases of the Ingalls life. The Laura Ingalls Wilder Park and Museum in Burr Oak features the Masters Hotel, which Charles helped run and in which the entire family lived and worked for about a year after the death of baby Freddie. http://www.lauraingallswilder.us/

In Vinton, the Iowa College for the Blind where Mary attended college is still in use (although its name has changed), and houses a few artifacts from the time of Mary's stay. Prior arrangements required to visit. http://www.iowa-braille.k12.ia.us/

Spring Valley: Almanzo and Laura, with Rose, spent several months in Spring Valley, Minnesota with his parents. The farm is now privately owned, but the church the family attended now houses the Spring Valley Methodist Church Museum, with many interesting facts and artifacts of the Wilders and their time here. http://springvalleymnmuseum.org/

Malone: The boyhood home of Almanzo, the Wilder Homestead at Malone, New York, is run by the Almanzo & Laura Ingalls Wilder Association. The restored home at this site has the distinction of being the only original, extant home about which Laura wrote. (The other original homes were built after the end of the stories in the books). They also have a replicas of the Wilder barns and the school Almanzo attended. http://almanzowilderfarm.com/

Notes

In the Beginning

1. There are two known Masonic aprons of George Washington extant, one of which is owned by the Grand Lodge of Pennsylvania and may be viewed at their museum in Philadelphia. The other is in the possession of Alexandria-Washington Lodge No. 22 in Alexandria, Virginia.

See also "George Washington Papers at the Library of Congress 1741-1799," *Library of Congress*, February 15, 1999, http://memory.loc.gov/ammem/gwhtml/.

2. There are many websites which list famous Masons; an Internet search will turn up more than you can read in a day. I have been unable to find again the first one I saw, as described. Perhaps it no longer exists or perhaps (hopefully) it has been updated with more accurate information.

Chapter 1 - History

1. Michael Haag, *The Templars: The History and the Myth* (2008; reprint, New York: HarperCollins Publishers, 2009), 11.

2. Malcolm Barber, *The Trial of the Templars* (New York: Cambridge University Press, 1978), 1.

3. From the Constitution of York, dating from 926 A.D. (with modern spelling for your reading pleasure): "Soon after the Decease of St. Albones, there came diverse wars into England out of diverse nations, so that the good rule of Masons was disturbed and put down until the time of King Adilston. In his time there was a worthy King

in England, that brought this land into good rest, and he builded many great works and buildings, therefore he loved well Masons, for he had a son called Edwin, the which loved Masons much more than his father did, and he was so practiced in geometry, that he delighted much to come and talk with Masons and to learn of them the Craft. And after, for the love he had to Masons and to the Craft, he was made Mason at Windsor, and he got of the King, his father, a charter and commission once every year to have assembly within the realms where they would within England, and to correct within themselves faults & trespasses that were done as touching the Craft, and he held them an assembly at York and there he made Masons and gave them charges, and taught them the manners and commands the same to be kept ever afterwards. And took them the charter and commission to keep their assembly, and ordained that it should be renewed from King to King, and when the assembly were gathered together he made a cry, that all old Masons or young, that had any writings or understanding of the charges and manners that were made before their lands, wheresoever they were made Masons, that they should show them forth, there were found some in French, some in Greek, some in Hebrew, and some in English, and some in other languages, and when they read and saw well the intent of them was understood to be all one. And then he caused a book be made thereof how this worthy Craft of Masonry was first founded, and he himself commanded, and also then caused, that it should be read in any time when it should happen any Mason or Masons to be made to give him or them their charges, and from that time until this day manners of Masons have been kept in this manner and omen, as well as men might govern it, and furthermore at diverse assemblies have been put and ordained diverse charges by the best advice of Masters and fellows." This and other similar documents have been made available online by the Masonic High Council the Mother High Council of the World of the Most Ancient and Honourable Fraternity of Free and Accepted Masons (an informational Lodge, not a Grand Lodge).

"The Old Charges," *The Masonic High Council the Mother High Council*, 2005, http://www.rgle.org.uk/RGLE_Old_Charges.htm.

4. The *Regius Poem*, or *Halliwell Manuscript*, is the best known Old Charge. It contains 15 articles of moral and ethical behavior for the master (from attending church to properly training apprentices) and 15 articles for the craft masons, along with stipulated punishments for breaking the articles. It also includes direction for annual conferences, a moral story, and a prayer. There are over 100 other Old Charges existing as well, each with similar content. The

moral and ethical requirements are often quite detailed, entailing such things as not sabotaging your competitor, not taking advantage of workers, and who should be held responsible in case of defects in workmanship. For example, section 144 of the Edict of Rothari, 643 A.D., states, "If a Comacine [a particular Italian guild of masons] Master with his colleagues shall undertake to restore or build the house of any person whatsoever, after an agreement shall have been closed as to payment, and it chances that someone should be killed, by reason of the house, through the falling of either material or stone, no claim shall be lodged against the owner of the house, because who after having contracted to do work for his own advantage, must assume, not undeservedly, the damage done." This and other similar documents have been made available online by the Masonic High Council the Mother High Council of the World of the Most Ancient and Honourable Fraternity of Free and Accepted Masons (an informational Lodge, not a Grand Lodge).

"The Old Charges," *The Masonic High Council the Mother High Council*, 2005, http://www.rgle.org.uk/RGLE_Old_Charges.htm.

5. Elias Ashmole, *The Diary and Will of Elias Ashmole,* ed. R. T. Gunther (1817; reprint, Oxford: Butler & Tanner, 1927), 209.

6. Arthur Heiron, "The Moderns & The Antients," *Manchester Association for Masonic Research,* May 1924, http://www.rgle.org.uk/RGLE_18th_century.htm.

7. Douglas Knoop, *The Genesis of Freemasonry* (1947; reprint, London: Q.C. Correspondence Circle Ltd., 1978), 159.

8. Dr. James Anderson, *The Constitution of the Free-Masons, containing the History, Charges, Regulations, &c of that most Ancient and Right Worshipful Fraternity, for the use of the Lodges* (London: William Hunter, 1723), 47.

9. Mark A. Tabbert, *American Freemasons: Three Centuries of Building Communities* (New York: New York University Press, 2005), 34.

10. The 1893 *Proceedings of...Canada* contains a copy of letters written by the men who discovered the stone. According to the Grand Lodge of Canada, the stone was given to the Canadian Institute of Toronto in about 1887, and it was to be used as a feature in the construction of the building at that time. The rock has since

disappeared; the Director of the Institute wrote that it had been covered with plaster.

Proceedings of the M. W. Grand Lodge of Ancient Free and Accepted Masons of British Columbia (Victoria, BC: Munroe Miller, 1893), https://archive.org/stream/cihm_14584#page/n7/mode/2up.

"The masonic stone," *Grand Lodge of British Columbia and Yukon*, November 7, 2006, http://freemasonry.bcy.ca/history/masonic_stone.html.

11. Benjamin Franklin, *Pennsylvania Gazette no.108*, 5 December 1730, quoted in Francis Vicente, "An Overview of Early Freemasonry in Pennsylvania," *Pietre-Stones Review of Freemasonry*, April 1, 2008, http://www.freemasons-freemasonry.com/pennsylvania_freemasonry.html.

12. John C. Miller, *Sam Adams: Pioneer in Propaganda* (Boston: Little, Brown and Company, 1936), 179.

13. Esther Forbes, *Paul Revere and the World He Lived In* (1942; reprint, Boston: Mariner Books, 1999), 197.

14. Brian J. Schimian, "Freemasons & the Military," *Midnight Freemasons*, November 11, 2013.

15. "Revolution: 1750-1805," *Africans in America*, PBS and WGBH Interactive, April 26, 2004, http://www.pbs.org/wgbh/aia/part2/2p37.html.

16. Ibid.

17. Jack Buta, *Black Freemasons White America: The History of Prince Hall Freemasonry*, (Jack Buta, 2011), Kindle edition.

18. George Draffin, "Prince Hall Freemasonry," May 13, 1976. The article is reprinted on the website of *The Phylaxis Society*, November 30, 2013, http://www.thephylaxis.org/walkes/draffen/php.

19. Sidney Kaplan, *The Black Presence in the Era of the American Revolution,* (Boston: University of Massachusetts Press, 1989), 209.

Chapter 2 - Modern Masonry
1. "Freemasons in Statistics," *About Freemasons*, August 5,

2013, http://www.aboutfreemasons.com/Freemasons_in_Statistics.

2. Grand Lodge of Texas A. F. & A. M, *Monitor of the Lodge: Monitorial Instructions in the Three Degrees of Symbolic Masonry as Exemplified in the Grand Jurisdiction of Texas, A. F. & A. M.* (Waco: Grand Lodge of Texas A. F. & A. M., 1982), 89.

3. Laura Ingalls Wilder, *Little House on the Prairie*, 37, 241.
Wilder, *The Long Winter*, 127.
Wilder, *On the Banks of Plum Creek*, 184, 188.

4. Wilder, *Little House in the Big Woods*, 83-85, 96.

5. Wilder, *Plum Creek*, 187.

6. Wilder, *Little Town on the Prairie*, 12.

7. Wilder, *Pioneer Girl*, 146.

8. Ibid, 143.

9. Wilder, *Farmer Boy*, 152.

10. John Hamill and Robert Gilert, ed. *Freemasonry, A Celebration Of The Craft* (Massachusetts: J.G. Press, 1998), 231.
Transactions: The American Lodge of Research Free and Accepted Masons, Vol. iii, no. 1 (New York: 1939), 182.
"Our Ministers," *The Great Synagogue Sydney*, 2010, http://www.greatsynagogue.org.au/OurCongregation/OurMinisters.aspx.
"A Survey of the Archbishop's Masonic Career," *Freemasons' Quarterly Review.* First quarter, 1835.
Pete Normand, *The Texas Mason* (College Station: Texas Lodge of Research, 1986), quoted in "R.E.B. Baylor, Pro Ecclesia Pro Texana," *Grand Lodge of Texas Ancient Free and Accepted Masons*, October 30, 2012, http://www.grandlodgeoftexas.org/content/reb-baylor-pro-ecclesia-pro-texana.
William R. Denslow, *10,000 Famous Freemasons,* Vol. III (Columbia: Missouri Lodge of Research, 1957), 297.

11. Benjamin Franklin, *Pennsylvania Gazette no. 108*, 5 December 1730, quoted in Francis Vicente, "An Overview of Early Freemasonry in Pennsylvania," *Pietre-Stones Review of Freemasonry*, April 1, 2008, http://www.freemasons-freemasonry.com/pennsylvania_

freemasonry.html.

12. According to Christopher Hodapp in *Freemasonry for Dummies* (Hoboken: John Wiley & Sons, Inc., 2013, p. 83), an estimated 80,000 - 200,000 Freemasons were thrown into concentration camps and murdered Nazi Germany.

13. Joseph Fort Newton, *River of Years* (New York: J.B. Lippincott Company, 1946), 26.

14. Allen E. Roberts, *Freemasonry: A House Undivided* (The Minnesota Lodge of Research, December, 1962), 1.

15. Jacob Jewell, *Heroic Deeds of Noble Master Masons during the Civil War from 1861 to 1865 in the U.S.A.* (Pueblo: The Franklin Press. 1916) quoted in Michael A. Halleran, *The Better Angels of Our Nature: Freemasonry in the American Civil War* (The University of Alabama Press: 2010), 114.

16. Dennis V. Chornenky, "Introduction to Freemasonry" (Masonic Restoration Foundation, 2005).

17. Grand Lodge of Texas, *Monitor*, 33.

18. Ibid, 34.

19. Wilder, *By the Shores of Silver Lake*, 174, 217.

20. Wilder, *Little Town*, 89.

21. Wilder, *Little Town*, 55.

22. Grand Lodge of Texas, *Monitor*, 122.

23. Ibid, 18.

24. Joseph Fort Newton, *The Builders: A Story and Study of Masonry* (Cedar Rapids: The Torch Press, 1915), 258.

25. "Grand Lodge Masonic Charity," *The Grand Lodge of Ancient Free & Accepted Masons of Virginia*, August 28, 2013, http://www.grandlodgeofvirginia.org/masonic_charity.htm.

26. "Disaster Relief," *Masonic Service Association of North America*, 2013, http://www.msana.com/msadisasterrelief.asp.

27. Christopher Sowrs to Conrad Weise, quoted in Benjamin W. Bryant, "Freemasonry and Toleration in the Colonies," *The Builder*, 1915.

28. This quote, or parts of it, are often misattributed to John Adams, probably because it was first publicized in the book *The Works of John Adams, Second President of the United States: with a Life of the Author, Notes and Illustrations, by his Grandson Charles Francis Adams, Vol. 6* (published by Little, Brown and Co. of Boston in 1856). The book, however, contains letters both to and from John Adams, and the quote is from a letter clearly signed by Samuel Adams, having been written to John Adams on 20 Nov 1790. The letter was also reprinted in *The Life and Public Services of Samuel Adams: Being a Narrative of His Acts and Opinions, and of His Agency in Producing and Forwarding the American Revolution. With Extracts from His Correspondence, State Papers, and Political Essays, Volume 3* by William Vincent Wells (Boston: Little, Brown and Company, 1865), beginning on page 308.

29. W.E.B. DuBois, *The Souls of Black Folk* (Rockville, MD: Arc Manor Publishers, 2008), 30.

30. Item #1 from Kenneth E. Hendrickson, *Chief Executives of Texas: From Stephen F. Austin to John B. Connally, Jr.*, (Austin: Texas A&M University Press, 1995), 37.
Item #2 from Bennett Wood, *Rhodes 1848-1998: A Sesquicentennial Yearbook* (Little Rock: August House Publishers, Inc., 1998), 16.
All other information on this list is from a flyer that was put out by the Grand Lodge of California. There is no date or other identifying information on the flyer.

31. Wilder, *Plum Creek*, 138.

32. Wilder, *Long Winter*, 143.

33. Wilder, *These Happy Golden Years*, 68, 86.

34. Grand Lodge of Texas, *Monitor*, 37.

35. John Paul Jones to the Countess of Selkirk, May, 1778 quoted in Edward Livermore Burlingame, *Scribner's Magazine, Vol. 24* (New York: Charles Scribner's Sons, 1898), 22.

John Paul Jones to French Minister of Marine quoted in Edward Livermore Burlingame, *Scribner's Magazine, Vol. 24* (New York: Charles Scribner's Sons, 1898), 22.

Dennis M. Conrad, "John Paul Jones" in E. Gordon Bowen-Hassell, Dennis M. Conrad, and Mark L. Hayes, *Sea Raiders of the American Revolution: The Continental Navy in European Waters* (Washington, DC: Naval Historical Center, 2003), 51.

36. George Washington to Robert McKenzie, October 9, 1774, *George Washington Papers at the Library of Congress, 1741-1799: Series 5 Financial Papers,* February 15, 1999, http://memory. loc.gov/cgi-bin/ampage?collId=mgw5&fileName=gwpage004. db&recNum=193.

37. Maurizio Viroli, *For Love of Country: An Essay on Patriotism and Nationalism* (Oxford: Clarendon Press, 1997), 1.

38. Herman Goering to Gustave Gilbert, quoted in G. M. Gilbert, *Nuremburg Diary* (New York: Farrar, Strau, 1947), 278.

39. Wilfred G. Soutiea, Jr. and Phillip G. Elam, "Undelivered Grand Oratory for the 179th Annual Communication of the Grand Lodge of Missouri," *Freemasonry and Patriotism* (Grand Lodge of Ancient Free and Accepted Masons of the State of Missouri, 2000).

40. "About the National Sojourners," National Sojourners, 2009, http://www.nationalsojourners.org/about.php?sid=1.

41. Wilder, *Farmer Boy*, 179.
Wilder, *Little Town*, 64, 73.

42. The information in this chapter has been handed down through the centuries. The following three books are a few among many that delineate it:

Malcolm C. Duncan, *Duncan's Masonic Ritual and Monitor* (New York: Dick & Fitzgerald, 1866).

Grand Lodge of Texas A. F. & A. M, *Monitor of the Lodge* (Waco: Waco Printing Company, 2002).

Albert MacKey, *MacKey's Revised Encyclopedia of Freemasonry* (Chicago: The Masonic History Company, 1929).

Chapter 3 - Order of the Eastern Star

1. "Dr. Rob Morris, Master Builder of the Order of the Eastern Star," *Grand Chapter of California, Order of the Eastern Star*, 2005, http://web.archive.org/web/20070708101023/http://www.oescal.org/2005/2005RobMorris.htm.

2. Paul Rich, "Recovering a Rite: The Amaranth, Queen of the South, and Eastern Star," *Heredom - The Transition of The Scottish Rite Research Society, Vol. 6,* ed. S. Brent Morris (Washington D.C.: The Scottish Rite Research Society, 1997).

3. Jean M'Kee Kenaston, *History of the Order of the Eastern Star* (Iowa: The Torch Press, 1917), 222.

4. "History of IOGT: A Noble Past," *International Order of Good Templars,* 2004, http://www.iogt.us/iogt.php?p=35.
"Temperance Orders," *Phoenix Masonry*, 2013, http://www.phoenixmasonry.org/masonicmuseum/fraternalism/temperance_orders.htm.

5. Rob Morris, *Origination of the Eastern Star*, August 1, 1884.

6. Ibid.

7. Kenaston, *History*, 138.

8. Ibid, 262.

9. Ibid, 266.

10. Ibid, 124.

11. "Our History," *General Grand Chapter, Order of the Eastern Star*, 2013, http://www.easternstar.org/our-history/.

12. "About Order of the Eastern Star," *General Grand Chapter, Order of the Eastern Star*, 2013, http://www.easternstar.org/information/about-order-of-the-eastern-star/.

13. Ernst Lehner, *Symbols Signs and Signets* (New York: World Publishing, 1950), 107.
Carl G. Liungman, *Dictionary of Symbols* (Denver: ABC-CLIO,

1991), 333.

Leonid Ouspensky and Vladimir Lossky, *The Meaning of Icons* (Boston: Boston Book and Art Shop, 1952), 213.

14. General Grand Chapter Order of the Easter Star, *Ritual of the Order of the Eastern Star* (Washington DC: General Grand Chapter Order of the Eastern Star, 1956), 27.

"About Order of the Eastern Star," *General Grand Chapter, Order of the Eastern Star*, 2013, http://www.easternstar.org/information/about-order-of-the-eastern-star/.

15. No record exists as to why Morris chose this name. The name Adah appears twice in scripture, neither in connection with the story of Jephthah and his daughter. One of these is as the wife of Esau, and the other as wife of Lamach and mother of Jabal and Jubal. Perhaps this is a clue, as Jabal and Jubal are significant within Masonic ritual. However, Jephthah's daughter clearly never had children, and her story appears much later in the biblical timeline than Jabal and Jubal, so she was certainly not meant to be the same person, although she could be the inspiration for the name. The meaning of the name Adah, from the Hebrew, is "adornment," but some sources also cite a Germanic origin meaning "noble one." This meaning could also have been an influence in choosing the name, as it fits the lessons of this degree. Morris' reason in choosing the name Adah for Jephthah's daughter will remain a mystery of the Order.

16. Judges 11: 30-39, King James Version, Holy Bible.

17. Ruth 1: 1-18; Ruth 2: 2, KJV.

18. Book of Esther, KJV.

19. John 11: 1-44, KJV.

20. 2 John 1: 1, KJV.

21. General Grand Chapter, Order of the Easter Star, *Ritual of the Order of the Eastern Star* (Washington DC: General Grand Chapter, Order of the Eastern Star, 1956), 60.

22. "Did You Know," *The Sheaf, Vol. 12 Issue 1* (Wallingford, CT: Eastern Star Charity Foundation of Connecticut, Inc., Spring 2013), 3.

Chapter 4 - Early Years

1. Donald Zochert, *Laura: The Life of Laura Ingalls Wilder* (New York: Avon, 1977), 5.

2. Martha Carpenter to Laura Ingalls Wilder, October 9, 1925, Rose Wilder Lane Papers, Box 17, Herbert Hoover Presidential Library, West Branch, Iowa.

3. Zochert, *Laura*, 10.

4. According to records of the Grand Lodge F. & A. M. of Wisconsin, Dousman, Wisconsin.

5. John E. Miller, *Becoming Laura Ingalls Wilder: The Woman Behind the Legend - Missouri Biography Series* (Columbia: University of Missouri Press, 2006), Kindle edition.

6. Zochert, *Laura,* 15.

7. Frances W. Kaye, "Little Squatters on the Osage Diminished Reserve: Reading Laura Ingalls Wilder's Kansas Indians," *Great Plains Quarterly,Vol. 20, #2* (Lincoln: University of Nebraska-Lincoln, 2000).
Miller, *Becoming*.

8. Miller, *Becoming*.

9. Fred Kiewit, "Stories That Had to Be Told," *Kansas City Star*, May 22, 1955 quotes Laura as saying, "The only reason I can think of being able to write at all was that father and mother were great readers and I read a lot at home with them."
William Anderson, *The Literary Apprenticeship of Laura Ingalls Wilder* (South Dakota State Historical Society, 1983), Ebook.

10. Miller, *Becoming*.

11. Zochert, *Laura*, 78.

12. Laura Ingalls Wilder, *On the Banks of Plum Creek*, 191.
Miller, *Becoming*.

13.Laura Ingalls Wilder, *Pioneer Girl*, 80.

14. William Anderson, *Laura Ingalls Wilder: A Biography* (New York: HarperCollins, 1992), 16

15. Wilder, *Pioneer Girl*, 98.

16. Zochert, *Laura*, 117.

17. Laura Ingalls Wilder to Rose Wilder Lane, March 23, 1937, Rose Wilder Lane papers, Box 5, Herbert Hoover Presidential Library, West Branch, Iowa.

18. Zochert, *Laura*, 117.

19. According to the records of the Grand Lodge of Minnesota, A. F. & A. M., Bloomington, Minnesota.

20. Wilder, *Pioneer*, 137.

21. Zochert, *Laura*, 117.

22. According to the certificate on display at the Laura Ingalls Wilder Home museum in Mansfield, MO.

23. Charles W. Howe, *A Half Century of Progress, Walnut Grove, Minnesota and Vicinity - from 1866 to 1916* (The Walnut Grove Tribune, 1916), 4.

24. Wilder, *Pioneer*, 153.

Chapter 5 - De Smet

1. Laura Ingalls Wilder, *These Happy Golden Years*, 138.

2. Wilder, *Pioneer Girl*, 181.

3. Caryl Lynn Meyer Poppin, *De Smet Yesterday and Today By Those Who Stayed* (De Smet, SD: The De Smet News for the De Smet Bicentennial Committee, 1976).
George Alden Ogle, ed. *Memorial and Biographical Record: An Illustrated Compendium of Biography*, (Chicago: Geo. A. Ogle & Co, 1898), 1023.

4. "Ingalls Was First Resident De Smet: Family of R.R. Timekeeper Lived at Silver Lake in 1879; Moved to Town," *De Smet News*, June 6, 1930.

Ogle, *Memorial*, 1023.

Poppin, *De Smet*.

Wilder, *By the Shores of Silver Lake,* 218.

Wilder, *Little Town on the Prairie*, 71.

Wilder, *The Long Winter*, 157.

Laura Ingalls Wilder Memorial Society, *Explore De Smet, South Dakota: A Driving Guide to Sites from the Little House Books* (De Smet, South Dakota: Laura Ingalls Wilder Memorial Society, 2002), 29.

5. John E. Miller, *Becoming Laura Ingalls Wilder: The Woman Behind the Legend - Missouri Biography Series* (Columbia: University of Missouri Press, 2006), Kindle edition.

LIW Memorial Society, *Explore De Smet*, 14, 17.

6. Wilder, *Pioneer Girl*, 222.

7. Wilder, *Long Winter*, 265.

8. Poppin, *De Smet*, 220, 265.

Wilder, *Pioneer Girl*, 233.

9. *Gleanings from Our Past, A History of the Iowa Braille and Sight Saving School* (Vinton, Iowa: The Iowa Braille & Sight Saving School, 1984), 23.

Katie Fraser Carpenter, "Mary Ingalls: Portrait of a Nineteenth Century Blind Woman," *Museum of the American Printing House for the Blind,* August 16, 2012, http://www.aph.org/museum/MaryScript. html.

"The Mary Ingalls Era 1877-1889," *Iowa Educational Services for the Blind and Visually Impaired*, 2014, http://www.iowa-braille. k12.ia.us/vnews/display.v/ART/4921ebc684123.

10. Miller, *Becoming*.

Wilder, *Little Town*, 35.

11. "A Capitol Railroad Job," *North Dakota Supreme Court*, ndcourts.gov/court/history/century/i.b.htm, accessed September 28, 2013.

Dr. D. Jerome Tweton, "Congress Creates Dakota Territory,"

The North Star Dakotan, n.d.

12. "Charles Ingalls, Active Town Citizen," *Lore, Volume 8 number 2,* Fall & Winter, 1982-83.

"Ingalls Was First Resident De Smet: Family of R.R. Timekeeper Lived at Silver Lake in 1879; Moved to Town," *De Smet News,* June 6, 1930.

John E. Miller, *Laura Ingalls Wilder's Little Town: Where History and Literature Meet* (Kansas: University Press of Kansas, 1994), 26.

Ogle, *Memorial,* 1023.

Poppin, *De Smet.*

William Anderson, *The Story of the Ingalls: A Biography of the Family from the Little House Books* (Anderson Publishing, 1971).

13. Dorothy Smith, *The Wilder Family Story* (1972. Reprinted, New York: The Industrial Press for Almanzo and Laura Ingalls Wilder Association, 2003), 7, 15.

14. Wilder, *Golden Years,* 237.

15. Mary Jo Dathe, *Spring Valley: The Laura Ingalls Wilder Connection 1890* (1990. Reprint. N.P. 2007), 31.

Smith, *Wilder Family,* 25.

Wilder, *Golden Years,* 219.

16. Anthony Grafton, Glen W. Most, and Salvatore Settis, *The Classical Tradition* (Massachusetts: Harvard University Press, 2010), 682.

Robert Muchembled, *A History of the Devil From the Middle Ages to the Present* (Cambridge, UK: Polity Press, 2003), 16.

17. Wilder, *On the Banks of Plum Creek*, 187.

18. Miller, *LIW's Little Town*, 26.

19. Grace Ingalls, Diary, March 26, 1887.

20. Carpenter, "Mary Ingalls."

Gleanings, 23.

"The Mary Ingalls Era 1877-1889."

21. Grace Ingalls, Diary, August 27, 1889; November 17, 1889.

William Anderson, *The Ingalls Family of De Smet* (SD: Laura Ingalls Wilder Memorial Society, Inc., 1995).

22. Wilder, *The First Four Years*, 93.

23. Grace Ingalls, Diary, July 23, 1887.

24. Rose Wilder Lane, Introduction to Laura Ingalls Wilder, *On the Way Home: The Diary of a Trip from South Dakota to Mansfield, Missouri in 1894* (New York: Harper & Row, 1962), 2.
Wilder, *Four Years*, 87.

25. William Anderson, *Laura Wilder of Mansfield* (1974. Reprint, N.P., 2012), 2.

26. *De Smet Leader*, August 10, 1889.

27. Grace Ingalls, Diary, August 27, 1889.

28. Grace Ingalls, Diary, August 27, 1889; January 2, 1890.

29. Dathe, *Spring Valley*, 10, 19.

30. Dathe, 30.

31. Wilder, *Long Winter*, 23, 170, 193.

32. Wilder, *Little Town*, 111.

33. Grand Lodge of Texas A. F. & A. M, *Monitor of the Lodge: Monitorial Instructions in the Three Degrees of Symbolic Masonry as Exemplified in the Grand Jurisdiction of Texas, A. F. & A. M.* (Waco: Grand Lodge of Texas A. F. & A. M., 1982).

34. "Tranquility Lodge No. 2000," *The Grand Lodge of Texas Ancient Free and Accepted Masons*, 2013.
http://www.grandlodgeoftexas.org/content/tranquility-lodge-no-2000.
"Tranquility Lodge History," *Tranquility Lodge No. 2000*, 2005.
http://www.tl2k.org/history.htm.

35. U.S. Department of the Interior, Census Office, *Twelfth Census of the United States, 1900,* Superior, Douglas County,

Wisconsin.
Wilder, *Golden Years*, 217, 282.

36. LIW Memorial Society, *Explore De Smet*, 21.
Ogle, *Memorial*, 250.
Wilder, *Golden Years*, 183.

37. Noel V. Bourasaw, "George W. Hopp, pioneer editor of Dakota Territory, Washington & Sedro, and his publisher brothers," *Skagit River Journal of History & Folklore*, 2008, http://www.skagitriverjournal.com/WA/Library/Newspaper/HoppBrothers.html.
Wilder, *Little Town*, 196.

38. George Washington Kingsbury, *History of Dakota Territory, vol. 3: South Dakota It's History and Its People,* ed. George Martin Smith (Chicago: S.J. Clarke Publishing Company, 1915), 374.
LIW Memorial Society, *Explore De Smet*, 18.
Poppin, *De Smet*.
Wilder, *Long Winter*, 16.

39. Kingsbury, *History vol. 5, 32.*
Supreme Council for the Southern Jurisdiction, Ancient and Accepted Scottish Rite of Free-Masonry, *Transactions of the Supreme Council, 33°, for the Southern Jurisdiction of the United States of America* (Charleston: Gr. Orient of Charleston, 1901), 123.

40. Kingsbury, *History, Vol. 2*, 373, 398, 544, 663, 809, 1663.
Ogle, *Memorial,* 285.
Poppin, *De Smet,* 72.
Privately held family information.
Wilder, *Long Winter*, 170, 193.
Wilder, *Golden Years*, 183.

41. LIW Memorial Society, *Explore De Smet*, 41.
Private.
Wilder, *Long Winter*, 90, 320.

42. Poppin, *De Smet,* 400.
Private.

43. Wilder, *Golden Years*, 13.

44. Wilder, *Little Town,* 23.

45. Ogle, *Memorial*, 1023.
Poppin, *De Smet*.

46. Dathe, *Spring Valley*, 25, 43.

47. Grace Ingalls Dow's obituary, *De Smet News*, November 13, 1941.
Poppin, *De Smet,* 377.

48. Arlene M. Warnock, *Laura Ingalls Wilder: The Westville Florida Years* (MO: Laura Ingalls Wilder Home Association, 1979), 8.
Janet Benge and Geoff Benge, *Laura Ingalls Wilder: A Storybook Life (Heroes of History)* (Washington: Emerald Books, 2005), 172.

49. Carpenter, Mary.
"Mary Ingalls Timeline," *Museum of the American Printing House for the Blind*, August 16, 2013,
http://www.aph.org/museum/MaryTimeline.html.

50. Benge, *Storybook,* 174.
Miller, *Becoming*.
Rose Wilder Lane, Introduction to Laura Ingalls Wilder, *On the Way Home: The Diary of a Trip from South Dakota to Mansfield, Missouri in 1894* (New York: Harper & Row, 1962), 4.

51. Poppin, *De Smet*.

52. Wilder, *Little Town,* 144.

53. Anderson, *Story*.

54. Denise M. Karst Faehnrich, "Edward Louis Senn's Half-Century on the Last Frontiers" (SD: South Dakota State Historical Society, 1999), 6, 19.

55. Edith Eudora Kohl, *Land of the Burnt Thigh* (1938, Reprint. Saint Paul, Minnesota Historical Society Press, 1906), 37.

Chapter 6 - Keystone

1. David Swanzey's obituary.
Privately held information from personal friends of David and

Carrie Swanzey.

2. According to the records on the Environmental Working Group website, http://www.ewg.org/mining/owners/overview.php?cust_id=2015519 (accessed 13 December 2013), from 1893 to 1920 David Swanzey claimed 5 mines under this program for a total of 450 acres.

3. Tom Domek and Robert Hayes, *Mt. Rushmore and Keystone* (Arcadia Publishing, 2012), Ebook.

4. Chuck Childs, *Lodge History, Mt. Aetna Masonic Lodge* (Keystone: 1992).

5. Ibid.

6. Childs, *Lodge History*.
To be considered "rich," a vein must yield at least two ounces of gold per ton of ore. The vein hit in the Holy Terror produced about 20 ounces of gold per ton of ore - ten times the amount of a "rich" mine. The mine regularly produced 500 ounces of gold per week; one week the yield was a record setting 3,500 ounces. In 1899, Holy Terror produced about 28,500 ounces of gold, for a value of around $1,225,000 in 1899 dollars, or about $34,000,000 in today's value.

7. Childs, *Lodge History*.

8. Ibid.
Carrie Ingalls Swanzey, "History of Mt. Aetna Chapter," records of the Grand Chapter of South Dakota, Order of the Eastern Star, 1935.

9. Faehnrich, "Senn's."

10. Domek, *Keystone*.

11. William Anderson, *The Story of the Ingalls: A Biography of the Family from the Little House Books* (Anderson Publishing, 1971).

12. "Mary Ingalls Was a Real Pioneer," *De Smet News,* October 26, 1928.

13. Private.

14. Ibid.

15. Childs, *Lodge History*.

16. Rex Smith, *The Carving of Mt. Rushmore* (New York: Abbeville Press, 1985), Kindle edition.

17. Domek, *Keystone*.
Faehnrich, "Senn's."
Gilbert Courtland Fite, *Mount Rushmore* (Norman: University of Oklahoma Press, 1952).
Smith, *Carving*.

18. Domek, *Keystone*.
Smith, *Carving*.

19. Ibid.

20. Ibid.

21. Private.

22. Ibid.

23. Childs, *Lodge History*.

24. Ibid.
The mines: The Big Hit Mining Company was organized in 1891. Its assay showed rich ore, but it was nothing like the Holy Terror. The Big Hit Group of six mines was patented in 1913. The Tykoon Group, founded in 1897, consisted of the four mines, with a fifth added in 1902. The Turtle Group consisted of two lodes. This group was patented in 1902. The unpatented mines were in the Blue Ribbon group, which had been located by David in 1909 and 1910.
The Environmental Working Group has performed an analysis of the Land and Mineral Records held by the Bureau of Land Management. According to their website (http://www.ewg.org/mining/owners/listcases.php?cust_id=2015519, accessed 10 December 2013), David Swanzey held five patents, the earliest in 1893 and the latest in 1920, and gained title to an estimated 450 acres of land from the public, more than about 93.2% of all other mining interests and 97.8% of other patent holders. Some of his mines were patented after his death, and would not be counted in these figures. Despite this,

the Swanzey were not wealthy. None of David's mines ever produced the big strike he was looking for. In fact, during the Depression the Swanzeys did not have enough money to pay the property taxes on the mines and had to get financial help from Laura to do so.

The mines listed above are what David owned at his death and Carrie inherited; David had bought and sold many others through the years. One of these was the Bull Run #1, which he owned with Thomas A. Edison. Edison eventually purchased David's share of Bull Run #1. Yes, that Thomas Edison. And yes, he was also a Freemason.

Chapter 7 - Mansfield

1. Laura Ingalls Wilder, *On the Way Home: The Diary of a Trip from South Dakota to Mansfield, Missouri in 1894* (New York: Harper & Row, 1962).

2. Ibid, 59.

3. Ibid, 74.
Larry Dennis and Debbie Arnall, *Mansfield, Missouri: The First One Hundred Years 1882 - 1982* (Mansfield, MO: Centennial Book Committee, 1983).

4. A. J. Wilder, "The Story of Rocky Ridge Farm," *Missouri Ruralist*, July 22, 1911. (Although the byline says A. J., it is believed by many that Laura was the author.)

5. Wilder, *Missouri Ruralist*, July 22, 1911; June 1, 1912; February 20, 1918.
William Anderson, *Laura Ingalls Wilder: A Biography* (New York: HarperCollins, 1992), 152.

6. Wilder, *Missouri Ruralist*, July 22, 1911; June 1, 1912; February 20, 1918.

7. Anderson, *Laura Wilder of Mansfield* (1974. Reprint, N.P., 2012), 4, 7.
Rose Wilder Lane to Jasper Crane, December 13, 1926, Box 4, Rose Wilder Lane Papers, Archives, Herbert Hoover Presidential Library, West Branch, Iowa.

8. John E. Miller, *Becoming Laura Ingalls Wilder: The Woman*

Behind the Legend - Missouri Biography Series (Columbia: University of Missouri Press, 2006), Kindle edition.

9. Ibid.
Anderson, *Mansfield*.

10. Miller, *Becoming*.

11. Anderson, *Mansfield, 4.*

12. Records of the Grand Lodge of South Dakota, A. F. & A. M.

13. Dan L. White, *Laura Ingalls' Friends Remember Her: Memories from Laura's Ozark Home* (Missouri: Ashley Preston Publishing, 2009), Kindle edition.

14. This will be a condensed but accurate meeting. None of the secret work is revealed.
General Grand Chapter Order of the Easter Star, *Ritual of the Order of the Eastern Star* (Washington DC: General Grand Chapter Order of the Eastern Star, 1956).

15. White, *Remember*.

16. Anderson, *Mansfield*, 8.

17. Miller, *Becoming*.
William T. Anderson, *The Literary Apprenticeship of Laura Ingalls Wilder* (South Dakota State Historical Society, 1983), Ebook.

18. Miller, *Becoming*.

19. Rose Wilder Lane, Afterword, *On the Way Home: The Diary of a Trip from South Dakota to Mansfield, Missouri in 1894* (New York: Harper & Row, 1962), 118.

20. *Mansfield Mirror*, June 19, 1913; August 2, 1913; August 14, 1913; August 24, 1913; September 25, 1913; October 2, 1913.

21. *Mansfield Mirror,* September 24, 1914; October 22, 1914; August 24, 1916; August 2, 1917; May 2, 1918.

22. *Mansfield Mirror,* July 29, 1915; November 18, 1915; August

24, 1916; October 12, 1916; August 2, 1917; November 8, 1917.

23. *Mansfield Mirror*, June 1, 1912; September 7, 1916; October 31, 1918; December 4, 1919; December 2, 1920.

24. *Mansfield Mirror*, May 21, 1914, April 4, 1921; April 21, 1921; June 9, 1921; November 3, 1921; April 20, 1922; October 19, 1922; January 13, 1927; May 5, 1927; June 9, 1927.
Wilder, *Farmer Boy*, 371.

25. White, *Remember*.

26. John Case, "Let's Visit Mrs. Wilder," *Missouri Ruralist*, February 7, 1918.
Wilder, "Poultry Raising as an Occupation for Women," *The American Food Journal*, September 13, 1910, 27.
Miller, *Becoming*.

27. *Mansfield Mirror*, September 7, 1916.

28. *Mansfield Mirror*, December 22, 1921.
Pamela Smith Hill, *Laura Ingalls Wilder: A Writer's Life* (Pierre: South Dakota State Historical Society Press, 2007), Kindle edition.
Wilder, *West From Home: Letters of Laura Ingalls Wilder, San Francisco, 1915*, ed. Roger Lea MacBride (New York: HarperCollins Publishers, 1974).

29. Anderson, *Mansfield*, 19.
Mansfield Mirror, July 5, 1917; August 23, 1917; January 16, 1919; February 6, 1919; September 21, 1922.
Miller, *Becoming*.

30. *Mansfield Mirror*, May 1, 1913.
Wilder, *These Happy Golden Years*, 39.

31. *Mansfield Mirror*, August 2, 1917; March 21, 1918; April 1918; May 5, 1919; August 14, 1919.
Miller, *Becoming*.
Missouri Ruralist, November 20, 1917; February 20, 1918; April 20, 1918; May 20, 1918.

32. *Mansfield Mirror*, August 14, 1919; February 10, 1921; February 26, 1925.

Miller, *Becoming.*

33. *Mansfield Mirror*, February 4, 1915; September 19, 1918; January 16, 1919; August 7, 1919.
White, *Remember.*

34. *Mansfield Mirror*, June 29, 1916; June 12, 1919; April 15, 1920; September 29, 1921; June 22, 1922; December 23, 1926.
White, *Remember.*

35. *Mansfield Mirror,* December 2, 1920; February 2, 1928.

36. *Mansfield Mirror*, January 11, 1917.

37. *Mansfield Mirror*, April 23, 1925.

38. Anderson, *Mansfield*, 23.

39. Laura Ingalls Wilder to Martha Carpenter, June 22, 1925, Box 17, Rose Wilder Lane Papers, Archives, Herbert Hoover Presidential Library, West Branch, Iowa.
Miller, *Becoming.*

40. Anderson, *Apprenticeship.*
Anderson, *Mansfield*, 21.
Miller, *Becoming.*

41. Anderson, *Mansfield*, 24.
Hill, *Writer's Life.*
Miller, *Becoming.*
Stephen W. Hines, editor, *Laura Ingalls Wilder, Farm Journalist: Writings from the Ozarks* (Columbia, MO: University of Missouri Press, 2007), 306.

42. Anderson, *Apprenticeship.*
Hill, *Writer's Life.*

43. Anderson, *Mansfield*, 26.
Hill, *Writer's Life.*
Miller, *Becoming.*

44. Anne T. Earton, "New York Times Book Review," *New York Times*, April 24, 1932.

45. Hill, *Writer's Life*.

46. Anderson, *Laura*, 13.

47. Miller, *Becoming*.

48. Hill, *A Writer's Life*.

49. Wilder, *By the Shores of Silver Lake*, 127.

50. Hill, *Writer's Life*.

51. Amy Sickels, *Laura Ingalls Wilder* (New York: Infobase Publishing, 2007), 104.
Anderson, *Mansfield*, 31, 35.

52. Anderson, *Mansfield*, 40.
Miller, *Becoming*.

53. Jim Tedder, "Laura Ingalls Wilder, 1867-1957: She Wrote Nine 'Little House' Books About Pioneer Life," *Voice of America*, May 26, 2011.
Kendra Meinert, "Little House stars relive days on the prairie during Laura Ingalls Wilder Days," *The Green Bay Press Gazette*, July 24, 2010.

Bibliography

By Laura Ingalls Wilder:

Published by Harper & Brothers of New York:
Little House in the Big Woods (1932)
Farmer Boy (1933)
Little House on the Prairie (1935)
On the Banks of Plum Creek (1937)
By the Shores of Silver Lake (1939)
The Long Winter (1940)
Little Town on the Prairie (1941)
These Happy Golden Years (1943)

Published by Harper & Row of New York:
On the Way Home (1962)
The First Four Years (1971)
West from Home (1974)
A Little House Traveler (2006)

Various articles, *Missouri Ruralist* (1911 - 1923). On microfilm at the State Historical Society of Missouri in Columbia, Missouri and collected into several books, including *Little House in the Ozarks: The Rediscovered Writings: Laura Ingalls Wilder: Farm Journalist*, and *Writings to Young Women*, all edited by Stephen W. Hines and the *Before the Prairie* books edited by Dan L. White.

Pioneer Girl - unpublished manuscript, forthcoming.

Anderson, Dr. James. *The Constitution of the Free-Masons, containing the History, Charges, Regulations, &c of that most Ancient and Right Worshipful Fraternity, for the use of the Lodges.* London:

William Hunter, 1723.

Anderson, William. *The Ingalls Family of De Smet*. South Dakota: Laura Ingalls Wilder Memorial Society, Inc., 1995.

Anderson, William. *Laura Ingalls Wilder: A Biography*. New York: HarperTrophy, 1995.

Anderson, William. *Laura Wilder of Mansfield*. 1974. Reprint, N.P., 2012.

Anderson, William. *The Literary Apprenticeship of Laura Ingalls Wilder*. South Dakota State Historical Society, 1983. Ebook.

Anderson, William. *The Story of the Ingalls: A Biography of the Family from the Little House Books*. Anderson Publishing, 1971.

Ashmole, Elias. *The Diary and Will of Elias Ashmole*. Edited by R. T. Gunther. 1817. Reprint. Oxford: Butler & Tanner, 1927.

Barber, Malcolm. *The Trial of the Templars*. New York: Cambridge University Press, 1978.

Bourasaw, Noel V. "George W. Hopp, pioneer editor of Dakota Territory, Washington & Sedro, and his publisher brothers," *Skagit River Journal of History & Folklore*, 2008. http://www.skagitriverjournal.com/WA/Library/Newspaper/HoppBrothers.html.

Bryant, Benjamin W. "Freemasonry and Toleration in the Colonies." *The Builder*. 1915.

Buta, Jack. *Black Freemasons White America: The History of Prince Hall Freemasonry*. Jack Buta, 2011. Kindle edition.

"A Capitol Railroad Job." *North Dakota Supreme Court*. ndcourts.gov/court/history/century/i.b.htm.

Carpenter, Katie Fraser. "Mary Ingalls: Portrait of a Nineteenth Century Blind Woman." *Museum of the American Printing House for the Blind*. August 16, 2012. http://www.aph.org/museum/MaryScript.html.

"Charles Ingalls, Active Town Citizen." *Lore, Volume 8 number 2.* Fall & Winter, 1982-83.

Charles River Editors. *American Legends: The Life of Laura Ingalls Wilder.* Charles River Editors: n.d. Kindle edition.

Childs, Chuck. *Lodge History, Mt. Aetna Masonic Lodge.* Keystone: 1992.

Dathe, Mary Jo. *Spring Valley: The Laura Ingalls Wilder Connection 1890.* 1990. Reprint. N.P. 2007.

Dennis, Larry and Debbie Arnall. *Mansfield, Missouri: The First One Hundred Years 1882 - 1982.* Mansfield, MO: Centennial Book Committee, 1983.

Denslow, William R. *10,000 Famous Freemasons, Vol. III.* Columbia: Missouri Lodge of Research, 1957.

"Did You Know." *The Sheaf, Vol. 12 Issue 1.* Wallingford, CT: Eastern Star Charity Foundation of Connecticut, Inc., Spring 2013.

"Disaster Relief." *Masonic Service Association of North America.* http://www.msana.com/msadisasterrelief.asp.

Domek, Tom and Robert Hayes. *Mt. Rushmore and Keystone.* Arcadia Publishing, 2012. Ebook.

"Dr. Rob Morris, Master Builder of the Order of the Eastern Star." *Grand Chapter of California, Order of the Eastern Star.* 2005. http://web.archive.org/web/20070708101023/http://www.oescal. org/2005/2005RobMorris.htm.

Draffin, George. "Prince Hall Freemasonry." *The Phylaxis Society.* http://www.thephylaxis.org/walkes/draffen/php.

Du Bois, W.E.B. *The Souls of Black Folk.* Rockville, MD: Arc Manor Publishers, 2008.

Duncan, Malcolm C. *Duncan's Masonic Ritual and Monitor.* New York: Dick & Fitzgerald, 1866.

Earton, Anne T. "New York Times Book Review." *New York Times.*

April 24, 1932.

Faehnrich, Denise M. Karst. "Edward Louis Senn's Half-Century on the Last Frontiers." SD: South Dakota State Historical Society, 1999.

Fite, Gilbert Courtland. *Mount Rushmore*. Norman: University of Oklahoma Press, 1952.

Forbes, Esther. *Paul Revere and the World He Lived In*. 1942. Reprint. Boston: Mariner Books, 1999.

General Grand Chapter Order of the Easter Star. *Ritual of the Order of the Eastern Star*. Washington DC: General Grand Chapter Order of the Eastern Star, 1956.

"Gleanings from Our Past, A History of the Iowa Braille and Sight Saving School." Vinton, Iowa: The Iowa Braille & Sight Saving School, 1984.

Grafton, Anthony, Glen W. Most, and Salvatore Settis. *The Classical Tradition*. Massachusetts: Harvard University Press, 2010.

"Grand Lodge Masonic Charity." *The Grand Lodge of Ancient Free & Accepted Masons of Virginia*. http://www.grandlodgeofvirginia. org/masonic_charity.htm.

Grand Lodge of Canada. *Proceedings of the Grand Lodge of Ancient Free and Accepted Masons of Canada*. Toronto: Hunter, Rose & Co., 1892.

Grand Lodge of Texas A.F.&A.M. *Monitor of the Lodge*. Waco: Waco Printing Company, 2002.

Haag, Michael. *The Templars: The History and the Myth*. 2008. Reprint. New York: HarperCollins Publishers, 2009.

Halleran, Michael A. *The Better Angels of Our Nature: Freemasonry in the American Civil War*. The University of Alabama Press, 2010.

Hamill, John and Robert Gilert, Editors. *Freemasonry, A Celebration Of The Craft*. Massachusetts: J.G. Press, 1998.

Heiron, Arthur. *Ancient Freemasonry and the Old Dundee Lodge No. 18 (1722-1920)*. London: Kenning & Son, 1921.

Heiron, Arthur. "The Moderns & The Antients." *Manchester Association for Masonic Research*. May 1924. http://www.rgle. org.uk/RGLE_18th_century.htm.

Hendrickson, Kenneth E. *Chief Executives of Texas: From Stephen F. Austin to John B. Connally, Jr.* Austin: Texas A&M University Press, 1995.

Hill, Pamela Smith. *Laura Ingalls Wilder: A Writer's Life*. Pierre: South Dakota State Historical Society Press, 2007. Kindle edition.

Hines, Stephen W., Editor. *Laura Ingalls Wilder, Farm Journalist: Writings from the Ozarks*. Columbia, MO: University of Missouri Press, 2007.

"History of IOGT: A Noble Past." *International Order of Good Templars*. 2004. http://www.iogt.us/iogt.php?p=35.

Hodapp, Christopher. *Freemasonry for Dummies*. Indianapolis: Wiley Publishing, Inc., 2005.

"Ingalls Was First Resident De Smet: Family of R.R. Timekeeper Lived at Silver Lake in 1879; Moved to Town." *De Smet News*. June 6, 1930.

Jewell, Jacob. *Heroic Deeds of Noble Master Masons during the Civil War from 1861 to 1865 in the U.S.A.* Pueblo: The Franklin Press. 1916.

Kaplan, Sidney. *The Black Reserve in the Era of the American Revolution*. Amherst: University of Massachusetts Press, 1989.

Kenaston, Jean M'Kee. *History of the Order of the Eastern Star*. Iowa: The Torch Press, 1917.

Kingsbury, George Washington. *History of Dakota Territory, Vol. 1-5: South Dakota It's History and Its People*. Edited by George Martin Smith. Chicago: S.J. Clarke Publishing Company, 1915.

Knoop, Douglas. *The Genesis of Freemasonry*. 1947. Reprint, London: Q.C. Correspondence Circle Ltd., 1978.

Kohl, Edith Eudora. *Land of the Burnt Thigh*. 1938. Reprint. Saint Paul, Minnesota Historical Society Press, 1906.

Laura Ingalls Wilder Memorial Society. *Explore De Smet, South Dakota: A Driving Guide to Sites from the Little House Books*. De Smet, South Dakota: Laura Ingalls Wilder Memorial Society, 2002.

Laura Ingalls Wilder Park and Museum. *Laura Ingalls Wilder: The Iowa Story*. Iowa: Laura Ingalls Wilder Park and Museum, 1989.

Lehner, Ernst. *Symbols Signs and Signets*. New York: World Publishing, 1950.

Liungman, Carl G. *Dictionary of Symbols*. Denver: ABC-CLIO, 1991.

MacKey, Albert. *MacKey's Revised Encyclopedia of Freemasonry*. Chicago: The Masonic History Company, 1929.

"The Mary Ingalls Era 1877-1889." *Iowa Educational Services for the Blind and Visually Impaired*. 2014. http://www.iowa-braille. k12.ia.us/vnews/display.v/ART/4921ebc684123.

"Mary Ingalls Timeline," *Museum of the American Printing House for the Blind*, August 16, 2013, http://www.aph.org/museum/ MaryTimeline.html.

"Mary Ingalls Was a Real Pioneer," *De Smet News*, October 26, 1928.

"The masonic stone." *Grand Lodge of British Columbia and Yukon*. November 7, 2006. http://freemasonry.bcy.ca/history/masonic_ stone.html.

Meinert, Kendra. "Little House stars relive days on the prairie during Laura Ingalls Wilder Days." *The Green Bay Press Gazette*. July 24, 2010.

Miller, John E. *Becoming Laura Ingalls Wilder: The Woman Behind the Legend - Missouri Biography Series*. Columbia: University of Missouri Press, 1998. Kindle edition.

Miller, John E. *Laura Ingalls Wilder's Little Town: Where History and Literature Meet*. Kansas: University Press of Kansas, 1994.

Miller, John C. *Sam Adams: Pioneer in Propaganda*. Boston: Little, Brown and Company, 1936.

Morgan, Giles. *Freemasonry*. Edison: Chartwell Books, Inc., 2007.

Morris, Rob. *The Mosaic Book of the American Adoptive Rite*. New York: J.B. Taylor, 1857.

Morris, Rob. *Origination of the Eastern Star*. August 1, 1884.

Muchembled, Robert. *A History of the Devil From the Middle Ages to the Present*. Cambridge, UK: Polity Press, 2003.

Muraskin, William A. *Middle-class Blacks in a White Society: Prince Hall Freemasonry in America*. California: University of California Press, 1975.

Newton, Joseph Fort. *The Builders: A Story and Study of Masonry*. Cedar Rapids: The Torch Press, 1915.

Newton, Joseph Fort. *River of Years*. New York: J.B. Lippincott Company, 1946.

Normand, Pete. *The Texas Mason*. College Station: Texas Lodge of Research, 1986.

Ogle, George Alden, Editor. *Memorial and Biographical Record: An Illustrated Compendium of Biography*. Chicago: Geo. A. Ogle & Co, 1898.

"The Old Charges." *The Masonic High Council the Mother High Council*. 2005. http://www.rgle.org.uk/RGLE_Old_Charges.htm.

"Our History." *General Grand Chapter, Order of the Eastern Star*. http://www.easternstar.org/our-history/.

"Our Ministers." *The Great Synagogue Sydney*. 2010. http://www. greatsynagogue.org.au/OurCongregation/OurMinisters.aspx.

Ouspensky, Leonid and Vladimir Lossky. *The Meaning of Icons*.

Boston: Boston Book and Art Shop, 1952.

Poppin, Caryl Lynn Meyer, Editor. *De Smet Yesterday and Today By Those Who Stayed*. De Smet, SD: The De Smet News for the De Smet Bicentennial Committee, 1976.

Proceedings of the M. W. Grand Lodge of Ancient Free and Accepted Masons of British Columbia. Victoria, BC: Munroe Miller, 1893. https://archive.org/stream/cihm_14584#page/n7/mode/2up.

"R.E.B. Baylor, Pro Ecclesia Pro Texana." *Grand Lodge of Texas Ancient Free and Accepted Masons*. October 30, 2012. http://www.grandlodgeoftexas.org/content/reb-baylor-pro-ecclesia-pro-texana.

"Revolution: 1750-1805." *Africans in America*. PBS and WGBH Interactive. http://www.pbs.org/wgbh/aia/part2/2p37.html.

Rich, Paul. "Recovering a Rite: The Amaranth, Queen of the South, and Eastern Star." *Heredom - The Transition of The Scottish Rite Research Society, Vol. 6*. Edited by S. Brent Morris. Washington D.C.: The Scottish Rite Research Society, 1997.

Roberts, Allen E. *Freemasonry: A House Undivided*. The Minnesota Lodge of Research, December, 1962.

Sickels, Amy. *Laura Ingalls Wilder*. New York: Infobase Publishing, 2007.

Smith, Dorothy. *The Wilder Family Story*. 1972. Reprint. New York: The Industrial Press for Almanzo and Laura Ingalls Wilder Association, 2003.

Smith, Rex Allen. *The Carving of Mount Rushmore*. New York: Abbeville Press, 1985. Kindle edition.

Supreme Council for the Southern Jurisdiction, Ancient and Accepted Scottish Rite of Free-Masonry. *Transactions of the Supreme Council, 33°, for the Southern Jurisdiction of the United States of America*. Charleston: Gr. Orient of Charleston, 1901.

"A Survey of the Archbishop's Masonic Career." *Freemasons' Quarterly Review*. First quarter, 1835.

Tabbert, Mark A. *American Freemasons: Three Centuries of Building Communities.* New York: New York University Press, 2005.

Tedder, Jim. "Laura Ingalls Wilder, 1867-1957: She Wrote Nine 'Little House' Books About Pioneer Life." *Voice of America.* May 26, 2011.

"Temperance Orders." *Phoenix Masonry.* 2013. http://www.phoenixmasonry.org/masonicmuseum/fraternalism/temperance_orders.htm.

"Tranquility Lodge History." *Tranquility Lodge No. 2000.* 2005. http://www.tl2k.org/history.htm.

"Tranquility Lodge No. 2000." *The Grand Lodge of Texas Ancient Free and Accepted Masons.* 2013. http://www.grandlodgeoftexas.org/content/tranquility-lodge-no-2000.

Transactions: The American Lodge of Research Free and Accepted Masons, Vol. iii, no. 1. New York: 1939.

Tweton, Dr. D. Jerome. "Congress Creates Dakota Territory." *The North Star Dakotan,* n.d.

U.S. Department of the Interior. Census Office. *Twelfth Census of the United States, 1900.* Superior, Douglas County, Wisconsin.

Various articles. *De Smet News.* De Smet: South Dakota.

Various articles. *Mansfield Mirror.* Mansfield, Missouri.

Vicente, Francis. "An Overview of Early Freemasonry in Pennsylvania." *Pietre-Stones Review of Freemasonry.* April 1, 2008. http://www.freemasons-freemasonry.com/pennsylvania_freemasonry.html.

Warnock, Arlene M. *Laura Ingalls Wilder: The Westville Florida Years.* MO: Laura Ingalls Wilder Home Association, 1979.

Washington, George. "George Washington Papers at the Library of Congress 1741-1799." *Library of Congress.* February 16, 1999. http://memory.loc.gov/ammem/gwhtml/.

LITTLE LODGES ON THE PRAIRIE

Wells, William Vincent. *The Life and Public Services of Samuel Adams: Being a Narrative of His Acts and Opinions, and of His Agency in Producing and Forwarding the American Revolution. With Extracts from His Correspondence, State Papers, and Political Essays, Volume 3*. Boston: Little, Brown and Company, 1865.

Wesley, Charles Harris. *Prince Hall: Life and Legacy*. Charleston: United Supreme Council Southern Jurisdiction Prince Hall Affiliated, 1977.

White, Dan L. *Laura Ingalls' Friends Remember Her: Memories from Laura's Ozarks Home*. Hartville, MO: Ashley Preston Publishing, 1992. Kindle edition.

Wood, Bennett. *Rhodes 1848-1998: A Sesquicentennial Yearbook*. Little Rock: August House Publishers, Inc., 1998.

Zochert, Donald. Laura: *The Life of Laura Ingalls Wilder*. New York: Avon, 1977.

Made in the USA
San Bernardino, CA
05 October 2014